To Mary
Thanks for all you do
@ Bryen — you make a
difference!

ADAPT
OR DIE

ADAPT OR DIE

LT GEN (RET) RICK LYNCH

WITH MARK DAGOSTINO

For information about this title or to order other books and/or
electronic media, contact the publisher:

LTG (R) Rick Lynch
www.rlynchenterprises.com
ricky.lynch55@gmail.com

ISBNs:
978-1-7378833-2-6 (Hardcover)
978-1-7378833-0-2 (Softcover)
978-1-7378833-1-9 (eBook)

Printed in the United States of America

Cover and Interior design: 1106 Design

To Sarah,
for all of your love and support through the years.

CONTENTS

AUTHOR'S NOTE

When I first sat down to write this book in 2012, I was right in the middle of one of the biggest transitions I'd ever made in my life: leaving behind a successful thirty-five-year career in the Army and trying to start all over again in the civilian world. Talk about an adapt-or-die situation. There was a statistic floating around at that time that showed lifelong military folks who didn't find purposeful, meaningful work after retirement tended to wither away and die in as little as five years. *Five years!*

Well, I'm happy to tell you that I've outlived that fate times two. Ten years have come and gone since my transition, and I'm still here. Far from withering away and dying, my career is busier than ever, my family has grown by multiple grandchildren, and the work I'm doing—the very life I'm living—feels more important and more meaningful to me than ever. Instead of "retiring," I saw the opportunity I had in leaving the Army to use my military experience to make a difference in the world, specifically through my passion for developing leaders. And after all this time, I'm able to speak from a new perspective: I'm not the retired general anymore; I'm a corporate executive and leadership trainer who just *happens* to be a retired general.

My goal back then was to build more concerned, caring, compassionate, and adaptive leaders—the kind of leaders who could stare down a crisis, change course as needed, and do the right thing not only for a company's bottom line but also for their people and their families, too—and that's what I've done.

It's all been based on the principles found here in this book. Principles that are more relevant in corporate America today than ever before, which is why I felt it was so important to release an expanded, Tenth Anniversary Edition of *Adapt or Die* at this moment.

In the eighteen months prior to finishing this edition, our nation and the world endured a global pandemic that changed everything. It changed the way we work. The way we *live*. It changed our expectations, our sense of trust, and our sense of "normalcy," whether we wanted it to or not. And honestly, if the concept of adaptive leadership didn't matter to you before, it sure as hell should matter to you now. Why? Because we've *all* had to learn to adapt. We didn't have a choice! And for the kinds of folks who might have been drawn to this book (or any leadership book) in the years preceding the pandemic, our particular sense of urgency and purpose ticked up as well—because if the pandemic proved anything, it's the profound difference strong leadership makes during troubled times, whether it's in the boardroom, in your living room, on Main Street, on Wall Street, or up in the highest offices in the land.

While the core principles and examples I shared in the original version of *Adapt or Die* remain intact here, what you'll find toward the end of this book is a brand-new Part 5, dedicated specifically to the experience and examples of adaptive leadership in action that I've lived and witnessed in corporate America in the last decade. The new chapters deal especially with adaptive leadership in times of crisis, spurred primarily by the questions corporate leaders and their workforces have been asking me throughout the pandemic and the early days of its aftermath. From questions about setting priorities, to time management, to conflict resolution, to embracing new technologies, and more, I've done my best to answer as many as possible here.

And my answers come from experience.

One of my first roles after leaving the Army (and writing this book) was to become Executive Director of UTARI—the multimillion-dollar Research Institute at the University of Texas at Arlington—where I spent four years developing robotics and other new technologies for the purpose of helping humanity. Which means technology doesn't scare me. So, adapting to virtual meetings and other pandemic-induced technological shifts came easy to me—and I'll teach you how to make it a little easier for you.

I followed that experience by founding R Lynch Enterprises, my consulting firm that's actively providing keynote addresses, leadership training, and historical leadership retreats to nineteen companies (and counting) all across America, including nine pharmaceutical companies, various IT companies, construction companies, an award-winning hotel, and one of the nation's largest retail grocery chains.

During it all, I've also spent a significant portion of my time working with nonprofit organizations to ensure that our wounded warriors have the technology, housing, and support they need in the years that follow their great service to our country. Which means I'm still in touch with the roots of my Army career, but filtering that experience through a different lens now, putting all of my skills to use to make life better for people I care about.

And taking care of people is my Priority One.

Leaving the Army wasn't an ending for me. It was just the beginning. I saw it as an opportunity, not an obstacle, and that is one of the key takeaways from this book. That's the way it works with adaptive leaders, and why, for many, the shake-ups caused by the pandemic provided tremendous opportunity for positive change. If it didn't go that way for you, well, guess what? There will be other life-changing, world-shaking events in the future, too. Change happens. It's not a question of *if*, but *when*. And one of the most positive changes any leader can make is to never stop learning and to prepare for the unknown, so you'll be unstoppable, no matter what the future may bring your way.

For that reason, even if you've already read the first edition of this book, I hope you'll dig in here—because the principles I talk about in these pages are worth reviewing more than once. I know this because the message of *Adapt or Die* has reached tens of thousands of people in the last decade, and the demand for these lessons has only grown stronger. I've not only sold thousands of books via two editions (and a paperback version, too), but I've been called to deliver an average of two speaking engagements per month since 2013. With even a lowball estimate of audience size of around 300 people per speech, that's 72,000 people in corporate America who've heard me talk about these principles in person, many of whom have followed up and asked me to return and advise their organizations again and again.

Why is this book still so relevant ten years later? Because these principles matter—and they won't ever change.

Instead, as you take the time to review them and make them a part of your daily existence, what *will* change, what *will* become stronger, what *will* become better-prepared to adapt to any challenge in the future—is *you*.

INTRODUCTION

If you picked up this book, chances are pretty good that you've made up your mind: You want to be a leader. Or maybe you're already a leader, and you want to be a better leader. A stronger leader. Either way, that's a very good thing.

We need more leaders. True leaders. Leaders who know what it means to "lead" and not just "manage."

America's got problems. Our governments (both national and local), our businesses (both big and small), our education systems (both private and public), even our churches and community organizations are facing budget cuts and shortfalls, global competition, shifting demographics, loss of morale and of moral direction, and a never-ending series of rapidly changing technological challenges that seem almost too big to bear. Yet all of this can be solved. I believe the solution to almost every problem we face is strong leadership—leadership built on the ability to adapt.

Adaptation, as history shows us, is the key to survival not only in business or out on the battlefield but also in life. The phrase "Adapt or die" exists for a reason, and the best leaders, the strongest leaders, live by it.

The world moves fast today—faster than a lot of seemingly capable leaders and even some well-oiled machines and top-notch organizations can handle. But true leaders know how to adapt and how to get those around them to adapt to any situation.

Think you've got what it takes to be that kind of a leader? I think you do. I believe in the power of individuals to change their circumstances, to change their environment, to change the course of their home life and workplaces, and to change for the better. You have the strength it takes to do that, using the tools that God blessed you with. The question is whether *you* have the *belief* that you have what it takes to get it done, and whether you can recognize how to use the tools you've been given.

My aim in writing this book is to help you do just that.

The thing is, once you know your foundation, once you have your guiding principles in place, leading is basically a matter of digging deep and choosing to do the right thing—no matter how big or how small the challenges before you may be.

So, what are those challenges? After thirty-five years in the Army, leading groups of American heroes as small as 100 soldiers and as large as 120,000 civilian employees, chances are I've not only faced it but survived it, overcome it, and come out the other side better for it. In fact, no matter how big your challenges might seem, I bet I've got a story that'll help put it all into perspective for you.

Got a budget to trim? I was required to trim $5 billion from one of my budgets over a two-year period without cutting back on any of the services we were tasked to deliver. Facing a tough negotiation? In Iraq, I sat across the negotiating table from sixteen heavily armed Sunni insurgents who were hell-bent on killing me, with no one but a translator to back me up on my side of the table—and won. How did I do that? The same way I've adapted and pushed through every decision and struggle in my life: by seeing opportunities instead of obstacles; by acting as an engaged leader; by standing up as a lifestyle evangelist who leads not just with words but by example; and by knowing my priorities and standing on a solid foundation that allows me—and, therefore, those around me—to adapt and persevere with resilience.

It took me a lifetime to learn how to master those principles. In the pages of this book, I'll share stories and examples from a variety of points in my life and career in the hopes that you'll learn a little faster than I did, and start leading with courage and conviction right away, no matter what challenges come your way.

In life and work, it's almost a certainty that you'll face challenges you don't see coming. In fact, one of the toughest foes to ever face me down in my entire career was a young woman—an Army wife—who stopped me on the street with tears in her eyes three days after I took over command at Fort Hood, Texas, the largest Army base in the free world.

"You generals are lying to us!" she said to me.

I was taken aback. "Ma'am, I don't understand," I said.

"You tell us that you're bringing our husbands home between deployments. You say it, but you don't mean it. Here at Fort Hood, my husband comes home every night after our kids go to bed. He's always working weekends," she said. "Just keep him. You're teasing my family. My kids understand why Daddy's gone when he's in Iraq or Afghanistan, but they don't understand why they never get to see him when he's right here in Texas."

A manager might hear a complaint like this, show some sympathy, and basically go back to whatever he or she was doing before. "Tough," might be the internal response. "There's work to be done, and our soldiers are here to do it." But neglect and denial just aren't my style. What this young woman was telling me was something that had been churning in my gut for some time: We, as the Army, hadn't done enough to adapt our systems, schedules, and routines back home to a war that was now stretching toward a decade in length. The war, with its multiple back-to-back deployments, was taxing our soldiers and their families to the brink. We knew it, but we weren't doing enough about it. We needed to adapt to this new reality before the whole system simply died under our watch.

As a leader, I realized it wasn't anyone else's responsibility. It was my responsibility to do something about it and to do something about it right away.

That very day, I demanded that all 63,000 soldiers at Fort Hood be home by 6:00 to eat dinner with their families. It's a demand I would enforce from that day forward. Five days a week. I also insisted that every soldier and officer (the equivalents of "supervisors" and "bosses" in my organization) leave work at 3 p.m. on Thursdays for mandatory family time—to join in afternoon ball games and bonding activities that had been set up prior to my taking over Fort Hood but which were never truly enforced. I also declared that no soldier would be allowed to work weekends without my personal approval. (And guess how many soldiers were willing to seek approval from a general for *that?*)

I know there are CEOs all across the country laughing at the very idea of ever demanding that their employees leave early, shaking their heads at the ridiculous notion that a workday could end at 3 p.m. even one day a week without destroying productivity.

I'm here to tell you CEOs that you're just plain wrong.

This sweeping order not only resulted in a significant drop in incidences of domestic violence, divorce, and failed relationships, but Fort Hood, which held the dubious distinction of having the highest suicide rate of any base in the Army, exhibited the *lowest* suicide rates in the Army just a year later.

By guiding people toward better balance in their lives, morale went up. Productivity went up. We didn't lose anything. In fact, just the opposite. Work got done and then some. Our soldiers became more efficient, more productive, more effective during the course of the day, and we all enjoyed the benefits. Traffic accidents, which were rampant—we had traffic fatalities every fifteen to twenty days on base—nearly disappeared. At one point, we went 245 days without a single fatality, thanks to a broad spectrum of directives I put into place to improve work/life balance, and by insisting that platoon leaders (my "middle management," as it were) pay more attention to the personal safety of our soldiers at every level.

It's a documented example of "family first" policies that made a major difference in a lot of people's lives, including my own. I walked the walk. If I told my soldiers to be home for dinner by six o'clock, you'd better believe I was home for dinner by six myself. If I told them to leave at three o'clock on Thursdays, I left at three on Thursdays. And if I said, "We're not working on weekends," I wouldn't work on weekends. Period.

I did find myself getting up at four in the morning to work two and a half hours before heading into the office most days because I didn't want to sacrifice the time with my family the night before. So you do have to work hard as a leader—harder than anyone else on your team at times—but you don't have to sacrifice your family or anyone else's family time in order to do that.

My bold move resonated across the entire army, and a long-entrenched culture began to change almost overnight. In 2009, the *Austin American Statesman* wrote an article dubbing me "The Family First General," and I couldn't have been more proud.

You might be asking yourself, *What on Earth does that story have to do with leading "my company" or "my department" or "my university" or "my organization"?* It has to do with treating your subordinates, your workforce, your team—the individual members of whatever group it is that you're tasked with leading—as if they were your very own children. And that may sound like a lot of soft talk coming from a three-star general, but I hope you'll see by the end of this book that it's actually just about the toughest talk I could lay on you. I hope you'll learn that the only way you're going to get ahead, the only way you're going to get on course, the only way you're going to move your company forward, and the only way to move this country forward—in education, in business, in politics, in everything—is to live by one very important rule: Treat your people well, and they'll treat you well in return. I've followed that rule from life-or-death situations on the battlefield to nine-to-five obligations back home, and the results have always, always been positive.

Of the many examples of my personal leadership style I'll share in this book, one tenet that undergirds everything is that our people are our most important resource. If we don't take care of them, they won't have the ability to adapt. And what happens when you don't adapt? That's right: *You die.* Your organization dies. Your government dies. Your business dies. On the battlefield, your people themselves will die. Today in America, if we don't take care of our people first through the example of strong leadership, I'm afraid the very spirit that keeps this country thriving is going to die, too.

I don't mean to sound overly dramatic here, but in life, you worry about the things you love. And I love our nation. We've got some big problems, and I don't see a way out of these problems without strong leadership on our side.

Our leaders have to know that our people are what matter. When leaders forget that, I believe it is to our great peril.

I ask that you keep this in mind as we forge ahead. It's at the root of everything I have ever done as a leader. Everything I hope that you, the leaders of today and the leaders of tomorrow, will embrace for the sake of us all.

Part One

OPPORTUNITIES, NOT OBSTACLES

Have I not commanded you? Be strong and courageous.
Do not be afraid; do not be discouraged, for the Lord
your God will be with you wherever you go.
*—*Joshua 1:9

Obstacles are a part of life, and great leaders see obstacles for what they really are: opportunities. Nurturing your ability to see through obstacles is one key to becoming a great leader. The fact is, if you're not facing obstacles in your life and work, if you find yourself gliding along in your comfort zone all the time, you're probably working in the wrong place. Push harder. Look for opportunities to work outside your comfort zone. Face obstacles head on, find the strength to push through them, and you'll find that the rewards on the other side are almost always greater than you could have expected. It takes some strength and a whole lot of faith to push through sometimes. But do you know what it all comes down to? Your attitude. It's up to you to choose: Is this obstacle the thing that'll do you in? That'll shut you down? That'll stop you dead in your tracks? Or is this obstacle simply a challenge that's going to cause you to grow and learn, and become better at whatever it is you do?

I choose to see opportunities, not obstacles. What do you choose to see?

– 1 –

NO MONEY

Growing up as a kid in Hamilton, Ohio, potato soup was the highlight meal of my week.

Needless to say, my family had no money.

Our household included not only me, my mom, my dad, and my younger brother, but since Dad had been married previously, I had two half-brothers who were there sometimes as well—and, all together, we rarely had a nickel between us.

Like a lot of other parents in our small city, Mom and Dad both worked shift work at the paper mill: seven to three, three to eleven, or eleven to seven, day in and day out, and, despite working all those hours, neither of them brought home much of a paycheck. They provided for the family as best they could. I'm not complaining. I'm eternally grateful for their hard work, but there was simply nothing left over at the end of the week. That posed certain challenges. It didn't matter that things cost less then. It didn't matter that my parents could give me a dollar to run to the store for a half gallon of milk, a loaf of bread, and a pack of cigarettes, and I'd bring 'em back change. We were still barely scraping by.

It was clear to me by the age of thirteen that, if I wanted to have nice school clothes or have my own transportation or be able to go to

McDonald's with my buddies, Mom and Dad weren't going to hand me a ten-dollar bill and say, "Go have a nice time."

So, at thirteen, I went looking for work.

That was a pretty big turning point and a springboard into many life lessons learned. Even before that, I was ambitious. I worked on my cousin's dairy farm in Indiana, pulling in sixty cents an hour as a kid. But the first real job I found as a teenager was painting houses. There was a guy who worked with Mom at the paper mill who had a side business painting houses, inside and outside. So I threw myself into it and started putting money away for the things I wanted.

Over the next few years, I migrated from that to the restaurant business. I was a busboy and then a grill cook—like a lot of kids. And by the time I was a senior in high school, I was working as the assistant manager of a pet store in Hamilton.

Nobody ever said, "Hey, Rick, you gotta get a job." It was just clear to me that if I didn't get a job, I wasn't going to have what I wanted. And if I give my parents credit for anything, especially my mom, it's instilling this profound work ethic: Working hard is the right thing to do, and if you ever find yourself not working hard, then you're probably not in the right position.

There are people in life (and a lot of people in today's America) who would look at my thirteen-year-old self and see the whole situation as something negative. As if it were a burden that I had to get a job. But I didn't see it that way then, and I certainly don't see it that way now. The fact that my parents didn't have money and didn't hand me everything I wanted wasn't an obstacle. It was an opportunity—an opportunity of a lifetime, because it set me up for a lifetime of success.

When I got my first job, I got my first sense of independence. For the first time in my life, I wasn't relying on my mom or dad. I had my own money. I could buy my own clothes. I could go to McDonald's whenever I wanted without relying on anyone else's handouts. And when I turned sixteen, I bought my own motorcycle: a Yamaha 175 Enduro. That's how I got back and forth to school, and it's also how I got back and forth to work in the restaurant business.

Many years later, when I became a lieutenant in the Army, I read an article on career development that pointed to one very important trait of success: Do every job superbly. I already knew that firsthand because of my early work experience as a teenager, and because it was something my mom had taught me. *Whether you're a house painter, a dishwasher, a grill cook, or a lieutenant, do the best job you can, and you'll always be successful*, Mom used to tell me. Of course, the article also said that another aspect of success is to make sure people know that you're doing a good job: Be visible and widely known! That would get easier for me over time. I wasn't much of a people person early on. I was more of an introvert. But in time, I would grow to enjoy talking to people and getting to know everyone, no matter where I worked.

Seeing opportunities instead of obstacles is about having the right mindset. For me, beginning at age thirteen, part of that was a realization that your current set in life does not have to be permanent. You have a choice, and you can change whatever it is that's holding you back. You can make those changes with a positive attitude, and, as a result of that positive attitude, you can work through it. If you don't do that—and, unfortunately, I see this all the time—you can fall into a state of resignation: "It is what it is. It ain't gonna get any better than this." Think of the state of the nation these days and the overwhelming sense of resignation that's swept across America. People talk as if everything just is what it is: Unemployment is the way it is, the deficit's the way it is, governmental paralysis is the way it is, and there's nothing we can do about any of it.

That's letting the obstacle blur the opportunity.

I go back to Joshua 1:9 all the time: "Do not be afraid; do not be discouraged." That conviction and determined spirit alone gives me the strength and courage to plow on today. But I didn't have the Bible and those teachings in my life when I was thirteen years old. I didn't get that until I started going to church almost twenty years later. So where did I get that conviction and spirit from?

I think I got it from my mom. I love my dad, but he wasn't the nurturer. He was the guy with the belt. Mom was the nurturer: caring and loving, with an infectious laugh. Her name was Dorothy, but everyone called her Dotie. It was a fitting nickname because, in fact, she doted on my brother and me all the time. She doted on us so much that it was a major bone of contention between her and my dad. He would always complain that she was "trying to spoil those kids." Maybe she *was* trying to spoil us, by spending more time with us. Every year she would go into debt to buy us Christmas presents, and then we'd see her work even harder just to pay off that debt. Because of the extra time that she gave and the affection she showed, she has proven to be the most influential person in our lives.

I never saw my mom complain. The lot in life that she had was good enough for her—even if she knew it wasn't good enough for my brother or me. She wanted more for us, and she made that clear. To be fair, so did my dad.

My father, Calvin, graduated from the seventh grade, and that's as far as he got in school because he didn't think he needed any more than that. Mom graduated from the eleventh grade, so neither one of them were high school graduates. But Mom was the gal who always advocated that we needed to get straight A's if we wanted to get ahead in life. She pushed us in her kind and gentle fashion. Dad, on the other hand—if you didn't get straight A's, you had some explaining to do when you got home. It was that level of discipline with him: Even though he had only a seventh-grade education, he wouldn't have tolerated anything but the best from my brother and me.

It's funny to think about, but the roots of your upbringing run deep. There is something that happened there in Hamilton, Ohio, in all of those lessons and all of that pushing from my parents during my formative years that really carried me to where I am today. There was something in all of it that gave me the foundation of optimism—this steadfast belief that I could overcome obstacles and turn them into opportunities, every time.

Colin Powell says, "Optimism is a combat multiplier." I believe that's true. When you look at lists of famous people's quotations, especially famous leaders, you see a lot about optimism. Abraham Lincoln said, "A man is about as happy as he makes his mind up to be." I believe that's true, too.

As you're confronted with difficult circumstances, your outlook is everything. Your outlook is going to help you overcome the obstacles and turn them into opportunities. Every time. But you need to have a positive attitude—otherwise, you risk shutting down. Otherwise, you miss seeing the opportunity that's right there in front of you, or asking for advice that just might lead you to an opportunity you never knew existed.

– 2 –

BEAST BARRACKS

Getting over the "no-money" obstacle was pretty easy as a teen. I found work. I made money. Problem solved. But I was a junior in high school when that obstacle grew into a problem that I thought was wholly insurmountable: There was no way that my parents could ever afford to send me to college, and even though I was working, I knew in my heart there was no way I could ever afford to pay a bill as big as college tuition.

I was a good student. My parents saw to that, and I saw to it. I got all A's. It wasn't like I was a genius or anything. I just worked hard. I worked hard at whatever I did, be it schoolwork or house painting. But what good would that do me if I couldn't go to college? If I couldn't find a way to pay for school, I thought, I might wind up working at the paper mill, just like my parents, and I knew I didn't want to do that.

How on Earth could a kid go to college if he didn't have a way to pay for it?

Since my parents didn't have an answer, and my peers didn't have an answer, and I couldn't seem to come up with an answer myself, I went to see the guidance counselor at my high school. "Ma'am," I said, "I'm getting all A's, as you well know. I'm on the honor roll here, I'm in the National Honor Society, but my parents can't afford to send me to college. Is there any way I can still go to school?"

Her response? "How about a military academy?" I had no idea what a military academy was, so I said, "What's that?" Her answer just about blew my mind: "Well, that's a place where they *pay you* to go to school."

No one had ever told me that such a place existed! Ever since the inkling of an idea of a college education was put into my head, I had been told that it was something that cost a whole lot of money. All it took was asking the right question to the right person with the right knowledge, and the whole notion that college wasn't affordable was no longer a concern. "Okay!" I said. "Let's try that!"

So basically, the fact that I didn't have any money suddenly turned into another amazing opportunity: Not only could I still go to school, but there were schools out there that would pay me to go! Talk about a win-win situation.

Of course, my interest in going to a military academy had nothing to do with an aspiration to join the military.

My dad was a private E1 in 1945, when he was drafted into the Army—that's the lowest rank on the totem pole, so to speak—and he was a private E1 when he was kicked out of the Army two years later, in 1947. He was the world's worst soldier, a fact he's very proud of to this day. So the inspiration certainly didn't come from him.

To tell the truth, I didn't really think a whole lot about the military part of the equation. All I saw was the possibility of my getting a free college education, and the unbelievably big bonus of getting paid for the chance to go get it.

That guidance counselor's advice marked a significant moment in my life, that's for sure. She also said I should look at Reserve Officer Training Corps (ROTC) scholarships to non-military schools because they could provide for a four-year education as well. That was a whole other way to get the education I desired with no money out of my own pocket. I could hardly believe it! So I applied for and received a four-year ROTC scholarship and wound up applying to ten different schools that would've taken it. I went to visit only one, though: Ohio State. That school seemed really appealing, and I thought in my heart that's where I was going to go and put that scholarship to good use. But this was 1972. If you recall, in 1972, people didn't like the United States military very much. On the heels of Vietnam and the incident at Kent State, I stepped foot onto the campus in Columbus and quickly realized that if I went there in uniform, I was sure to be a persona non grata. So I said to myself, "I might as well go to the military academy, where everybody's the same and nobody's throwing stuff at you!" The military academy was the clear choice.

I went through the application process to both West Point and Annapolis. I got my West Point acceptance on a Tuesday and my Annapolis acceptance on a Wednesday. The only reason I chose West Point was that its acceptance letter came in first. The postman determined my fate.

"West Point? Are you crazy?!" my dad said when I told him that I was accepted there. "That's the Army!"

By that point, there was no way he could have deterred me. My independence had pretty much been established. So I ignored his warnings about how tough it would be and how much I would hate it, and I packed my bags with no idea what lay ahead.

Money was still an issue, of course. I had to buy a pair of black shoes before they'd let me step foot onto that campus. And I had to have $300 set aside in order to open the account where the Army would deposit my pay while I was in school. Luckily, my grandmother lent me the money for both. There's nothing like family to back you up when you're first stepping foot into the world.

I still remember vividly the sight of Coco, our family poodle, looking out the door after me as I got into the car and drove off to the airport. I was scared to death that day. I had no idea what I was getting into. Everything I was fixing to do was going to be a first for me. I cried when the car pulled away from the house, and I cried when I got on the plane. This young, green kid flew to New York City all by himself, and I cried when the plane landed! I had rarely been out of the state of Ohio, and there I was plopped in that sprawling metropolis with no one to guide me. I was literally the country boy in the big city. All the new recruits had to stay at a particular hotel, and after I checked in, I basically spent the night by myself. I'm an introvert by nature, and I was particularly introverted early in my adult life, so it was very difficult for me to talk to strangers or to make new friends. I remember going to see a James Bond movie instead of trying to get to know anyone.

It was July 2, 1973.

Representatives from West Point came and picked us all up the next morning and drove us down to that beautiful high-ground campus overlooking the Hudson River. But as soon as we got off the bus, the yelling, screaming, harassment, and drills began. I vividly remember thinking that everything at West Point was uphill, because they made you run all the time, and it seemed like everywhere you ran was uphill—there wasn't a downhill stretch to be found!

Even something as simple as eating dinner was a challenge. The way West Point is organized, the mess hall has these ten-man tables. The upperclassmen are all at the head of the table, and at the foot are three plebes (that's what freshman were called). One plebe is designated the "cold beverage corporal." He's required to know what everybody wants to drink. One is the dessert cutter. And one guy is there just to take all the wrath of the upperclassmen. The long and short of it was that those three plebes—of which I was one—never got a chance to eat. I would leave that mess hall just about starving every single day.

If you've ever seen a movie depicting the sort of harassment that goes on in these places, you have some idea of what I'm talking about here. But believe me, you have no idea what it feels like to be chastised and yelled and screamed at for hours and hours for days on end until it actually happens to you. And it is miserable.

There's a name for this six-week indoctrination period at West Point. They call it "Beast Barracks," and there couldn't be a more fitting name. I think I went in weighing 175 pounds, and, six weeks later, I was down to 145. And remember, I had no idea what I was getting into before I got there. I hadn't prepared for that experience at all. I only went there because I couldn't afford to go to any other college. Nobody had prepared me for this extreme entry into adulthood.

Three weeks into it, I felt defeated. I thought, *This is not going to work for me.* I was completely overwhelmed.

I called my dad and said, "You were right. I can't do this. The Army's not for me. I'm coming home."

Guess what my dad's reply was?

"Oh, yeah?" he said. "Where are you gonna sleep?"

Tough love.

I didn't appreciate it much at the time, as you might imagine. But that tough love was exactly what I needed in that moment. The fact is, the Army wanted to break me down. And they had. They did a good job! They wanted to break me down to build me up, instill a discipline that would be lifelong and unforgettable. We don't do that so much anymore in the Army because, candidly, that was just pure, unadulterated harassment. We don't want our officers to treat their subordinates that poorly in the field, so why were we treating them like that at the academy? But good, bad, or indifferent, Beast Barracks was a part of what it took to get to the glorious education that awaited me on the other side. Only I was so broken down that I nearly succumbed to the obstacle, right there. I nearly gave in. I was overwhelmed by the negativity of it all. I couldn't see the bigger picture, couldn't see the opportunity that getting through this harassment and pain and suffering was going to bring my way. I needed my dad's tough love, his refusal to let me quit, in order to get through it.

"You started it—you're going to finish it." That was his message. So I hung up the phone and went back to Beast Barracks. After another three weeks of hell, it was over. Then it started to feel more like school—a really good school with fantastic teachers and students who wanted to succeed. Sophomore year was called our Yearling Year, and by the time I was halfway through it, I started to hit my stride. I went back to what I knew: Hard work yields results. I did all of the things that cadets were supposed to be doing. I saw the rewards of that hard work in my grades. I became a Star Man, which meant I was in the top 5 percent of my class. I was also selected to command one of four regiments at the school. Becoming a regimental commander is one of the highest achievements at the academy! And before long, I found myself truly enjoying my time at West Point.

If I had given up, if I had given in to the obstacles they threw at me in those first six weeks, I never would have found that sense of enjoyment. I never would have discovered the passion for leadership that would launch me into a thirty-five-year career. It was a great lesson in the power of commitment.

Applying that sort of tough love to myself is something that would take years to master. Heck, I still haven't mastered it! There have been plenty of other times in my career when I wanted to quit—I'll talk about those in upcoming chapters. But not giving in, not giving up, and following through until you get to the other side of the challenge are important first steps in learning how to lead—not to mention learning how to adapt and move forward when the going gets tough.

Resist the urge to quit—and do your best to instill that resistance in those working under you. You won't regret it. There's opportunity in the obstacle. Every time. You just have to work a little harder to see it.

REMINDER

Focus on opportunities, not obstacles.

★ ★ ★

"It can be done!"

★ ★ ★

− 3 −

SPEAK UP!

I graduated from West Point as an engineer officer. In broad terms, the Army defines an engineer officer as someone who provides support for all of the engineering duties in the Army. That support could come in the form of construction (roads, bases, bridges), conducting reconnaissance and demolition duties, or in training the force with new engineering technologies. Any way you look at it, it was all about one word: support. Engineers are always answering to someone else. Engineers are always playing a supporting role. And I knew very early on that wasn't the role I wanted to play. But this was the Army. You do what you're told. You follow orders. So I settled in to my new home in Fort Hood, Texas—the largest Army base in the free world—and got to working.

A couple of years into this new career of mine, the Army looked at what a hard worker I was and decided to promote me. They made me a first lieutenant, appointing me the adjutant for the Seventeenth Engineer Battalion. That may sound like a good thing on paper, but to put it bluntly, the job sucked. I was the perpetual middleman, the cleanup guy, the go-to secretary who solved everybody else's problems. I would show up to work with an agenda, and, within two minutes, the phone would ring, and that entire agenda would be blown to bits.

Every day I wound up faced with somebody else's crisis and had to spend all day chasing my tail trying to deal with that crisis.

I got so fed up, I finally went to the battalion commander and told him straight up, "I'm going to have to resign my commission. This is not what I want to do."

What *did* I want to do? I wanted to lead. I wanted to be a company commander. I knew I had what it took to be a leader, and yet the Army was burying me in this job I couldn't stand. I was so fed up with the whole thing, I was fully prepared to quit and go find another career.

My battalion commander sensed just how serious I was, and since he didn't want to see me leave, he suggested I try something else. "How about you go interview to be Doc Bahnsen's aide?" he said.

Doc Bahnsen was a legend. He was serving as the one-star assistant division commander of the Second Armored Division at the time. But it's his history that made soldiers stand a little taller when he walked into a room. This is a guy they wrote a book about with the rather bold title *American Warrior*. He's a man who won a distinguished service cross and five silver stars in Vietnam, who commanded a cavalry squadron when he was just a major—you're supposed to be a lieutenant colonel to do that. He was about as intimidating as a guy could be, but he seemed like the kind of leader I could learn from. *Being an aide is better than being the adjutant,* I thought, so I decided to interview, even though I still had a great big chip on my shoulder.

I walked into Bahnsen's office. "Lieutenant Lynch reporting," I said.

He cut to the chase: "What are you here for, Lieutenant?"

"Sir, I'm here to interview to be your aide."

"Why do you want to be my aide?" he asked.

Here's where I decided to show a little courage—and perhaps a bit of brash stupidity. "I don't want to be your aide," I told him. "I just don't want to be the adjutant anymore. What I really want to be is a company commander."

It's hard to describe just how angry General Bahnsen turned in that moment. Nobody talked to Doc Bahnsen that way. Nobody! Let alone some lowly lieutenant. "Get out of my office!" he yelled.

Well . . . that's that, I figured. *My career is over.*

As I made the long walk back from division headquarters to battalion headquarters, I started thinking seriously about what I could do to make a living after I left the Army. I was absolutely positive I had just thrown any chance of staying in the Army right out the proverbial window.

I couldn't have been more wrong.

While I was busy beating myself up for my behavior, General Bahnsen picked up a phone and called my battalion commander—not to have me punished, but to give him an order that would change my role in the Army from that day forward. An order that would change everything for me, which my rather dumbfounded battalion commander would relay to me the moment I stepped foot back into his office.

You know what Doc Bahnsen ordered the battalion commander to do after our short, blunt, rather heated meeting? "Make Lynch a company commander."

I was shocked! "Why would he do that?" I asked.

And the battalion commander told me exactly what Bahnsen told him: "Anybody with that much fire and passion deserves to be a company commander."

I signed for my first company the next day. In a matter of seconds, Doc Bahnsen had made me the leader I wanted to be all along. All because I spoke up and spoke my mind.

If that event had not taken place, I would not be where I am today.

SPEAK FROM THE HEART

Sometimes you have to exhibit the moral courage, the personal courage to do what you think is right, and to *say* what you think is right—even if you run the risk of getting into some trouble for saying it.

If you're not happy with your circumstances, don't just accept them—go out there, and try to change them.

Far too often, people have a sense of resignation: *This is my lot in life, and it's as good as it's going to get, and that's it.* You cannot do that. You can't. Doc Bahnsen saw something in me because of what I did in his office. And two years later, after I commanded the company he put me in charge of for two full years, I reported to General Bahnsen's office once again—this time as a captain.

"What are you here for, Lynch?" he asked.

"Sir, I've commanded my company now for two years. I've been at Fort Hood for four and a half years, even though it's normally only a three-year tour, and the Army's saying I've got to go take another posting somewhere else."

That's just the way things work in the Army. They move you around. They change your position. That's the rule. And the thing a lot of strong leaders know is that rules don't always apply to every individual in an organization. Sometimes rules have to be broken, or at least bent, in service to a greater good.

Bahnsen had grown to like me in those last two years.

He said, "You're not leaving here. I'm going to put you in another company."

I watched him make one phone call after another until he finally got hold of the two-star general and got permission for me to stay.

So I signed to take the reins of my second company and wound up staying at Fort Hood, Texas, for an unprecedented six years—all because a guy like Doc Bahnsen said, "I'm not going to take 'no' for an answer. I know what's right for this guy. He needs to be a company commander again, so we're going to allow him to command for three continuous years."

Just so you understand what a bending of the rules that was, a company commander served an average of only twelve months total in that position back at that time in the Army. So Bahnsen's actions tripled my time in that role.

And it all traces back to my bold but truthful words: "I don't want to be your aide." As I look back on that moment, I don't think it was a case of my being young and stupid. Not at all. I see it as something that was part and parcel of my desire to become a leader: the ability to show professional, personal, and moral courage.

I think that's how Doc Bahnsen saw it, too. And that was a valuable lesson: If you find yourself in an uncomfortable circumstance, don't just throw up your hands and say, "It is what it is." Figure out a way to work your way out of it. You don't have to be rude to do it, but you can state your mind in a thoughtful, tactful fashion. However you do it, it's certainly better than just throwing up your hands because nobody's listening. You've got to keep trying. You've got to find the right person to talk to. I had been telling everyone what I wanted to do all along. I had been saying, continuously, to anyone who would listen, that I wanted to be a company commander.

General Doc Bahnsen turned out to be the guy who was willing not only to listen but also to take action to do something about it.

If I hadn't spoken my mind, if I hadn't told him what I really wanted to do, there is just no way I would have gotten what I wanted. If I hadn't spoken up, I never would have found the opportunity that existed in the obstacle of that terrible job the Army had stuck me with. Turns out, having that awful job of adjutant drove me to bold action—to taking one big and necessary step toward being the leader I wanted to be.

Looking back on that period, what I really learned by doing and watching was that, in order to be a successful company commander, I needed to be aggressive, I needed to be enthusiastic, I needed to be strong but fair, and I certainly shouldn't take "No" for an answer. All of those lessons would apply in all sorts of areas as I moved forward.

Of course, I was still an engineer in the Army, which meant I was still playing a supporting role, by definition. I'd have to keep fighting to get to a position of true leadership, which was an uphill battle against all kinds of forces that wanted me to stay where I was.

Winning that battle would take me a few more years.

– 4 –

SAYING "NO" TO "NO"

Sarah Cockerham was the recreation supervisor for the city of Killeen, Texas, when I first laid eyes on her in the spring of 1982. I have a passion for sports, and she was the woman they said I had to go see in order to register my softball team in the local league. People say love at first sight is a myth, but it sure isn't a myth to me. It was clear to me in that initial encounter that I could spend the rest of my life with this woman.

There was just one problem: She wouldn't go out with me!

It turned out that Sarah came from a military family. Her dad was a master sergeant when he left the Army, and her mom was a sergeant E-5 in the Women's Army Corps. Sarah had grown up in Texas since she'd been six months old, but her four older brothers and one older sister had moved all over the world with the military. It was tough, and they always let her know what a tough life it was. And the one thing her dad told her throughout her entire life, and especially right before he died at age fifty, when Sarah was just twelve, was, "Whatever you do, don't date a GI!"

Getting over that obstacle was pretty difficult, but I was getting pretty good at not taking "No" for an answer. I figured the same lessons would apply in my personal life, but it would just take some

23

persistence. Boy, did it ever. I spent $690 on flowers trying to get Sarah to go out with me! It was a nonstop effort of flowers and phone calls until finally she agreed to come to my house for a Fourth of July party. It wasn't even a real date. My roommate and a whole bunch of other people were there, but standing next to Sarah, watching the fireworks that night, I remember thinking, *This feels right.*

My efforts were worth every penny. Sarah finally relented, and we went out on some real dates. I fell in love with everything she is, and she made me feel love like I'd never known. That October, I took her down to South Padre Island. Everything seems right to me when I'm at the beach, so I decided that was the place. We were standing knee-deep in the ocean when I pulled a ring out of my swim trunks and asked her to marry me. She said "Yes."

We got married that December 4, and life changed for me in that instant. Sarah became my top priority. My career was going great. I was in command of my second company there at Fort Hood. But every decision I made from that point forward would require her counsel, and everything I did would take her and our marriage into consideration first.

That change in priorities would grow even deeper the following October, when our daughter, Susan, was born. From my perspective, nothing mattered more than my family at that point. Nothing. Sarah and Susan would always come first. Before me. Before my career. Before everything. I was beginning to set the priorities in my life that would provide a solid foundation for me to stand on once I became a leader.

Of course, I still had quite a ways to go.

After six years at Fort Hood, I found out the hard way that I had extended my welcome just as far as it could be extended. The Army doesn't like its soldiers to stay in one place, and it was time for me to move on. I tried to preempt some placement I didn't want by call-ing the engineer branch and telling them how thrilled I would be to command another company. But the Army wasn't having it. They wanted to put me into a new role. And the role they decided to put me in was that of an Army recruiter in Dayton, Ohio.

I don't mean any disrespect to the powers that be, but that seemed like a really, really dumb decision for my career—and an even worse decision for my family. We were an Army family. We were prepared to go wherever the Army sent us. We just didn't want to go to Dayton.

My apologies to the great people of Dayton, Ohio, but the idea of moving my family to that Midwestern city so I could spend my time as a recruiter sounded like a death sentence to my twenty-something ears. I offered to move almost anywhere else. Heck, I was willing to go overseas if I had to in order to command another company or take on a more interesting, leadership-oriented role. But the Army simply said, "No." It was time to move on.

I had established a pretty good track record by this point for not taking "No" for an answer in any part of my life. So I kept on asking, over and over. I basically begged the Army for another option—any option—until they finally presented me with a choice: "Well," they said, "instead of being a recruiter, you could go study this thing called robotics at either Stanford, MIT (the Massachusetts Institute of Technology), or Carnegie Mellon."

What was that? I could hardly believe my ears. After listening to my repeated pleas, the Army finally told me they would be willing to put me back in school—to send me to get my graduate degree instead of sending me off to be a recruiter. They were very interested in pursuing new technologies at that time, and the fact that I was an engineer officer—a role I didn't want to be in, don't forget—put me in the perfect position to do that. Obstacles/opportunities. You gettin' this?

I put down the phone, picked up the dictionary, and looked up *robotics*. Like a lot of people who grew up in the 1970s, the only robots

I'd ever really heard of were the science-fiction kind. But what "robotics" meant as a field of study was to pursue the use of machines to perform tasks traditionally performed by human beings—especially repetitive tasks or tasks that needed to be performed in areas that could be hazardous, of which there were plenty to be found in the Army. It sounded intriguing.

The idea of going back to school and being a student again hadn't really occurred to me at that stage of life, but I thought it would be a whole lot better than becoming a recruiter in Dayton, Ohio. Sarah agreed! So I went ahead and applied to MIT.

I was accepted six weeks later. I moved my young family up to Boston, Massachusetts, which is one heck of a far cry from Texas both in terms of culture and weather. But my wife saw the opportunity that lay before me and fully supported the move.

The school seemed pretty excited to have military officers in their midst. First of all, they didn't have to worry about financial assistance. The Army was paying our tuition. And second, they knew they could count on the fact that officers do a pretty good job at completing assigned tasks (which corporate America knows a little something about, too. That's why there are so many ex-military officers serving in mid- to top-tier management positions at corporations all over this country). MIT was happy to have me, and, at first, I was happy to be there.

There was just one problem: I had no idea how tough MIT was going to be.

I was used to being a big man on campus at West Point, at the very top of the class academically, and I received all A's in high school. But I got to MIT, and the highest grade I managed to eke out of a test was a 52. I was always the lowest in the class. The bottom. The pits. It wasn't that I wasn't working hard. I was! It was just that I was hanging out with all of these professional students, and I couldn't seem to hold a candle to their performance in that world.

Remember all of the kids in your high school who wore pocket protectors and sat in the front row? They went to MIT. Academics meant everything to these students. They didn't do anything else. Never went anywhere else. In fact, I was convinced they only came out at night. They were like moles! And, oh, by the way, most of them had no idea about life outside of the university. Here I was with a wife and a seven-month-old daughter, having made it through Beast Barracks and West Point and six years at Fort Hood, while most of these students had no life experience outside of school and dorm life. But every one of them crushed me in the classroom.

It was such an ego blast to me after working so very hard. In fact, the one time I got a 52 on a test, my advisor accused me of cheating. He didn't think I was capable of doing even *that* well. I hadn't cheated, of course. What I had done was gone to the library and reviewed all of the previous tests in that subject, written down all of the answers, and memorized as many as I could. I worked hard to find a solution to the problem of continuously failing tests. And even then, it resulted in only a 52 out of 100.

To say I was discouraged is an understatement. Every time I'd get a test back, I'd take the posture of giving up.

"I quit," I'd say to myself. "I'm going to the ROTC department and calling the Army. I just quit."

Of course, I'd usually walk by a pay phone on the way to the ROTC offices, and since Sarah had followed me up there, I felt the need to tell her I was gonna quit before I went ahead and actually did it.

Lo and behold, each and every time I called her to tell her I was quitting, she'd say, "No, you're not. You brought me all the way up to Boston, I'm freezing cold, and you're gonna finish!"

Tough love. Just when I needed it most.

Both times in my early life that I was tempted to give in to the obstacle, someone else came through and pushed me forward. First it was my dad, with his tough love at West Point. And then there was Sarah, reminding me of my commitment at MIT. My dad and Sarah, telling me, "You're not gonna quit." And I'm grateful to both of them.

Sometimes we need that extra push in life. Sometimes we need that helping hand. You need to be willing to listen to the people you trust, to accept the help that they're offering in your times of struggle, even if they're telling you something you don't necessarily want to hear.

Many years later I participated in the Bud Light series of triathlons—a combination one-mile open-water swim, twenty-six-mile bike race, and six-mile run. And in each of those grueling races, my training partner was the one person who kept me from quitting. Believe me, no matter how passionate you are about sports—and I am—in the middle of that test of human endurance, you want to quit! In fact, I almost drowned during the Chicago triathlon. There were six-foot waves, and the water was 60 degrees. It was miserable. But even in those conditions, my training partner got me through. He pushed me to finish the race. It was a fitting metaphor for facing down obstacles in my life, for sure.

Whenever I've come up against an obstacle, it seems, somebody's been there to help me over the hurdle. I think God puts those people in your life for a reason. And as life has proceeded, I've helped plenty of people over their own hurdles in return. That's just the way it works. The results of those extra-effort, getting-over-the-hurdle moments in life are filled with opportunity. Almost by definition.

Just as West Point turned from Beast Barracks into the launching pad for my entire Army career, enduring the low grades and repeated blows to my self-esteem in order to complete my master's degree in robotics at MIT would turn into an immeasurably large opportunity for me as well. Robotics was the wave of the future. My knowledge in the field would separate me from my peers in the Army and push me to the forefront—not only during my Army career, but in my post-Army career as well, as I moved on to consult for major robotics-centered technology firms. My knowledge and expertise in that field, which would be bolstered through years of further experience in the Army itself, would also lead to my landing a job at the University of Texas at Arlington, where I was appointed to the position of executive director of the University at Arlington Research Institute, just a few months after my retirement from the Army in January of 2012.

When I trace back to the roots of my current position in life, it boils down to this: I listened to my wife. I didn't quit. And—oh, yeah—I refused to sit back and take "No" for an answer when I knew that answer wasn't what I wanted or needed in my life and/or career.

– 5 –

CHANGING CAREER PATHS

Soon after graduating from West Point, in year three of serving in the Army, I started pushing to transfer to a different branch. It was clear as day to me that as an engineer officer, I would spend my entire career working for somebody else. That's not what I wanted. I wanted to be the guy in charge. The only way to do that, as far as I could see, was to branch-transfer. My first choice was to be an armor officer, but nobody wanted me to branch-transfer.

"No. You can't do that" was the answer from on high. "There's a shortage of engineer officers. We don't need you as an armor officer."

For nine years after West Point, I accepted "No" for an answer. But I never stopped asking for it. I never gave up trying.

People tend to want to keep you in a box. Whatever role you started out in, somehow, structured organizations of all shapes and sizes—from the Army to colleges to big corporations—want to keep you there. If you're on a certain career path, there's this inherent pressure built into the system to keep you on that career path whether you like it or not. I've never understood where that comes from, and I've simply never stood for that behavior. In life, we need to choose our paths to follow our call, to go after whatever it is we want to go after, or we're never going to be fulfilled.

That belief was driven home for me even further prior to wrapping up my studies at MIT. In August of 1985, my wife gave birth to our beautiful son, Lucas. Just as my marriage had refocused my purpose in life, and just as the birth of my daughter, Susan, had refocused my priorities, the birth of Lucas sharpened my desire to do right by my family first, in everything I did. As you know, I didn't have much of anything growing up. I wanted to give my kids so much more than my parents gave me. Not the material things, so much, but the backbone and guidance they needed to succeed in life, whatever they chose to do.

After graduating with my master's degree from MIT, I was assigned to and stationed at Fort Knox, Kentucky. I remember driving down there from Boston in a little Toyota Corolla with my wife, our young daughter, a six-week-old son, and a mini-dachshund named "Squirt," all stuffed into that compact car. We slept on the floor of our new home the first night because we didn't have any furniture!

It was there at Fort Knox where I was given a new title: Robotics Project Officer. I was still an engineer. I still worked for the engineer branch of the Army. It was a forward-thinking position, on the cutting edge of new technologies in the field that would slowly change the way we do business on the battlefield—looking ahead to the unmanned vehicles and drones that are in operation all over the world as part of our armed forces today. But the title did little to put me on the leadership track I wanted to be on. And now, for my family as much as for me, I wanted to be on that track more than ever.

Luckily for me, I went to work for a major general named Tom Tait—a man who would become one of my mentors. Tom was a guy who recognized my strengths and abilities, and was willing to go the extra mile for me.

One day General Tait and I flew from Fort Knox over to Fort Monroe, Virginia, to brief another general on an armored cavalry program. I presented the standard overview that you might present in a boardroom, to which the other general commented, "Hey, that's a great brief."

He then turned to General Tait and said, "Why do you have an engineer officer working this?"

General Tait said right then and there, "I can fix that."

On the flight home, Tait turned to me and said the words I'd almost given up hope of ever hearing: "You want to be an armor officer?"

"Sir, I've been trying to be an armor officer for *nine years*," I said.

We landed. He picked up the phone. He called the armor branch chief in Washington, DC, and said, "If you don't get Lynch branch-transferred, you're fired."

A lot of wheels went into motion, and the next thing I knew, the branch transfer was approved. Just like that, I was an armor officer. For all those years, I had kept the faith and continued to strive. I felt like I was finally getting my reward. It brought to mind Matthew 25:21: "His master replied, 'Well done, good and faithful servant! You have been faithful with a few things; I will put you in charge of many things. Come and share your master's happiness!'"

The thing is that everybody—and I mean *everybody*—told me not to make that transfer. Let me explain why everyone was so against it.

I was an established engineer officer. In general terms, the Army promotes you according to years of service. But we have a system in place that dictates that, if there's someone who's clearly a cut above, we can select him or her for promotion early. My entire career, I was selected for promotion early. By the end of my career, I was one of the youngest three-star generals in the Army because I worked hard, prayed hard, and got promoted early time and time again.

The fact that I was already nine years in as an engineer officer meant I was pretty far along on a well-established career path in that branch, so everybody assumed that if I branch-transferred, my career would be over. That's in-the-box thinking at its worst. The general consensus was that, by jumping over to armor, I would be erasing my nine years of career progress and starting from scratch. "They're never going to let you command a tank battalion because you were never a tank-platoon leader or a tank-company commander," they said. "You just don't have the experience!" That was a risk I was willing to take.

Pushing outside the box was certainly going to present more obstacles, but I expected those obstacles to soon become opportunities. My first assignment as an armor officer was in the Eleventh Armored Cavalry Regiment. The regimental commander there, knowing I'd never been a tank-platoon leader or tank-company commander, decided to make me the regimental logistics officer. That's purely a support position, not operations. This felt like a huge step backward.

I got why the assignment was made. All of my peers in the armor branch had been tank-platoon leaders and tank-company commanders. They had spent ten years working their way up to the position. And here I was, this new guy putting on armor brass without any kind of professional background. I could have easily said right there, "Okay. I didn't branch-transfer so I could be the guy counting toilet paper. That's not what I came to do." I could've quit. But I had learned a thing or two about not quitting by that time in my life, and I didn't need an outside voice to tell me to stick with it. Just like it had been at MIT and West Point, I knew that this was only an obstacle. Nothing more. Rather than just give up, I said to myself, "Okay, I'm going to work my way through this."

I did the best I could. I followed my own rules: I worked hard, just like my mom taught me, and I didn't complain; I made myself widely known, so that the higher-ups knew me and could see what a good job I was doing. And it worked. Just three months later, I was selected to become an operations officer for the First Squadron, Eleventh Armored Cavalry Regiment. Operations officer was just where I wanted to be as a field officer. Much like the chief operating officer at a corporation, the operations officer generally runs the unit. They plan activities, allocate resources, and maneuver forces on the battlefield. It is the job all aspiring commanders want in order to prepare them for command. It was perfect.

My wife made a pretty big move in her own career while we were stationed in Kentucky. She decided to go back to school, eventually earning her master's degree in education from the University of Louisville. And she did this while juggling a home, two kids, a dog, and me! If that's not proof that you can get it all done and get what you want if you're willing to put in the hard work and dedication, I don't know what is. Sarah never fails to amaze and impress me.

We both made bold moves, and those moves paid off.

Because I was moved into the armor branch, I would be stationed in Germany when the Warsaw Pact crumbled and the wall came tumbling down. I was there in the Fulda Gap when the East Germans came into West Germany and experienced freedom for the first time. I witnessed that great moment in history firsthand because I had made the decision to branch-transfer from engineer to armor and accept that risk. I made that decision even though the Army and everyone I knew threw all of those obstacles up and said, "You ought not do it!"

My branch-transfer decision was not only a success, it was also the jump-start I needed to set me on the path toward a successful career that would culminate in my becoming a general.

If I had given in to that pressure and not followed my heart, I never would have moved up to become a flag officer, I never would have been a division commander or corps commander. It was a life-changing experience. All because of this guy named Tom Tait, who had the audacity to pick up the phone and say, "You're branch-transferring Lynch, or you're fired."

Could my career have come to a screeching halt after I made that transfer? Yes! In some ways, making that branch-transfer was the ultimate risk. But I knew that it was something I needed to do, and I was determined not to let that transfer stop the momentum of my career, no matter what. I simply wasn't comfortable being the support guy. I knew that. I wanted to be the guy in charge. I knew I didn't like to be the guy in the back of the room who hoped nobody would ask him a question. That wasn't me. I wanted to be the guy in the front of the room. The guy who asks the questions, and whom people would ask questions *of*.

Eventually I would get a chance to do that on a far bigger scale than I ever could have imagined.

– 6 –

THE DIGITAL BATTLEFIELD

The speed at which technology advances gets faster and faster each year. It's a daunting thing when you think about it. Our kids and grandkids today take for granted the kind of technological advances that were pure science fiction back when you or I were in high school and college! When Epcot Center opened at Disney World in Florida, in 1982, they had "futuristic" displays that incorporated "video phones" from some distant time when we might actually be able to see the person we're talking to on a big television-like screen in addition to hearing them. Today it seems like every six-year-old has been on Skype on their mommy's tablet or notebook, or FaceTimed their grandma on the iPhone in the palm of their hand—as naturally as if it's always been there. Heck, those cell phones themselves, those handheld wireless communication devices that we all carry around and curse about when the signal drops, the very thought of their existence was equated with spaceships and far-out planets on *Star Trek* as recently as the 1970s. We've already eclipsed that sci-fi handheld wireless communicator vision with smartphones, high-speed wireless Internet connections, and who knows what'll come next?

Technology flies. The best leaders not only embrace that fact, but jump right into the pilot's seat during the test-flight stage of any new technology that might benefit their organization and stay far ahead of the competition—even if that means taking some pretty big risks along the way.

Of course, when it comes to adopting technology or just about anything else that's "new," any leader or forward-thinking employee at any company in America can tell you this fact: The hardest thing about getting a new idea *in* is getting the old idea *out*.

Back in the mid-1990s, the Army decided to create a digital brigade, the 1st Brigade, 4th Infantry Division. Because of my background at MIT, I had established myself as a leader who was comfortable using new technology. So the Army decided to make me the commander of that brigade.

What the Army realized was that we were struggling on the battlefield. We weren't even at war then, but we were using this area at the National Training Center in Barstow, California, to conduct military training and explore the complexities of a potential battle with the Soviet Union or anyone else in the modern era. This was 1997. And one of the problems we had on the battlefield, especially in a place like the Mojave Desert (which was a pretty good approximation of what we'd find on the sands of Iraq a decade later), is that it was pretty easy to get lost. We'd be out there fighting, and we didn't know where we were.

Now, I know there are plenty of old-school military guys who will puff up their chests and tell you they always had their bearings, but it just wasn't true. There were battlefields throughout history, let alone in those war-game scenarios, where we didn't know where we were, we didn't know where our buddies were, and we sure as heck had no stinking clue where the enemy was.

We'd have these formations: If you're a tank-platoon leader, you've got four tanks; if you're a tank-company commander, you've got ten tanks; if you're a battalion commander, you've got forty-five tanks, and in the heat of battle, you'd lose track of who went where. So we decided to use digitization as an opportunity to promote "situational awareness," which we defined as knowing where you are, knowing where your buddies are, and knowing (at least approximately) where the enemy is.

That all started in the mid-1990s, and they tested this in one experimental brigade—the brigade that I commanded.

The biggest obstacle to this whole thing working was that nobody wanted to give up their maps. Nobody wanted to throw out the way it *used to* be in anticipation of how it *could* be. I wound up in a situation where there were more people watching me with clipboards in their hands, taking notes about all the things that didn't work, than there were people working for me. It was so brand-spanking-new, everyone was nervous and just looking for any reason to give up and stick to the way things had been. But there were those of us who knew what the future might hold, and we were just trying to figure it all out. We didn't know if it would work, or how it would work, but we knew the world was changing—and we wanted to be on the forefront of that change.

Technology's a tricky animal. I remember one time as a full colonel, I was doing a major training exercise with this brigade, and the corps commander, a three-star general, came walking in and said, "Rick, brief me on your situation." Right then, in that moment, everything stopped working. I call it Murphy's Law of Technology: It's not *if* the technology's going to fail, but *when* it's going to fail, and it *always* fails at the worst possible time. Since it was fairly early on in the development of this new tracking technology, I didn't have any backup system in place, which meant I stood there looking pretty silly to the corps commander. I learned the hard way that I needed an analog backup to the digital systems we were introducing, because those digital systems were occasionally going to break down.

Nowadays, when everybody's got GPS devices in their cars and on their smartphones, this seems like pretty simple stuff. But we put systems on all of our vehicles that allowed us not only to track them from a central location but also allowed those systems to talk to each other and talk to headquarters. I could look at a digital screen and see where everybody was, and everybody on the battlefield could determine where everybody else was, too. You can imagine how many lives that could be saved just by avoiding friendly fire situations alone. We also had reporting mechanisms in place so we could report where the enemy was, and then we used algorithms to extract where the enemy was going to be at any given time.

Back in 1997, this was a big deal. Most homes that had Internet service were still using dial-up connections, and Internet providers were trying to sell customers on higher bandwidth. It could easily take fifteen minutes to load a single high-quality digital photo onto the screen on your desktop. And here we were playing real-time digital warfare in the desert in California. It was awesome!

Fast-forward six or seven years beyond this trial-and-error stuff, and we actually had situational dominance in Iraq—situational dominance being "situational awareness" combined with "situational understanding." It allowed us to win, to reduce casualties, and more.

The digital brigade was a clear example of an opportunity, not an obstacle. But not everyone felt that way, and thankfully those of us who did feel that way prevailed. If we'd have looked at the early tests and just said, "This is too hard. These systems aren't working, and it ain't worth the effort," then we wouldn't be as dominant on the battlefield as we are today. The art of applying advanced technology to improve your capability is not always easy and not always clear, especially since it always continues to evolve. But it's a necessary part of adaptation in the modern world and continues to be of paramount importance in the Army even now, after I've retired. Unmanned systems are the next wave—robotics that will be used to take human soldiers out of dirty, dull, or dangerous tasks, and will help save hundreds if not thousands of individual lives. I'm working on all sorts of projects with that end-goal in mind as we speak. And all of it traces back to those early challenging days in the mid-1990s.

The digitization of our armed forces was an act of courage. We were boldly going where no man had gone before. Taking the risk of trying these new systems and knowing that, potentially, they weren't going to work was important. Having the audacity to try this new capability, but at the same time having enough common sense to retain some analog capability as well truly mattered. There were forces in play that wanted to put an end to it, that insisted it was a waste of time and money. We certainly know better today.

It's the same sort of forces that leaders in corporate America come up against all the time. The thing is, it's up to leaders to know when it's worth it to take the risk. You have to trust your gut and your experience, and be willing to take calculated risks in the name of progress, of advancement, of adaptation to the rapidly changing world around you. You have to be willing to try something that may or may not work as part of a long-term look at progress for your organization.

Using all of the Army's new digital systems down in Barstow toward the end of my two years, I commanded a brigade of 5,000 soldiers in a mock battle against a force using traditional measures— guys with maps, basically—and I'll admit to you here and now that we got our butts kicked. The digital brigade lost, and lost big. It was a laser-tag battlefield. Nobody was dying, but it was quite a blow. We accepted the fact that some of our systems worked and some didn't. But I never stopped looking at that last statement with an optimist's eye: "Some of the systems worked." So it wasn't a loss. Not to me, and not to any other champion of the digitization of the Army. It was the early stages of trial and error. The research and development phase, if you will. And those early tests allowed us to move forward to finally get to the point we're at today.

Where are we today? Talk to any soldier, and he or she will tell you: The difference between winning and losing on today's battlefield is situational awareness. When I led the surge in Iraq in 2007, my battle space was the size of the state of West Virginia. Thanks to the technology I helped launch a decade earlier, I knew where my people were at all times. Not just a few people, but 25,000 soldiers. That's 25,000 American heroes with their lives on the line. I knew where our equipment was, too. Billions of dollars' worth of equipment. I could toggle down on a single vehicle anywhere in that battle space and tell you who was in that vehicle at any moment. If we hadn't done the work of experimentation in the late 1990s, this situational awareness would have been an impossibility.

It took us a decade to work through all the bugs of what we were doing. Thankfully people had the foresight and fortitude to work through it—and to push back against the forces that would have kept us from moving forward. Lives were saved because of it. Lots of lives. On both sides.

Adapting to change, including technological change, is a major key to survival.

I'm happy that I was one of the people who pushed us forward, not one of the people who tried to stop progress from happening on the battlefield. I'm glad to have stuck around to see those changes in action, and to witness the rewards of our willingness to try, fail, learn, try again, and improve until we got it right.

Ten years from now, will you be able to say the same in your own field?

– 7 –

LEARNING FROM POOR LEADERSHIP

I was just a young captain the first time I found myself working for a lousy leader. Everything this particular guy did aggravated me. He was one of these leaders with an ego as big as the room, and everything he did was about himself. No matter what I spoke to him about, he just wouldn't listen. He didn't care.

Working for a boss who's incompetent, a horrible person, an unqualified dolt, or worse, is one of the most frustrating things any forward-thinking employee, volunteer, soldier, or want-to-be leader ever faces. Answering to someone who's maybe not as smart as you are, or who looks down on their workers, or who is only in the job to fulfill some ego trip or personal agenda that has nothing to do with the task at hand—boy, I can feel my blood pressure rising just thinking about it! Can't you? We've all been there. We've all had to deal with a bad boss or a lousy teacher or a hypocritical leader at one point or another. It's just a part of life.

The thing is, what you choose to do with that experience is up to you.

In the case of this particular leader, it came to a head one day when I went home to Sarah, saying, "I'm either going to hit this guy or quit!" The hotheaded young man in me thought it was just not

43

worth the pain to put up with this guy, and since I knew how much trouble I'd be in if I hit him, I honestly started thinking that the only way out of the situation might be to resign from the Army.

Well, Sarah managed to calm me down to the point where I didn't do either. "No, you're not going to hit him," she said, and, "No, you're not going to quit. You're going to continue to persevere." (Have I mentioned what a blessing it's been to have Sarah in my life? She's been my saving grace more times than I can count. Having that one person who always has your best interest at heart and who knows how to set you straight is important in life.)

So I went back to work. But the whole time I was under this guy felt like wasted time. I was fuming. I felt like my whole career was at a standstill. I couldn't wait until it was over.

As I look back on it now, I realize that I missed an extraordinary opportunity: I was so caught up in feeling angry and feeling sorry for myself for having to work under this lousy leader, I missed an opportunity that was staring me in the face.

I wouldn't miss it the next time.

A few years later, I wound up serving under another leader who made my skin crawl. He was one of these guys who loved to talk the talk, as if he were some moral superior we should all get down and worship. The thing was, he didn't follow any of his own philosophies. Everything he did was 180 degrees from the values he kept telling us to follow!

There is no quicker way to lose the trust of your subordinates than to say one thing and do another. This guy proved it every day. And one day, when I found myself on the verge of talking back to him, I stopped myself.

That's when I decided to make a very positive change in my life.

From fairly early on in my career, I had kept notebooks on leadership. I observed the things my leaders said and did, and kept notes on them. I figured, *If this guy's doing something that works, and he's in a position of leadership that I'd like to be in someday, the least I should do is make note of it and then do my best to emulate that behavior when I become a leader myself!* It seemed pretty logical. It made sense to me to try to learn to copy the behavior of leaders I admired.

Dealing with this lousy leader made me see something else that was worth taking notes on: behaviors that, as a leader, I would never, ever want to exhibit myself.

So, I started a notebook specifically dedicated to that subject. I used the negatives of this terrible leader's words and actions as a guideline. The way I would become a success myself was to do the *opposite* of everything this guy did.

Talking back to him at the time would have had no upside. He was my leader. I had to answer to him, like it or not. If I'd have been disrespectful or hurtful, or if I'd have called him names, I would have been relieved of my position. So I didn't do that. I tried to soldier on, to just get through it. And I did.

As a result, I learned a lot, and I told myself, "If I ever get to that level, I'm not going to be like that." Well, guess what? I did get to that level, and far beyond. And I think of that lousy leader all the time—as a simple self-check to make sure I do absolutely nothing that he ever did.

I've since advocated that approach to all of my subordinates. "Keep these notebooks. Watch what you're seeing. If you like it, and it works for you, write it down, and when you get to that position, do it. If it doesn't work, and you don't like it? Don't do it."

Having the ability to pay attention to what you're seeing and experiencing, and to listen and learn from what's right in front of you, is one way to take almost any obstacle—in this case, a horrible boss or a terrible leader—and turn it into an opportunity. Even if it means paying attention to what's wrong, and learning exactly what not to do because of it.

★ ★ ★

– 8 –

OBSTACLES OF OLYMPIC PROPORTIONS

After serving in Germany through the fall of the Berlin Wall, my career in the Army continued on a decidedly international track. I served in the first Gulf War on the ground in Kuwait. I'll talk more about my experience there later on. After a few years home, I went on to serve as the operations manager for Joint Forces Command, Naples, Italy, a NATO command overseeing missions in Bosnia, Kosovo, and Macedonia—all of which would eventually lead to my career as a general officer in a post-9/11 world and my multiple roles in the war in Iraq.

Let me tell you, for a kid from a paper-factory town in Ohio to wake up in the middle of a country like Kosovo is a shock on many levels. The language and cultural barriers you face in many of these foreign countries is enough to make even the smartest among us feel ridiculously under-educated. There's almost no amount of studying or preparation you can do that will ever make you feel like a native. There are so many cultural subtleties to try to grasp, and in the heat of war, or even in the aftermath of war, those cultural subtleties can sneak up on you when you least expect it.

The reason the Army sent me off to Kosovo was not only because they thought I was the right man for the job, but because they wanted me to get experience in understanding peace-support operations and multinational operations. Kosovo Force (KFOR), a multinational force of about 12,000 people that NATO created in order to keep the peace, was being commanded by a French lieutenant general when I arrived. His deputy was a German major general. I started out as deputy chief of staff for operations, and later, I became the chief of staff—overseeing a staff of six hundred from twenty-six nations. And I was the only American general on that staff!

I was pretty good at communicating by this point in my career. Or so I thought. I had daily meetings with my eight general officers on that staff. Two weeks into it, the French general came to me privately and said, "We all are required to speak English here, but we have *no idea* what you're saying!" It never occurred to me that my Texas colloquialisms didn't translate. When you're fixin' to talk to a multinational force, you can't use phrases like "fixin' to"!

It was a simple but important lesson: When you're working internationally, you have to learn to be precise in your communication. You can't risk having anyone in the room not understand what you're trying to say.

After working with NATO, I learned to keep my eyes open for cultural differences so I could prepare myself for conversations with enemies and allies alike. Attempts at keeping the peace required an understanding of cultural barriers and how to circumvent them. In fact, some of the cultural lessons I learned in Kosovo would come to serve me well in Iraq nearly a decade later.

One of the biggest realities I had to adapt to in multinational affairs overseas was accepting the fact that things just aren't always going to go our way, sometimes for very deep-seated cultural and political reasons. As Americans, we like to jump in, call the shots, and expect that everything's going to work out. Two problems we have as a country right now is that we have a short-term memory, and we want to rush to a conclusion. President Clinton got us into Bosnia thinking we'd be there for one year—and we're still there to this day! Heck, we're still a presence in Germany; we've been there since World War II!

We always seem a bit surprised and dismayed when things don't work out exactly the way we expect them to. But we shouldn't get discouraged. Instead, we as leaders need to step back and assess the situation from every angle. My work in Kosovo in a postwar peace-keeping capacity with NATO provides a stark example of what I'm talking about. In the simplest of terms, we were trying to get the Kosovar Albanians to work friendly with the Kosovar Serbians. The fighting in this latest conflict was over. They needed to rebuild. They *needed* to work together. Why couldn't we go in there, help keep the peace for a while, and get out? Well, think of it this way: The Kosovar Albanians had been persecuted by the Serbians for the past century. An entire century. They wanted freedom from that persecution, and they wanted Kosovo to be a separate country from Serbia rather than a province of Serbia. They wanted freedom—something we take for granted in America. Even with the current conflict over, the ongo-ing conflict and fight for freedom versus control wasn't going away. That caused tension, which caused continual violence. Serbs attacked Albanians, Albanians attacked Serbs. It was all we could do to watch out for hotspots and keep the peace as best we could while the politi-cal resolutions unfolded.

Many of us were frustrated by the violence. We could understand the historical significance of what was going on, but hadn't it gone on long enough? Wasn't it just time for these two sides to work out a resolution and be done with it?

One day, one of the leaders of the Kosovar Albanians came to me with a simple but much-needed lesson in perspective: "General, you don't understand. The Serbs killed three of my brothers and ten of my cousins, and if you think I'm going to forgive them anytime soon, you're mistaken."

Just like that, all the politics and posturing went right out the window. I realized there were troubles here that were immediate and deeply personal. Yes, the political strife was deeply rooted. It stretched back decades, the way conflicts in the Middle East stretch back decades and even centuries. It's hard for us to understand this kind of ethnic identification. It's foreign to us. But we're not talking only about "sides" here. We're talking about families. We're talking about loved ones. We're talking about brothers, sisters, mothers, cousins, spouses, children. Leaders can't lose sight of the fact that it's the people who matter. The fighting over land and power and control and politics isn't about any of those things. It's about people. And it's the same in the business world, politics, and elsewhere.

The world is much smaller today than it used to be. It's true! Anyone in corporate America knows it. Competition is global, as are the obstacles and opportunities that business leaders never had to think about tackling before the Internet came into its own. The smaller the world gets, the more complicated it becomes, and business leaders have to be ready to adapt in the global environment at a moment's notice—while understanding that it might take a very long time to make inroads or find resolutions when you're working in other parts of the world. But we can't lose sight of the fact that the root of every organization, every province, every country, is its people.

No matter what part of the world you're in, asking the right questions, listening to what you're being told, and seeing the cultural differences as clearly as you can make all the difference. For me, that early lesson of Kosovo ethnic identification would stick with me and come to serve me well in Iraq. My ability to identify with the deep-seated differences in the Shia and Sunni populations, and to see the

Iraqi people as just that—people—would allow me to make the most of my position in a very dangerous and difficult situation.

SAYING "YES!"

One of the biggest lessons I learned in my time spent overseas was that, sometimes, it pays to be the guy who says, "Yes."

Sometimes leaders need to be willing take on tasks nobody else wants and even to attempt to do what others might think is just about impossible. Isaiah 6:8 states: "Then I heard the voice of the Lord saying, 'Whom shall I send? And who will go for us?' And I said, 'Here am I. Send me!'"

That's certainly what I did in the summer of 2004.

Less than three years after the 9/11 attacks, the Summer Olympics were set to start in Athens, Greece, that August. As you can imagine, the fear of terrorist attacks happening during the games was extraordinarily high. And rightly so. The games were happening in a part of the world that was close in proximity to known terrorist cells operating in Afghanistan, Pakistan, and Iraq. Millions of people and any number of heads of state would be in attendance. And in what could only be seen as a bonus to the deviant minds inside al-Qaeda, the eyes of the world would be watching.

The pressure to keep the games safe grew so intense that the Greek government—at the very last minute—decided to ask NATO for help.

Somewhere along the line, someone decided that the best team to handle anti-terrorist security operations as a backup to the Greeks' own forces would be the NATO Response Force. The Response Force was historically a toothless tiger: soldiers who did drills and stayed prepared but never saw any action because the NATO nations could rarely agree unanimously on putting them into service. The force comprised a total of 16,000 people from across the NATO nations, including special forces, ground troops, ships at our disposal in the

Athens vicinity, air forces that could be called in if needed, and a sixty-person leadership staff that would serve from inside the Greek Pentagon. Nobody else wanted to take command of this outfit. A number of three- and four-star generals were asked to take on this mission before me, and all of them found some reason not to do it.

In some ways, I don't blame them: It was clear that, if something went wrong at the Olympics, this NATO Response Force would be to blame for it. And whoever was heading up the Response Force would receive the ultimate blame.

By the time this responsibility was presented to me, there were just three weeks before the torch was to be lit and the XVIII Summer Games began. Three weeks!

Confronted with the mission to deploy the DJTF (Deployable Joint Task Force) of the NATO Response Force to Athens for the Olympics on such short notice, I could easily have said, "This is too hard. Go get somebody else." But I didn't. I looked at it as an opportunity to finally train this staff in a real-world mission and a chance for me to lead a multinational force into action. So I said, "Yes."

We were finally going to give this toothless tiger some teeth.

I threw everything I had into prepping the Response Force to be a terrorist-watchdog group on the ground. We learned the ins and outs of the venue maps, knew where we wanted people positioned, prepped all kinds of possible scenarios and responses, and hit the ground running in Athens with confidence that we could pull this off—keeping athletes, dignitaries, politicians, and the public safe from harm. Our team was fired up because they were finally getting to do what they'd trained to do. There were a few glitches along the way, though. At one point, I realized that about half of my staff was simultaneously attending and "keeping an eye on" a certain Summer Olympics event: women's beach volleyball. Heck, we had so many eyes on those bikini-clad bodies in the beach volleyball stadium, a terrorist couldn't have moved one inch without getting taken out! Much to my men's dismay, I had to order a whole bunch of them to move on to other venues, making sure *all* of the Olympics venues were being watched just as keenly. When all was said and done, the Response Force did its duty. The games were safe. The only thing history will remember about those games is who won gold. Had we not been there, tragedy might have struck.

When the mission was over, I think it's fair to say that the NATO Response Force as an organization was more coherent than it had been in its entire history. The entire Response Force was proud of what they did: "Look what we can accomplish!" was the new mantra. They had real-world experience to back them up.

Putting that Response Force to work on the ground was a blessing. We got more accomplished for the Response Force as an organization than any amount of planning, training, meetings, and "talking" ever could. Military people want to move to the sound of the guns. Putting aside family separations and the wariness one feels over the possibility of memorial services, there's not a soldier, sailor, airman, or marine serving today who, if given a choice between being stateside or being in Iraq or Afghanistan, wouldn't want to be over there. Because that's what we're trained to do.

I think there's a lesson in that for the corporate world: Move to the sound of the guns. There's merit in the act of doing—of real-world experience versus planning, going to meetings, talking about stuff all the time, and then talking about it some more. Staleness sets in that way. "Let's have a meeting to plan the next meeting!" Leaders need to put a stop to it. Get your workforce into spring-into-action mode. Go get stuff done. Stop talking about it, and do it. Take a risk. Even if it goes wrong, at least it's going somewhere. And you'll all learn from the experience. Take a lesson from those Nike ads, and "Just Do It." We'll all be better for it.

Looking back on those Olympics now, I realize that rushing to get my staff ready to roll that quickly taught me a few great lessons on efficiency, time management, and preparedness that would serve me well three years later, when I found myself with only six weeks to prepare a unit of 25,000 men for the surge in Iraq—one of the largest military undertakings our country would attempt in recent memory.

I gained the experience I needed by saying, "Yes" and taking a risk.

– 9 –

FACING THE MEDIA

On the heels of my success in Athens, the Army sent me off to Iraq to serve as the deputy chief of staff for political, military, and economic affairs for the Multinational Force-Iraq (MNF-I). I said goodbye to my family once again and went to work in the United States Embassy in Baghdad. For two months in the spring of 2005, I adjusted to this new environment at the epicenter of the still-new war, and adjusted to my role as best I could. I attended Ambassador Zalmay Khalilzad's country team meetings. I would be deeply involved in attempting to build "capacity" in the Iraqi government and populations, which meant developing jobs, schools, industry, etc.

Iraq was in a state of despair. The people of Iraq, just like us, want freedom from fear. They want to have a job, they want to be able to provide for their families, they want to be able to send their kids to school, they want healthcare, and, at that point in time, they had none of that. It was a big job, a massive coalition team effort, and I felt like I was just starting to get a handle on things when General George Casey called me into his office.

"Rick, I know you came here to be the deputy chief of staff for political, military, and economic affairs, but, in addition, you're now also the spokesman for the force."

I was shocked. The spokesman for the force was the guy who stood in front of the television cameras and briefed the press on everything we were doing in Iraq. He was the guy you'd see on the evening news, the guy who had to answer everyone's questions. *Why on Earth would General Casey want me for that role?*

I expressed my doubts and reservations to him as strongly as I could. I explained to him that I didn't have any particular training to do that and didn't particularly *want* to do that—and he promptly reminded me that he was the man in charge. I had no choice.

The obstacle here was obvious: I had no training. I had never been a spokesperson before. Ever. The war in Iraq was one of the biggest military endeavors the United States had taken on in decades, and one that lately had been going south on us, which meant that being the spokesperson was akin to being on the firing line. I mean, there are people who like to deal with the media, but I had no particular affinity for doing that, under even the best of circumstances. And to be frank, I didn't really know what I was doing. I could not understand why Casey had selected me for this.

Let me paint the picture for you: The year was 2005. It was a challenging time in the Iraq War. Casualty rates were high, and costs were exorbitant, but we were making progress. Our basic bumper-sticker mission statement, which was put into place by Condoleezza Rice, was "Clear, hold, and build." Our Army could do that. We could clear an area of those who were fighting back, we could hold an area and essentially stop the violence, and then we could get about rebuilding the infrastructure and facilities to help get the Iraqis back on their feet. The only problem was, once we did any of that, we'd have to move on to the next area—and often we didn't have enough troops to leave a security force in place once we left. From my perspective and the perspective of just about anyone who was over there at that time, we didn't have enough troops on the ground.

Our enemies would come to see that as an opportunity they could exploit.

The insurgents were continually attempting to drive a wedge between the Sunni and Shia populations already, causing constant tensions. But in February of 2006, they took it so far as to blow up the Golden Mosque in Samara, the most sacred Shia shrine in Iraq. They started kidnapping and killing local businessmen and politicians. They did everything they could to keep the Iraqi people in a state of despair so they would be more pliable when it came to hating the Americans.

It got to a point where we would build a school or a bridge, and the very next day the insurgents would come and blow it up. They would target Iraqis who appeared to have helped us in our efforts, and either kill them or kill their families, destroying everything they loved. That drove a massive wedge into our ability to elicit cooperation from the people we needed most: the Iraqi population whom we were trying to help.

That whole situation was just beginning to develop when General Casey made me spokesman.

It took an awful lot of prayer for me to find a way to go into this with a positive attitude and even more prayer to find the "opportunity" in this tremendous obstacle that lay before me.

But I did it. Despite the obstacles at hand, I realized that an opportunity had presented itself: the opportunity to improve my communication skills. People had always told me that strategic communication and knowing how to deal with the media were important. The Army gave us all kinds of instructional talks about dealing with the media, and yet I hadn't been paying particular attention to it. I was hoping—nay, assuming—I'd never have to be the guy talking to the press!

After that conversation with General Casey, I could have thrown up my hands, said I'm not prepared, and possibly found some way out of it. After all, who wants to learn their lessons on dealing with the media *in front of the media*? But, instead, I prayed, I put my head down, I got to work, and found an even bigger opportunity in that obstacle—an opportunity to help tell the story of the very real progress we were making in Iraq. Having been the political-military-economic guy for those two months, it was clear to me that, even with the lack of sufficient troops, and even with the destruction caused by the insurgents, we were making some progress. Progress on the governmental side, the economic side, and also in building clinics and providing other various needs of the Iraqi people. It floored me that no one back home seemed to know about any of that. That very important story wasn't being told.

I can help communicate to the American people the progress we're making in Iraq, I thought. If that's not an opportunity, I don't know what is.

Of course, I wouldn't be talking to *just* the American people. And that presented another challenge: How could I effectively communicate our message, knowing that we were basically talking to three separate groups every time we went on television or talked to the papers? Every time I spoke, I would be talking not only to the American people, but also to the Iraqi people *and* to the insurgents. They would all be watching!

As spokesperson, my primary venue was live press conferences. Every Thursday I'd have to stand in front of this gaggle of reporters, all of whom were looking for bad news and looking to put the general on the spot. I would go back to headquarters and see myself on television—FOX, CNN, everywhere. What was said at this press conference was always considered newsworthy, because everyone was trying to figure out what was going on in Iraq at that time. So everything I said was transmitted instantly back to the States.

Talk about pressure. One misstep, and I'd be skewered!

I wound up on Jon Stewart's *The Daily Show* one time—and not in a good way. I was holding a press conference, talking about Abu

Musab al-Zarqawi, the infamous Jordanian terrorist. We had captured some video of Zarqawi basically acting stupid. He was wearing white tennis shoes, and he burned his hand on the barrel of a hot machine gun. He was clearly a nut job. So as part of our communication, I was trying to show the world—including the insurgents and the Iraqi people—"Look at this guy; he's an idiot!"

Jon Stewart wound up playing my entire piece that night, including my statement in front of the microphones: "Watching Zarqawi," I said, "is one of those things that makes you go 'Hmm.'" At which point Stewart stopped the clip and said directly to the camera, "It makes you go, 'Hmm . . . How come we haven't caught him?!'"

It's hard not to feel dumb when you've put your own foot in your mouth like that. It was a miscalculation on my part. In thinking about how those tapes would play to the insurgents and the Iraqis, I forgot to think through how it might make us look back in the States. But like all mistakes, it was (once again) something to learn from.

The entire experience was an opportunity to develop a new skill set that has served me very well. If I had not taken on that spokesperson role, I would not have been nearly as successful in my future roles as a division commander, corps commander, or IMCOM commander.

I've thanked George Casey numerous times in the years since for giving me that opportunity. I didn't thank him at the time, that's for sure! But his belief in me helped me develop a whole new skill set. And that spokesperson role gave me a good feeling as I helped try to turn the news around.

Of course, trying to turn the news around is a skill set all its own. Just as I thought it might, stepping into that role taught me firsthand about the art of strategic communication. What is strategic communication? "Consistent themes and messages delivered at high frequency over multiple media." And it's something every leader ought to be aware of and advocating for within his or her organization whenever necessary.

At one point, I had a senior editor of one of the most influential newspapers in the United States in my office in Baghdad, and I said to him, "I'm taking all of your reporters out to see good things and bad things. Why is it that the only thing that ever shows up in your newspaper is the bad things?" And he said to me, "Bad news sells newspapers."

I'd take the television affiliates out—NBC, ABC, CBS, FOX, BBC—with their camera crews, and I'd show them schools being built, clinics being built, kids in school, governmental process in action. They'd get good footage of all of that, and then all I'd ever see on television is footage of the most recent explosion.

"If it bleeds, it leads." That saying is terrible and true.

How could I get the real story out when the national media was so jaded and broken and clearly uninterested in writing about or airing anything that didn't "sell"?

It took me a little while, but what I finally realized is that the way to get the story out to the American people was not through the national media but through the local media. The local media was looking for "good news" stories of their men and women making a difference. So I had a great opportunity there, not only to do interviews myself, but also to empower our soldiers and others with information, so that, when they went home, they could go right to the local media and tell their stories of progress.

That same approach can work for corporations and other organizations. The opportunity is still there to get "good" stories out via the local media. It's not easy. You can't blanket the airwaves all at once with a single media hit. And yet the effectiveness of spreading the word on the ground through local media, one town, city, county, or state at a time, can make a significant difference in whatever message it is you're trying to send.

It's exhausting work, I've gotta say. I certainly wished there was one show, one newspaper I could have gone to. But even when I had big media coverage from Katie Couric or some other media giant, getting the word out on the good we'd done was a very tough road. That's all there is to it. It's tough!

Just to give you a sense of how tough it can be to get your message out, I'll share with you an impromptu moment that happened after I came home from Iraq and took over command at Fort Hood. This particular moment came many months after I had that run-in with the Army wife on the street—the run-in that prompted me to order all soldiers home for dinner with their families at 6:00 p.m. sharp. I had been featured in papers big and small, and all over local television and radio. Everyone was proclaiming me the "family-first general." We had become the family-first corps with all of the programs I'd put into place to help families reconnect and make the most of their time together on base.

News of my progress spread far and wide, and one time when General Casey and his wife, Sheila, came into town, they said, "Hey, since you're the family-first general, we'd really like to meet some of the families and see how it's going."

Now, I never stage these sorts of conversations. I never pick people in advance and say, "When asked this question, give this answer." I'd rather hear the truth, no matter how harsh it might be. So there was this group of families and soldiers sitting in this conference room, and Sarah and I were sitting in the back of the room, and George asked the question: "What do you think of the family programs here at Fort Hood?" A young private's wife stood up and said, "There aren't any family programs here."

I felt like I was gonna sink right through my chair. I had spent eighteen months building those programs, and yet in this one instance, this particular young woman didn't know about any of them. This just proves the point that you can have the best programs in the world, but if nobody knows about them, you might as well not even have them. Getting the word out is important stuff. Having some media savvy, I believe, is crucial for any leader.

As I moved on to other roles in my career, I always made it my business to learn everything I could about how people were getting their information, and then worked to get my message out to those outlets.

The thing some people forget is that both of those elements have to work together, in tandem, or the message simply won't be heard. When I was working at the Pentagon, I went out to visit one of our Army installations, and the garrison commander was so proud to show off this public-service announcement he'd put together on energy conservation, which had started airing on the local on-post television station. Later that day, he took me to speak to 500 family members, and, during my presentation, I asked the group, "How many of you watch the local on-post television station?" Only two people raised their hand! I didn't mean to embarrass the guy. I was just curious. Turns out, his message that he was so proud of wasn't being heard by anyone that he hoped would hear it. And that's a failure by any measure.

I ask that question all the time now: "Where do you get your information? Is it television, radio, the newspaper, or the Internet?" And the answer these days, from 90 percent of the people I talk to, is the Internet, usually through social media like Facebook, Twitter, etc. When you get into this a little bit, you quickly realize that, if you're going to communicate to people, you've got to communicate to them in a medium that they actually consume. Otherwise, you're just wasting your time.

As I talk to corporate America, that's an important point: "How are your potential customers or clients accessing their information?" It's not all the same.

Knowing enough to ask that question and seek out the answers will present new opportunities for you to get your message out. And then it's up to you to take advantage of that opportunity.

Actually, I suppose that's the real key to all of these obstacle/opportunity lessons, isn't it? Becoming a leader takes a whole lot more than just getting over the obstacles and getting the job done. It takes seeing the opportunities in the obstacles and taking advantage of those opportunities whenever you can. That's a big difference. And the difference will affect how far you get on the road to success—both your own success as well as the success of those around you and beneath you in whatever leadership role you take on.

Part Two

LIFESTYLE EVANGELISM

Let your light shine before others, that they may see your
good deeds and glorify your Father in heaven.
– MATTHEW 5:16

Leaders lead by example.

They don't just talk the talk; they walk the walk. In every aspect of life.

I have always tried to lead the way I would want to be led, and I hope you see examples of that throughout this book. I don't always succeed. I'm not perfect, and I don't even pretend to be. But I do my best to show my leadership style through my actions. To show strength by being strong; to show perseverance by persevering; to demonstrate work-life balance by balancing my work life and my family life, and so on.

"Lifestyle evangelism," the way I define it, has nothing to do with any particular religion. Yes, I am a man of faith, and my faith is the cornerstone of my strength as a leader. When it comes to prioritizing my life, God comes first, family second, and career third. How you prioritize your own life is, of course, up to you. But no matter how you prioritize your life, if you're going to be a leader, it's important that you become a lifestyle evangelist: that your actions match your words, and that the example you set in the way you lead and live your life helps to inform and inspire those you're leading.

When it comes to commanding troops—be they your workforce, your team, your community, your students, or your soldiers on a desert battlefield—leading by example is far more effective than all the preaching in the world. We can talk all we want. But it's the examples we set through our own deeds and actions that command respect and truly make a difference.

– 10 –

FINDING FAITH

My journey to God was a rather long one, by most standards. My parents never took me to church. Ever. We were a Christian household, and my mother and father were both believers. They just didn't believe in the tenets of organized religion, so the only time I ever stepped foot inside a church in my youth was when one of the neighbors asked my brother and me if we'd like to come along.

In fact, my most vivid "religious experience" back in Ohio was when I was maybe nine or ten years old. A Baptist minister knocked on our front door and wound up coming inside, where he sat in our living room and told my parents that they were going to hell because they smoked and drank.

"And your children are going to hell, too, because they aren't baptized!"

That was all my dad could take before he stood up, grabbed that minister, and physically threw him out the front door.

It's important to understand that I didn't grow up with a particularly strong belief system. I wasn't indoctrinated into a particular church from a young age. I found God and the beliefs that now serve as the foundation of everything I stand for a bit later in life as an adult and of my own free will.

My first experience attending church on any regular basis was at West Point. I was a member of the very first class of cadets who weren't required to go to chapel on Sundays. But we all went anyway. It was just sort of implied that you had to go, like it or not. So I went. And while I listened and learned on those Sunday mornings—absorbing a few lessons along the way—the real lessons I learned on morals and values at West Point were summed up in the Cadet Prayer that we all had to memorize and the Honor Code we were bound to live by.

The Cadet Prayer is this:

O God, our Father, Thou Searcher of human hearts, help us to draw near to Thee in sincerity and truth. May our religion be filled with gladness and may our worship of Thee be natural.

Strengthen and increase our admiration for honest dealing and clean thinking, and suffer not our hatred of hypocrisy and pretense ever to diminish. Encourage us in our endeavor to live above the common level of life. Make us to choose the harder right instead of the easier wrong, and never to be content with a half-truth when the whole can be won. Endow us with courage that is born of loyalty to all that is noble and worthy, that scorns to compromise with vice and injustice and knows no fear when truth and right are in jeopardy. Guard us against flippancy and irreverence in the sacred things of life. Grant us new ties of friendship and new opportunities of service. Kindle our hearts in fellowship with those of a cheerful countenance, and soften our hearts with sympathy for those who sorrow and suffer. Help us to maintain the honor of the Corps untarnished and unsullied and to show forth in our lives the ideals of West Point in doing our duty to Thee and to our Country.

*All of which we ask in the name of the Great Friend and
Master of all.*

Amen

The honor code is a little bit shorter, and slightly easier to memorize:

A cadet will not lie, cheat, steal, or tolerate those who do.

Religious beliefs aside, the themes and guidelines found in that
Cadet Prayer struck a deep chord in me. Long before I found God
in my life in any deeply personal way, I turned to those words for
guidance. When I think of those words—*a cadet will always choose the
harder right instead of the easier wrong . . . a cadet will have the cheerful
countenance . . . a cadet will never tolerate a half-truth when the whole
truth can be won*—that's how I've tried to live my life at every turn.

A leader has to have a foundation to stand on. There has to be
a moral code, a standard of principle from which he or she will not
turn. West Point gave me a head start on building that foundation.

And the honor code, to me, is simply a matter of black and
white—there are no shades of gray when it comes to honor. "A cadet
will not lie, cheat, steal, or tolerate those who do." That's how I've
lived my professional life at every turn. I think it's just as important
to say, "A *leader* will not lie, cheat, steal, or tolerate those who do."
In fact, imagine how quickly we could turn Washington around if
we swore our leaders to that code! What I ask myself often is, "Why
wouldn't our leaders want to lead with that kind of honor?"

There are plenty of delicate and difficult situations you face as a
commissioned officer, and I faced my share from Fort Hood to Bosnia
to Baghdad and back. Along the way, I realized that the honor code,
which was important to me as a cadet, was just as important if not *more*

important to me as a professional officer. It is an absolute cornerstone of my foundation, and, in many ways, it signifies the essence of what I am—perhaps because it was driven home so forcefully.

I was at West Point during one of the more difficult moments in the school's history. A moment when the honor code itself was put to the test. My class, the class of 1977, was at the center of the 1976 cheating scandal.

A professor in the department of electrical engineering noticed that one student had received "help" on a series of take-home problems that were supposed to be done individually. He then looked a little closer at some of the other students' papers, and realized that answers on many of them were too similar to have come from original work. In the end, 117 students were turned in under suspicion of cheating.

As you might imagine, the scandal rocked West Point to its very core. The ramifications of this thing spread all over, as parents, the press, even Congress reacted.

Sid Berry, the superintendent of the Academy at the time, formed an internal review panel consisting of three full colonels and two cadets to investigate the allegations.

I was one of those two cadets.

In my particular company, Company A-2, there weren't any indications of cheating. Since I had established myself as a leader within that company, I was in a good position to judge fairly as far as Sid Berry was concerned. I can honestly say that I had no knowledge of any cheating across any of the companies before the scandal broke, and to say I was shocked by it is an understatement.

As a part of this panel, we would look at every single allegation to determine how expansive this potential problem was, and then make determinations about what we should do about it. We fed our findings and recommendations not only to General Berry, but to General

Walt Ulmer, who was the commandant of cadets—and who would become a friend and mentor to me in the years following.

Here's where this process got tough.

I think most people know what kind of bonds and friendships are formed during your college years. At West Point, those bonds are amplified. In most cases, you stay with one company your entire time as a cadet. You go through Beast Barracks together, through Plebe Year together, you form relationships, and those relationships carry you through the rest of your life. But what we found in some companies is that those bonds had become so close that they had crossed the line into routinely violating the cadet honor code—as if the bond of friendship somehow overrode the honor system we had in place.

The fact is, other than that code, there was nothing keeping cadets from cheating. You could cheat if you wanted to cheat. You had access to folks who had already taken the same test you were about to take. The honor code demanded not only that you *not* cheat, but also that you not tolerate those who do.

Some of the cheating was so blatant that kids had copied each other's work verbatim—going so far that, when one kid doodled on his page during the test, the kids who copied it went ahead and copied the doodle, too (perhaps being foolish, or perhaps thinking it was a part of the answer). Other cases involved students simply talking about the test, or talking about the answers, when they shouldn't have been talking at all. And in some cases, a few of my classmates wound up being expelled from the school not because they themselves had cheated, but because they knew about the cheating and didn't report it as they were bound by the honor code to do.

They were found guilty of violating the honor code because they tolerated other cadets who broke the code.

This is a difficult thing for me to think back on, even today. Put yourself in their shoes: If you had been in a company that had been together for three years, if you did not cheat personally but knew that your best friend, the guy you'd been through Beast Barracks and Plebe Year and Yearling with, had cheated, you were supposed to turn him in. That's what the honor code says you are supposed to do, right? Would you have done it? Some folks chose not to do that, and as a result of not turning in their buddy, they were found guilty, and action was taken.

I thank God that I wasn't confronted with that decision myself. I was oblivious to anybody cheating, so I wasn't faced with what is—as far as I can tell—the closest thing there is to a gray area in the honor code. In my work life, my adult life, or my professional life, if I discovered a co-worker cheating, lying, or stealing—I don't think I'd have much hesitation at all in turning that person in to the proper authorities, or dealing with the situation in whatever the most appropriate manner might be. But in school? If my best friend had cheated and I was aware of it back then, would I have turned him in? I've asked myself that question often over the last thirty-five years, and I'm still not sure of the answer. That's the hard truth. I'm not sure. Being an eyewitness to the West Point cheating scandal taught me important lessons about honor and the ramifications of breaking the code of honor. It helped heighten my awareness of the right and wrong in just about every decision I would face. This was an important moment for me morally, but it would be more than a decade before my moral compass would find its true north in the church.

After Sarah and I married in 1982, we became what I would call "recreational Christians." We went to church basically because everybody else did. It was a social place, a place to find community. Sarah had been baptized as a child, but not me. I was still very much the outsider, listening, maybe absorbing a lesson now and then, but not really understanding or even seeking to understand.

That all changed in 1988.

I was stationed at Fort Leavenworth, Kansas, when I first met a chaplain named Joe Miller. Joe Miller had a way of talking to a congregation that I'd never experienced before. Direct. Honest. "Down-to-Earth" might be the best way to describe his oratory style.

I was thirty-two years old, and, for the first time in my life, I guess I was ready to truly listen. One day, Joe stood up in front of our church and gave a talk about something called "inner peace." He quoted from the Bible, referring to Philippians 4:6-7: "Do not be anxious about anything, but in every situation, by prayer and petition, with thanksgiving, present your requests to God. And the peace of God, which transcends all understanding, will guard your hearts and your minds in Christ Jesus."

I admit I was anxious about a lot of things in those days: my career, my finances, my kids. That's pretty common for a lot of thirty-two-year-old men, I suppose. So the idea he presented of *not* being anxious about anything certainly resonated with me. That evening at the dinner table, my wife and I got to talking about the whole notion, and we realized that neither of us had that "inner peace" in our lives that Joe had spoken about. It was something we both simultaneously felt we were missing and ought to pursue.

We wound up working with Joe Miller intensely for the next six weeks, and Joe helped bring us to Christ. At the end of those six weeks, I was baptized. And even though Sarah had already been baptized as a child, she was baptized again—and I was able to participate in that.

I won't go on too long about this. I realize this decision belonged to my wife and me as individuals, and not everyone believes that church is for them. My own father, who is still with us, refuses to attend church to this day. He still takes the Lord's name in vain, and it drives me nuts! But I do believe a relationship with God is important—even if it has little to do with what church you belong to. And that relationship is certainly an important part of my life.

Ever since I was baptized at age thirty-two, I've started each day in prayer. I've dedicated some time each day to Bible study. I believe what it says in Joshua 1:8: "Keep this Book of the Law always on your lips; meditate on it day and night, so that you may be careful to do everything written in it. Then you will be prosperous and successful." And I've done my best to live my life as an honest reflection of my faith.

Even though I had tried to live my life with honor since my West Point days, it was Joe Miller who truly drove home the notion of lifestyle evangelism to me. "Hey, you can't be a sit-on-the-sidelines Christian," he would say. "You've got to be a lifestyle evangelist."

He's not the only person I had heard that from. When I was a brigade commander at Fort Hood, Texas, I was fortunate enough to bring Dallas Cowboys Coach Tom Landry in for a luncheon. He drove all the way from Austin, and we had about 500 people come out to see him, thinking they were going to hear from Landry the coach. Instead, we heard from Landry the Christian. He told that group, "Being a Christian isn't about who you are. It's about what you do."

It was reinforcement from an unexpected place. And I've got to tell you, that notion has stuck with me ever since.

One of my favorite books is *A Life That God Rewards* by Bruce Wilkinson, and its basic message is this: God really doesn't care how many stars you wear or how much money you make; He cares about how many people you touch. That's how I want to live and how I've tried to live in my life of service in the United States military. And this conviction remains in my post-military career and will remain until the day I die.

My strength comes through my relationship with God. When I have difficult times, the first thing I do is drop to my knees and pray, "God, get me through these difficult times." I turn to Scripture, including 2 Timothy 3:16, 1 John 8:10, Psalm 119:11 (see appendix 2 for full texts), and other verses.

You will see reflections of my faith and a few more Scripture references in the coming chapters, as I tell you about some of the most difficult times I've faced as a leader, and how I got through them—finding opportunities in obstacles and adapting in the face of sometimes unimaginable pressures and difficulties.

My faith is the foundation on which I build my life. And as a leader, I hope you will take the time to ask yourself: *What is the foundation upon which I build my own life?*

★   ★   ★

– 11 –

THE CAPTAIN AND THE SHIP

I was awarded the Soldier's Medal in Doha, Kuwait, at the end of the first Gulf War. For those of you who don't know, the Soldier's Medal is the highest award you can receive in peacetime for heroism. It's like the peacetime version of the Medal of Honor, and, to get the medal, you have to risk your own life to save others.

I tell this story not to be boastful but to highlight my commitment to my subordinates—and my commitment to being a leader in the fullest sense of the word. I also hope to get you thinking about your own level of commitment—to ponder what you would do in a similar situation, as a reflection of just how much you care about the people you're leading, the people who are looking to you to lead.

It was 1991. I was the executive officer of this regiment, as a major, which means I was second-in-command of a unit of about 5,500 people. The war was over. We had sent Saddam Hussein's Republican Guard running back over the borders toward Baghdad, but had decided as a nation not to pursue them into Iraq. Since Saddam still had a viable army, my regiment remained as basically the last remaining American presence in the desert.

As a matter of organization at that time, we had asked and been given permission to consolidate all of our ammunition and vehicles together in one secure location. We basically collected a whole regiment's worth of trucks, tanks, and ammo that had been fanned out across the desert and put them in what amounted to a massive parking lot surrounded by a ten-foot concrete retaining wall.

One day, the aide to the one-star general called me and said, "Hey, we think you have a problem in your motor pool." There was black smoke rising from one of the vehicles.

The regiment's commander was out checking training, which meant the responsibility for whatever this was fell on my shoulders. We weren't under attack. I knew that. We were far from the enemy. So I hoped it was nothing as I got in my vehicle with my driver, Pete Bazek, and went down there. That's when I saw it: a fire in the engine compartment of one of our artillery vehicles. That might not have been much of a problem at all—if that vehicle weren't chock-full of ammunition and parked smack-dab in the middle of a tightly confined parking lot full of other vehicles full of ammunition.

Clearly I had to act fast. There was no time to call for help. No time to order someone else to do what had to be done. I crawled inside the vehicle and tried to put out the flames myself, but the fire was spreading too fast, and the vehicle started blowing up around me. I made a decision then and there to evacuate the motor pool. As disciplined as our soldiers are, any emergency evacuation will result in a bit of chaos. It's to be expected. So during those frantic seconds of the evacuation, fifty-two of my soldiers were injured—not from the flames, and not from the horror of what was about to happen, but because they had to get over that ten-foot retaining wall in a hurry. And they did.

As the flames spread and the first sparks of ammunition fired off in the back of that artillery vehicle, I quickly exited out of the vehicle and started running toward the retaining wall. Unfortunately, the wall was too far away to reach in time. I was stuck in the middle of that motor pool when, all at once, the artillery vehicle exploded—causing all of the other vehicles and ammunition around me to catch fire and explode as well.

The engine-access panel from that vehicle blew straight up in the air when it happened, landing with a crash within two feet of my head. Shrapnel flew everywhere, and yet, as I raised my head and picked myself up from the dirt, unable to hear anything but a high-pitched ringing that seemed to emanate from somewhere deep inside my brain, I knew I was okay. Somehow, by the grace of God, I had survived. And I knew what I had to do next.

I spent the next six hours rushing from vehicle to vehicle looking for those men who didn't evacuate or didn't have time to evacuate and were hiding. My mission was to find them and lead them to safety. I would not stop until I knew every one of those men was accounted for.

Six hours later, they were.

About $52 million worth of equipment was destroyed during that six-hour burn, including four M1-A1 battle tanks that were melted into useless hunks of molten steel. That's how horrendous the heat was. But no lives were lost. That's what mattered most.

As for the risk to my own life? Put it this way: I was in charge. In the face of disaster, if that meant I would go down with the proverbial ship, then so be it. As long as my crew was safe.

That's what a leader does. Or perhaps more accurately: That's who a leader *is*.

I can't say where all leaders get their strength when it comes to life-or-death situations. But the reason I was comfortable staying in that motor pool until everyone was safe is simply because I believed that God was going to protect me. I prayed and knew that, if God wanted me to die that day, I would die; if He wanted to protect me, He would protect me. So I went about my business, and that was that.

There, and in my multiple tours in Iraq, I was never once afraid of dying. Strong Christians, candidly, are not afraid of dying—they just don't want to do it anytime soon.

There's a book called *Heaven Is for Real*, which became a massive international bestseller when it was released, and with good reason. It tells the story of a four-year-old boy who underwent emergency surgery and hovered near death at a hospital, only to be revived and come back filled with stories of what heaven looked like, including unimaginably accurate details of the people he saw there during his brief visit to the afterlife. He knew things about people he had never known or been told about in life. Some critics have questioned whether the book could possibly be true, but I read it, and I believe everything that's in that book because it's based on the Bible. I believe that, when you die, you go to heaven, and you leave behind your Earthly trials and tribulations; you're there for all eternity. So I was never once afraid for my personal well-being, even when I was getting shot at all the time.

In Iraq, more than a decade after that motor-pool incident, many times when my helicopter flew, it got shot at. I had the best helicopter pilots in the division, so through the 624 hours I spent in the back of a Blackhawk during combat operations, I never once sat back there worried. I figured if it was my time, it was my time.

I wasn't looking forward to dying. I wasn't hoping to die. But I was prepared to die—and my wife and children were prepared for that potential as well, even though none of us wanted it to happen.

Perhaps it takes a certain fearlessness to truly lead. If you have no faith, I'm not sure where that fearlessness can come from. In fact, a lady came up to me recently after one of my speeches and asked, "If my son doesn't have the strength that you profess, where is he going to get his strength from?" I confess that I really don't know the answer to that question.

Outside of my faith, I think that fearlessness I exhibited in Kuwait just comes from the notion of loving your subordinates like you love your own children. If your own children were caught in a fiery deathtrap, you'd do anything you could to save their lives. Back in Kuwait, I saw those men as my children. I made sure they were safe. Nothing could have stopped me. End of story. Staying behind and doing the right thing for my men was an easy decision to make.

Chances are the decisions you make in corporate America are not going to be life-or-death decisions, but leading from that same point of view will make a difference—because every decision you make as a leader does have an impact on people's livelihoods. If you make a bad decision, people could ultimately lose their jobs. Lost jobs can result in people being unable to pay their bills, having their homes foreclosed on, or not being able to send their kids to college. Is that what you would want for your own children? Whether their lives are on the line in the heat of the moment or not, you hold those lives in your hands.

So you have to ask yourself: Where do you get your source of strength as you're looking to take care of your subordinates? Do you have the faith to make it through the fire, for their sake? When the chips are down, when the motor pool's blowing up around you, when you're put to the test, will you have the strength to stand up and do what's right, based on the priorities that matter most?

In life, you never know when you'll be tested. I never could have foreseen the lengths to which I would be tested that day in 1991. And regardless of the fact that General Norman Schwarzkopf flew in to personally pin that medal on my uniform, I am simply humbled and thankful that neither my life nor any of my subordinates' lives were taken away that day. And I stand proud knowing that I did the right thing under the toughest of circumstances—knowing full well that I would do it all over again if I were faced with a similar challenge tomorrow.

★ ★ ★

– 12 –

TIME MANAGEMENT

Before you get scared off, let me remind you that being a lifestyle evangelist doesn't mean you have to necessarily risk life and limb for your subordinates. In fact, I pray you never find yourself in a situation anything like the one I faced in Kuwait.

Most of the time, being a lifestyle evangelist just means sticking to your principles and perhaps showing a little tough love when necessary—especially when it comes to leading by example in the discipline of time management, a crucial area of focus for this fast-paced, overburdened world.

I firmly believe that the difference between an extremely successful individual or organization and a moderately successful one is time management. The reason? Without time management, organizations flounder. I think most business courses will teach you that. I think most managers and business leaders understand that. But the part that often gets overlooked is that, without proper time management, the individual members of any organization can be consumed and overwhelmed by their work. And if the individuals who make up an organization are overwhelmed and consumed by their work, they are either going to burn out or stop working to their full capacity. And if the members of an organization are not contributing at their full potential, that will, by definition, negatively affect the organization.

It all comes down to taking care of your people. Take care of them, and they will take care of you.

We all need to find a level of work-life balance that works for us. That includes both leaders and subordinates. For all the talk about work-life balance and the almost mythical achievement it seems to be in the eyes of so many individuals who are aimlessly searching for it, there really is just one key: time management. I've enjoyed the benefits of work-life balance for the last twenty or more years in my career. How did I get there? By applying time-management principles to my standard workweeks back home, as well as in the middle of combat operations in Iraq. I simply made time management a top priority, and that opened the door to the balance I needed.

You have to ask yourself: How much time do I need? Where can I carve out time not just for my work life, but also for my family life, my play life, and just for myself? Carving out time just for yourself is especially important for leaders. If a leader isn't having fun, nobody's having fun. Making time to let loose, to play, to enjoy yourself, and to relax will have a positive effect on you and on the lives you influence. But there's another reason, too: As a leader, with so many people in your ear and so many decisions to make, you have to make time for yourself just to think. Whether I was working in division command, corps command, Installation Management Command, or in the university system after leaving the Army, I've always carved out time on a daily basis just to think. Often it happened in the early hours of the morning, when I was sure no one would bother me.

The block of time that worked for me was between four and six-thirty every morning. For twenty years, that was my quiet time. It may seem extreme to rise so early, but it worked for me. The phone was not ringing, my wife was asleep, nobody was asking me any questions—it was a time for me to read reports, write letters, plan for the day, or simply to think. If you don't make time to think, whatever decisions you make over the course of the day are just going to be echoing somebody else's thoughts, not yours. Over the last twenty years, this is the way my day started, even in my post-military career—it's me in the office, the dogs by my side on the floor, my wife and kids still sound asleep. When you find something that works for you, stick with it.

At any Army base, PT (physical training) begins at 6:30 a.m., so that was how I marked the beginning of my workdays. Generally I was at work every day from 6:30 a.m. to 5:30 p.m. At 5:30 I'd head home for dinner and stay focused on the family until nine or so, when my kids (when they were younger) would head to bed. Then Sarah would do her thing, and I could work some more if necessary in preparation for the next day before going to bed myself. When the kids stayed up later, I'd remain focused on the family later. It evolved over time, and I had the freedom to evolve within a time structure I set for myself early on.

The rule I tried to follow was 15-7-2.

The "7" refers to sleep. You need to get seven hours of sleep. I certainly do. Everybody knows their own rhythms, but I don't function well on less than seven hours. I'm also a morning person. Some people aren't.

The "2" refers to physical training. I found, after a few years of trial-and-error and following other people's schedules and routines, that I've got to get seven hours of sleep and two hours of physical training in every day to keep my metabolism rate and my heart rate up—so I feel good enough to function at maximum capacity all day long.

That then leaves me the "15"—fifteen hours a day for everything else.

In combat, it was pure 15-7-2: a full fifteen-hour workday, balanced by seven hours of sleep and two hours of working out. (Yes, I worked out even in combat, which gave me the physical capability to have the endurance I needed to make it through each day. I couldn't risk not working out and seeing my muscles atrophy when I needed them most.)

And, by the way, I demanded that my subordinates follow a similar schedule. I needed them to be just as fit and efficient as I was in order for our organization to work.

Back home, that fifteen hours got broken into ten hours of work and five hours with the family. And the only reason I could pull that off was because of effective time management—including the managing of my subordinates' time at work.

Here's where the importance of time management comes within your organization. If your organization isn't managing time effectively, it will drain time from other important areas of your life. And that's when work-life balance gets lost.

DON'T MISS OUT ON YOUR LIFE

I'm pretty sure I first learned the importance of time management from Walt Ulmer, the West Point leader who would become a friend and one of the five big mentors in my career. (I'll talk more about my mentors, and the importance of mentorship, in Part 3 of this book.)

Walt Ulmer had one particularly effective rule that I just flat-out copied, called "The 7-minute Rule." Basically, what I tell my subordinates in every setting I've ever worked in is that, if we have a meeting that's supposed to start at 1:00 p.m., and it's 1:07 p.m. and I'm still not there, you all leave. I'm an effective time manager, so if I'm not there, then, obviously, I've been sidetracked by something important, and I don't want you wasting your time waiting on me.

Whenever I communicated this for the first time in any new leadership role, people didn't believe me! They worried they'd somehow get in trouble for leaving, when, in fact, the *last* thing I wanted was for anyone to be sitting around twiddling their thumbs. The fact is, I would not be late if I could have been on time. I showed that by repeatedly being on time. This is a simple but effective way to walk the talk. But there were times when I didn't have a choice, and if I were sidetracked by something I could not avoid, it made no sense for me to keep people waiting. That's simply not a good use of their time.

Conversely, I make it very clear how important it is that everyone arrive at a meeting on time. There have been numerous cases when I'd walk into the conference room on time and lock the door—leaving people on the other side of the door wishing they'd been on time—just to demonstrate the importance of being on time.

West Point generally taught you that "on time" meant ten minutes early. That's what "on time" looks like to me. I realize not everyone operates by the same clock, but in the workplace, we need to. The fact is, in the modern world, just about every one of us carries a synchronized clock in our pocket. It's called a cell phone. So there is no excuse; you show up on time. Period. Otherwise you're wasting other people's time and slowing down their productivity.

(A side note here: In private life it's not always that easy, and sometimes you have to adjust accordingly. If you're married to a person like Sarah, you're dealing with a different perception of time management. She tends to always be fifteen minutes late, even when I'm trying to be ten minutes early, so it's a game we play. If I know we've got to be ready at 1:00 p.m., I tell her we've got to be ready at 12:45. I build that into our schedule.)

In addition to arriving on time, I end meetings on time. If a meeting is supposed to end at 2 p.m., it ends at 2 p.m.—regardless of whether we're finished with the conversation. Once everyone in your organization knows that—and knows that they can't get away with belaboring a point or over-stretching a presentation—they all start watching the clock and using their time more effectively. When that clock struck 2, they knew I'd be standing up and saying my goodbyes as I headed off to tackle the next block in my schedule. And while it may come off as a bit anal-retentive, showing your workforce that discipline is extremely powerful.

I did hurt some people's feelings when I locked them out of the room or cut off the discussion rather than let the meeting run over. But they knew I was doing it for the sake of time management, and they knew I was doing it so that I could, indeed, live my life the way I described to them from day one: so I could be home for dinner by 6 p.m., and so they could be home for dinner by six, too.

I carried that "home-for-dinner" rule into every position I held in my career, including my work at the Pentagon, overseeing the management of every Army installation on Earth. I refused to sacrifice my family time for my work time, or my workers' family time, either—and, in the end, that was appreciated. I walked the walk. I lived by my words, and I acted upon them. I was never one of these bosses who would hold a long meeting promoting work-life balance, and then make everybody stay at work until 9:00 p.m. because of some big deadline that same week. (If you're working in corporate America, I have a feeling that sounds all too familiar to you!) My workers knew where I stood and respected it because I lived by it. Therefore, I got results.

You may disagree with the way I organize meetings or stick to a firm timetable. The point is, I walked the walk that I said I wanted others to walk. I demonstrated the importance of time management in my daily life, and I was able to take care of my jobs and my family at the same time as a result of that effort.

Despite the extreme nature of my career in the military, I didn't miss my son's football games or my daughter's plays unless I was deployed—unless I was physically gone. And unlike travel in corporate America, my deployments were compulsory. When I was forced to go to Kosovo, it wasn't a choice. When I was forced to go to Baghdad, it wasn't a choice.

I meet CEOs all the time who miss big family-life events. And it always saddens me, because I know that it doesn't have to be that way. They have a choice. They have a choice to be better time managers, and to give the time they need to their families if they want to. And if you've been listening to me, you understand why I think that's important.

I do my best to explain this to people all the time, and sometimes I wish everybody would just listen to more country-western music. There are so many lessons in those lyrics. There's a song out called "Don't Miss Your Life" by a guy named Phil Vassar. It's the story of a corporate executive flying from one place to another, and there's an old man sitting next to him, and he says he's off to another meeting and it's his daughter's birthday, and the old man warns him about the regrets he has from his own successful career: how he missed his daughter's first steps and his son's crossing home plate for the first time. He tells the young executive, "Don't miss your life."

I put it another way when I talk to groups of people all over this country: "Don't miss your dash."

You see, when you pass by a cemetery, you notice that just about every headstone has a birth date and a death date, and those two dates are separated by a dash. That dash represents your life. What you do with that life is up to you. Believe me, you don't want to miss it.

In the Army there were no ifs, ands, or buts: When I had to go, I had to go. And that time away, when I couldn't dedicate my allotted hours to my family, was extremely tough on me.

Funny enough, the bulk of my time away did start with a choice. My family was in Texas when the Army first decided to send me to Washington, DC. My daughter, Susan, was going into her junior year of high school. I thought I would be spending only fourteen months in Washington, and we sat down as a family and decided it would be too disruptive to the family to move everyone for a fourteen-month stay. So I went to DC by myself and commuted back and forth for as much family time as I could get.

It was tough, but we made it through. And the effort I made putting in all those hours on planes back and forth was worth every added stress to my time-management plans, for sure.

But then I got promoted to general officer and wound up staying in DC for two years. When I finally came back home, the army deployed me to Kosovo for a year—just as my son was entering his senior year. (My kids are just twenty-two months apart in age.) I missed too many of his football games because of that. I missed too many of those little moments in the afternoon when I could have helped him with his homework. I missed those moments sitting around the dinner table with him as he finished his high school career.

The Army wound up sending me to Italy after that, and then off to Iraq—back-to-back-to-back. That time lost with my son had a cost.

I missed my son's high school graduation because I was in Naples, Italy. I simply didn't have a choice, and, of course, my son didn't blame me for that. We were an Army family. We knew absences sometimes came with the territory. But I didn't realize how emotional it was for Lucas until one day, a few years later, when he said, "Dad, it really hurt me that you weren't there for my high school graduation." He didn't blame me—but that didn't mean it didn't hurt.

My daughter graduated from college in four years, but for my son, it took eight years. I think it was partly because I wasn't there to help him. Right then and there, as we talked, I committed to be the guest speaker at his college graduation. When he did finally graduate, not only was I there speaking, I was the one who got to hand him his diploma. At the end, I was finally *there*.

The thing is, you never get those moments back.

No matter how big or important the organization is that you're leading, your life and your family are bigger. Time management, focused on the priorities that you set, is the key to your being a part of your own life.

Don't miss your dash, people. Use your time wisely. And make sure your workforce follows your lead. They'll thank you for it in the end.

REMINDER

Achieve a work-life balance.

★ ★ ★

"How are you living your dash?"

★ ★ ★

– 13 –

FOCUS MANAGEMENT

While I credit time management with much of my success as a leader—and my adherence to time management as a prime example of how I've tried to behave as a lifestyle evangelist—I think my ability to focus comes in a close second.

I think, as a culture, and certainly as a country, we've all become too easily distracted from the tasks at hand. A little distraction now and then is somewhat understandable, but the worst part about what I see happening today is that the culprits, in most cases, aren't even worthwhile distractions. Instead, we're consumed by what I call "absurd distractions." (Thomas Friedman refers to this idea in his book *That Used to Be Us*.)

Think about our political landscape. Rather than focus on critical issues such as the deficit, unemployment, or our heavy reliance on foreign oil, our politicians are constantly focused on things that are absolutely absurd. Just one month before the 2012 presidential elections, all focus suddenly turned to Big Bird and whether we should cut the miniscule funding we give to PBS.

There was a time not long ago, in this post-9/11 world, when Congress couldn't pass a basic budget, let alone any major bill, but somehow managed to pass a bill regulating the audible volume of television commercials. How does that take precedence over, well, just about anything else? Or the absurd distraction I had to work around during my time at the Pentagon: revoking the military's "Don't Ask, Don't Tell" policy. We were fighting two wars at the time. Two! I remember sitting in the Pentagon as we're trying to figure out how to fight these wars in Iraq and Afghanistan with limited resources, and then all of a sudden, for political reasons, we decide to announce that we're going to revoke "Don't Ask, Don't Tell." This distraction was all anyone could talk about, from the evening news to the offices of the top brass, from the White House down to the dinner tables of soldiers and their families. I'm not saying these are issues that don't deserve being addressed at some point, but in the context of the crises that are enveloping our nation, they are absolutely absurd distractions.

We all can recognize absurd topics that are occupying our minds, we just choose not to do anything about them. I mean, everywhere you go, the water-cooler talk has been taken over by the Kardashians (*who?*) or which celebrity marriage is falling apart. And it's one thing to gossip at work, but when the gossip is all about the lives of so-called reality TV stars, there's clearly a national problem with our ability to focus on the real world.

Even in the business world, the distractions are never ending. In the summer of 2012, one guy from Chick-fil-A announced where he stood on the gay marriage issue, and he had the mayors of Boston and Chicago and elsewhere come out and lambast him for expressing his opinion. Suddenly it was all the media was talking about. Thousands of people were boycotting Chick-fil-A, and thousands more came out and protested the boycotts! A restaurant best known for their fried chicken sandwiches with the pickle on top was now the center of too many people's attention. And yet there's no uproar, no protest, no support shown over life-and-death issues that are staring us in the face. This is the very definition of an absurd distraction. And when the media and mayors and everyone else are focused on something so absurd, you can bet they're not focusing on the stuff that really matters.

My point is, you cannot focus on critical issues when you're consumed by absurd distractions.

It's up to you, as a leader, to take charge and tell your workforce what to focus on. To actually say, "Here's what you've got to focus on. We're not going to allow ourselves to be distracted by all these other things"—no matter how much distraction and how much pressure you're under to do otherwise.

Perhaps my biggest test of focus came when President Bush announced the surge in Iraq back in 2007.

To refresh your memory, the war in Iraq had been stretching on since March of 2003. The war was incredibly unpopular at that point: We had lost a lot of American lives for what seemed like fairly dubious reasons, and as far as the American people were concerned, this war had no end in sight.

I'm not going to get into the arguments about whether we should have invaded Iraq in the first place. That discussion is for a different book. We were there. We had a job to do—and it was pretty clear to everyone involved that we weren't doing the job the way it needed to be done.

From the very beginning of this war, we in the Army knew that we didn't have enough troops on the ground to tackle the tasks at hand. We had enough troops to get in, defeat Saddam Hussein, and get out. But that wasn't what we were tasked with accomplishing. There was a counterinsurgency at play. There was rebuilding to do. Our military was tasked with what should have been State Department work, with aid work, with peace-keeping, and policing work in a country fraught with ethnic conflicts of epic proportions.

In that regard, despite the many calls for us to simply get out and bring our troops home, a massive surge of troops was just what that war needed. It was a good decision under the circumstances—and one that should have come much sooner, in my opinion. But there was just one hitch when the surge was finally hatched: the rapid speed of troop deployment.

I was in charge of the Army's Third Infantry Division at that time, and, by January, we had already been planning to deploy to Iraq. The plan was this: We would have six months to train and prepare for a rebuilding mission in the northern part of the country. Well, you know what they say about the best-laid plans. That January I got a call from General Ray Odierno, who was the corps commander in Iraq at that time.

"Hey, Rick," he said, "don't think about coming in six months—think about coming in six weeks." *Six weeks?*

He wasn't through: "And don't think about going north," he said, "think about going south."

With President Bush's announcement, our six-month timetable was shortened to six weeks, and our plan to go on a rebuilding mission in northern Iraq was completely scrapped. The new mission? I would be placing my 25,000 soldiers into combat operations in a highly dangerous area just south of Baghdad known (for good reason) as the Triangle of Death.

The American Army has the ability to adapt. We've built massive amounts of flexibility into our operations and into our people; I'll talk more about what it takes to create an adaptable workforce in Part 4 of this book.

So the biggest challenge I faced in preparing an entire division—including our division headquarters—to dive into a combat operation in the most dangerous part of Iraq on a six-week timetable, was to keep everyone on-task and focused on what needed to be done. No distractions.

With a truncated timetable and such a serious and daunting task in front of us, the absurd distractions went out the window pretty easily.

There's nothing to eliminate foolishness and get you down to basics quite like facing the prospect of enemy fire in a foreign land. But there are also all sorts of distractions that set in when your organization is challenged—including the distraction of naysayers.

There were a number of people on my staff who reacted to that six-months to six-weeks news by shutting down.

"General," they said, "there's no way we can make such a major shift in that amount of time! You've got to call someone! You've got to tell them we can't do it!"

They immediately gave up. There are certain people in any organization who are so uncomfortable working outside of their current planning process that when someone throws them a curve ball, they immediately shut down. And that shutting down keeps anything from happening. It's up to a leader to point them in the right direction, to reassure them, and to show them that it can be done.

One of the reasons some of my staff shut down was that the Army had given us so many tasks to accomplish before we deployed—a number that could not physically be tackled in six weeks. The fact was, the Army had given my division headquarters 137 tasks to complete before we deployed. Those tasks included advanced training exercises that had to be perfected, setting up command-and-control linkages between the various brigades that would report to us in the field, allocating all kinds of resources—from personnel to equipment to money, and more. My staff was right. We couldn't tackle 137 tasks in six weeks. It *was* impossible. But that wouldn't keep us from deploying on time. It simply meant that we had to focus—and that ability to focus fell squarely on my shoulders.

I asked myself, "Of those 137 tasks, which are the most critical?" I pared the list down to thirty-eight tasks, and I focused on those thirty-eight tasks during that six-week training period, while simultaneously working to develop a timeline in which we could tackle the rest.

"Which are the tasks that we have to do now? Which tasks can we accomplish on the fly, as we move? Which tasks can we work on after we arrive in the field?"

We would still get through the 137 tasks. They would just be done on a different timetable, and many of them would be done after we hit the ground in Iraq.

Presenting my staff with just thirty-eight tasks to tackle in six weeks suddenly made the job seem doable. I would still have to work to keep them focused, of course, so no one would be sidetracked into working on the remaining tasks until those thirty-eight tasks were completed. But by my trimming the tasks down to the absolute most critical, suddenly the six-week shift seemed like less of a crisis and more of an "urgent development."

KEEP YOUR EYE ON THE GOAL

In my early-morning time, I looked ahead to the opening days of a major combat operation. *What would we need to know? What would likely happen?* For example: The Air Force would be heavily involved in bombing campaigns right from the outset, and in any heavy air operation, chances are we'd be tasked with downed-aircraft recovery. My men needed to be ready for that. So that's one of the training exercises we tackled at home. And guess what? Within a week of our arrival that March, we faced a downed-aircraft recovery mission—and my crew responded seamlessly.

Taking the time to think, taking the time to plan, taking the time I needed to lead with confidence rather than with urgency or panic made all the difference. I can't stress enough how important it is for leaders to decide when to decide. If you need to make a decision on the spot, that's one thing. But if you can take a few minutes, a few hours, a few days to decide, you need to set a timetable and stick to it. Use that time to consider your options thoroughly. But don't over-think. Sometimes too much information and weighing too many options can cause more confusion than clarity. Use your expertise, your experience, your faith, your knowledge, your beliefs, and your guiding principles to make your decisions, and then stick by them.

Listening to my gut, relying on my own expertise and experience in the field while culling suggestions from my staff and filtering them through my own thought process allowed me to make a conscious decision to say, "This is where we're going to focus." And even though there were lots of other folks around me who were trying to distract me, running around like chickens with their heads cut off, yelling, "We've got to do this!" or "We've got to do that!" I kept the focus on the critical tasks.

In all walks of life, if leaders would focus on the critical tasks and not the absurd distractions, we would all be better off. (The media could learn that lesson, too!)

Some of you may argue with me about this, but I have to say that one of the biggest distractions we face in our home and family time is the constant draw of email and other after-hours office communications. It is my belief that you have to have the mental discipline to shut that communication down at certain times for your own sanity, and, in the long run, this will improve productivity. There are multiple studies out there that show how devastating a single email chime on your phone can be when it comes to affecting your focus. Every time it vibrates or beeps, you stop what you're doing and answer it. It then takes time—sometimes lots of time—to get back to whatever you were doing, whether it's writing a report or playing with your kid. And that's not good for anyone.

There are some bosses who demand instant responses, who expect their subordinates to be online and reachable at all hours of the day. That needs to change!

A boss who demands urgent replies to emails at all hours of the day or night, including the weekends, simply isn't operating efficiently. That boss isn't focused on the right things. If you've studied any managerial coursework in the past, you've probably come across the Franklin Covey quadrants of productivity. I would say that boss is operating in quadrant 3, which is not where you want to be.

I'll paraphrase those quadrants here just to give you a better sense of what I mean. There are basically four quadrants your organization can operate in at any given time.

Quadrant 1 is when everything is urgent and everything's important. That's what it's like in the Pentagon, where everyone's rushing around from crisis to crisis, and there isn't time to deal with anything else.

Quadrant 2 is when you're focused on what's important but not urgent—which means you actually have time to focus and make good decisions about all kinds of things.

Quadrant 3 is when everything's urgent, but none of it is important. That's the "let's set up a meeting to talk about the next meeting" world that so many corporations are stuck in.

Quadrant 4 is when nothing's urgent and nothing's important— which basically means you're spinning your wheels and not getting anything done.

Clearly quadrant 2 is where you want to spend most of your time and where you want your organization to spend most of its time, no matter what it is you do for a living. Quadrant 2 is what happens when you focus and avoid unnecessary and especially absurd distractions.

Quadrant 2 is achievable even when the pressure is on, as we proved by staying focused and on-task in the six-week preparation for the surge.

How do you get there? By asking the right questions and demanding the right answers. When it comes to keeping my organizations focused, the three questions I ask all the time are:

1. "Are we doing the right things?"
2. "Are we doing things right?"
3. "What are we missing?"

If you want to keep your organization focused on the right things, then those questions have to be asked repeatedly and answered repeatedly. I worked in a few areas and organizations where generally the answer to those first two questions was "No," but we went ahead and kept doing what we were doing anyway, often without any consideration of question number three. (The Pentagon certainly comes to mind here!)

As a leader, I've made it my mission to answer those questions honestly. Whether going into combat or just keeping your business afloat, you want to be able to answer those first two questions with a "Yes," and the final question with, "Nothing at all." That's how you'll know that you're focused on doing the right things and doing the right things to stay focused.

REMINDER

Decide when to decide.

★ ★ ★

"Take the time to think."

★ ★ ★

– 14 –

WALKING THE WALK

Do you want to know one of the primary reasons I've been able to lead on my terms for the last twenty years—bucking convention, standing up for what I believe in, getting results, adapting at will, overcoming obstacles by turning them into opportunities, and never looking back while I climbed the ranks all the way to becoming a three-star lieutenant general in the United States Army? All while staying true to my personal mantra of putting God first, family second, and career third? I've been able to do that because I wasn't held back by the "A" word.

"What's the 'A' word," you ask?

Aspiration.

I know, I know. That sounds backwards. We've all been programmed to believe that aspiration is a positive thing—that aspiration is a motivator. And it is—to some degree. But drawing the line on reasonable aspirations can also give you a tremendous amount of freedom.

I know this because I accomplished my highest career aspiration all the way back in 1993.

Shortly after leaving West Point, I set one very particular goal for myself: I wanted to be a battalion commander. That was it. That was as high as I wanted to go in the Army. Once I accomplished that goal, I convinced myself I would be satisfied with my career.

The Army promoted me to Lieutenant Colonel Battalion Command in 1993. Everything after that was gravy. My time in the Army was pure service after that. I wasn't aiming for another promotion, and that gave me a certain amount of latitude I hadn't had before. If I was faced with a bad boss who wanted me to do things that were counter to my beliefs, counter to putting God and family first, I had the latitude to just say "No." If I couldn't live with a certain situation, I simply would have left the Army and moved on to another career. I had already accomplished my goal. I had achieved my mark of success.

That gave me freedom to follow my mantra, and to spread my mantra to others.

Leaders have to set the precedent. You have to draw the line. You have to have your priorities clear in life. My relationship to God, family, and then profession—in that order—became my mantra. If I was told to do anything that violated those priorities, I just wouldn't do it. I was okay doing that because I had already become successful. And that gave me power.

Everybody can get to that place in their chosen profession, unless they've got an overly ambitious sense of aspiration. If you've got the sort of aspiration that causes you to do things you know you shouldn't do in order to get from here to there, that's an issue you've got to deal with personally. You have to ask yourself, "What is good enough?" when it comes to your career, and then balance that with the all-important question, "What's the most important thing in my life?"

For me, putting God and family ahead of my career was paramount. That was the key to "living my dash."

On your deathbed, you're not going to wish you had worked more. You're not going to wish that you had worked harder. You're going to wish that you had spent more time with your loved ones. If people can acknowledge that, then they're probably going to be better at the work-life balance.

Just to hammer this point home, I want to tell you about a town-hall meeting I held with about 500 staffers at Fort Leavenworth, Kansas, during my time as head of Installation Management Command (IMCOM)—overseeing a worldwide workforce of 120,000 people, most of whom were civilians. Whenever I held a town-hall meeting with these employees—and I did that as often as I could—I would talk about the importance of work-life balance. At this particular presentation, I spoke at length about living your dash, and how important it was to use time management to get your work done during the day and spend your evenings and weekends with your family. I explained to the audience that, if you're not maintaining a work-life balance, you're working way too hard and sacrificing your family. "God didn't promise you tomorrow. He only promised you today—and that's why it's called 'the present,'" I said. "So you've got to reverse that behavior. You've got to focus on your family. You never know when it will be too late."

There happened to be a mother and her thirty-two-year-old daughter in the audience that day. They both worked in the same installation, and yet the two of them had indeed been so focused on work that they were never spending any time together. They had become estranged, even though they both lived there and worked together at Fort Leavenworth.

For some reason, on that particular day, my words got through to these two women. They approached me after the presentation was over and told me their story. That day they committed to spending more time with each other, to focusing on each other more, to telling each other that they loved the other. I was humbled and thankful that my words could have some effect.

One week later, that thirty-two-year-old daughter died. She died of natural causes. It wasn't an accident, though there was no way to see it coming, no way to predict it. She just died.

To this day, that mother still contacts me now and then to say, "Thank you. Thank you for that one week."

I'll say it again, people: Live your dash. If you love somebody, pick up the phone and call that person and tell them that you love them. If you've wronged somebody, go and fix that wrong. Don't assume you'll have another tomorrow to do that. Go do it today.

I'm thankful every day for the time I've been able to spend with my family, and that might never have been possible had I aspired to be a general. The fact that I kept my aspirations in check allowed me to live life on my terms—and, in an ironic twist, helped me climb the ladder of success even faster because I could walk the walk while standing on the solid foundation of my beliefs. Having the ability to do that made me capable of being a leader—of leading, rather than following. when it came to the principles I believe in.

I want to step back for a moment here, lest you think that I'm making myself out to be a little too perfect. The fact that I've been able to live out my own personal mantra, the fact that I have achieved what I consider to be a successful work-life balance, the fact that I've accomplished some great things and amassed a proud record of service to this country over the last thirty-five years doesn't mean I'm perfect. In fact, far from it. I think it's important that I share a bit about that here.

In the Bible, Paul says, "For I do not do the good I want to do, but the evil I do not want to do—this I keep on doing" (Romans 7:19). To paraphrase, Paul is basically asking a very poignant question of himself: "Why do I keep doing what I'm not supposed to do?"

I find myself asking that very same question all the time. As much as I try to walk the walk and live my life as an example to others, I do things that are 180 degrees different from what I preach. Sometimes so much so that I'm embarrassed by them.

On one hand, it's a good thing that I can acknowledge this. At least I know I'm screwed up! I tell people all the time, "If you're screwed up and you know it, you're less screwed up than if you're screwed up and don't know it."

But on the other hand, it can be frustrating and embarrassing, even if I can find strength in the Bible that allows me to chalk it up to being human. Romans 3:23 reminds me that "all have sinned and fall short of the glory of God."

I'll give you a couple of specific areas that always get me. The first one is anger management. I've been fighting anger management my whole life. I remember as a battalion commander (just after my highest aspiration was realized), one of my captains said something so unbelievably foolish that my reflex was to hit him! I knew better, of course, so rather than hit him, I hit the easel that I was using. I slammed that easel so hard that I dented it and busted my hand—and this was in front of my subordinates. It was a reflection of not being able to control my temper.

When I was a young captain, one of my soldiers aggravated me so badly that I actually took off my helmet and threw it against the armored-personnel carrier. I threw it so hard, I destroyed my helmet. Think about that for a second: This was a helmet—a solid apparatus meant to keep your head safe in combat. You've got to throw a helmet pretty hard in order to destroy it, but that's how mad I was!

I'm very conscious of the fact that, on any given day, I can flip. I can demonstrate absurd behavior. I'll do it at home sometimes, too—just get so mad about something that I lose it. So I'm conscious of that all the time. God wants you to control your anger. God doesn't want you to be an angry person. And it's certainly not "lifestyle evangelism" to be punching easels and destroying helmets. But it's hard to always stop and think, *Now, what am I demonstrating here?*

There's a phrase a lot of people use: "What would Jesus do?" That's in my mind all the time. But even Jesus got mad. There was a time he threw everything out of the temple! He got mad. And Paul—I like studying Paul, because he messed up all the time. That gives me hope.

Since that hand-busting moment in the early 1990s, I've mostly worked through that anger. I don't think there's a time since I was a flag officer through today that you'd find somebody who would say, "Hey, Lynch screamed at me," or "Lynch belittled me," or any of those kinds of responses. I've been able to acknowledge that I had that problem and have worked on it. I do my best to live the example I want to set. But it hasn't been easy.

The second area I tend to come up short in is swearing. It says in the Bible, "Don't use the Lord's name in vain." It also says, essentially, "Don't swear. Don't use blasphemy. Don't curse." Putting the Bible aside, I think it's pretty important to demonstrate graciousness and a sense of control as a leader, and a foul mouth tends to show something that's just the opposite of that.

For me, especially since I've been trying to act as a lifestyle evangelist since I was thirty-two years old, staying true to the no-swearing rule is pretty important. Once again, though, I've been embarrassed by my own behavior while leading. The time it hit me hardest was, again, back when I was a battalion commander. In addition to trying to be the best lieutenant colonel I could be, I was attempting to be a decent spiritual leader to my subordinates (at least to those who were interested in some spiritual guidance). So I hosted prayer breakfasts and prayer lunches, and would bring soldiers and their families together to talk about their spiritual fitness. At the very end of my time, after serving as a battalion commander for two full years, the day before I left, a staff sergeant came up to me and said, "You're a hypocrite. You profess to be a man of faith and live a life like Jesus, but you swear like a sailor."

That was a real gut-shot for me. Nobody had ever confronted me on that, but he was exactly right. Here I was saying one thing but doing something else. The audio didn't match the video.

If you've been around a bunch of soldiers, or even seen a war movie or two, you probably have some idea just how much swearing goes on every minute of every conversation. It's par for the course. Here I was trying to set a higher example, yet falling prey to that loose language like everyone else. It was unbecoming of a leader, and, from that point forward, I did my best to stop it.

I fail. Almost every day. I find that swearing is a part of my natural cadence, especially when I get passionate about an issue or angry about something. So, every day, I struggle with it. I slip, even though I know I shouldn't. That's a frailty. I am a frail man, as are each one of us. We all sin and fall short of the glory of God, as it says in the book of Romans. But making a conscious effort, trying to do your best, trying to walk the walk and be conscious of the example you're setting for others is better than nothing, and I believe that the bar leaders set for themselves should be as high as possible if they're going to be successful.

Trying to walk the walk is better than not walking the walk at all.

And don't forget, all of this applies to your family life, too. The impact of the way you act and how you live stretches far and wide. Sometimes much further than you think.

My daughter, Susan, got engaged a while back. And you know what she told me one day? She said she learned how a woman should be treated in a relationship by watching the way I treated her mom as she was growing up. Watching our relationship taught Susan what to look for in her own relationships as she grew into the incredible adult she is today—and she said "Yes" to a young man who treats her like gold.

She learned that by watching me! I didn't even realize she was paying attention. I wasn't purposefully trying to set an example. It's just the way it was. What would have happened had I been acting differently? What would have happened had I *not* shown my wife the love and respect she deserved, and that I wanted to give her? What would have happened had I worked all the time and not been home enough to give Susan any impression in that regard whatsoever?

That's emotional. That's powerful.

I made an impact on my daughter in an area where I wasn't even consciously trying to make an impact. I made an impact on one of the most important people in my life just by staying true to who I am.

As I think about that now, I can't help but think that that's what leadership is all about. At all levels.

Walking the walk is what matters the most.

– 15 –

VOICE AMPLIFICATION

With every promotion, with every rise through the ranks, with every new job title, your voice gets louder.

I didn't realize this fully until I became a general—and started seeing the reactions from my subordinates when they encountered the stars on my uniform.

There were times when I'd be having a conversation with one of our soldiers or officers, especially if it was about something critical, and they would perceive me as yelling at them (even though I wasn't even raising my voice). Yelling—something I almost never did after focusing on controlling my anger way back in the early '90s. After some further reflection, it occurred to me that the stars on my chest were acting as voice-amplification devices.

Because of my position and the perceived power that comes with that position, every word I said had more of an impact. And that goes for anyone with any big title in any organization: CFO, CEO, president, vice president, senior manager, etc.

Knowing that you're speaking through an amplification system comes with a newfound responsibility. Consider this: If you were walking around in your everyday life with a headset microphone strapped on, like one of those things Garth Brooks wears in concert, knowing that every word that came out of your mouth was going to be heard by thousands of individuals, or, at the very least, blasted full-force at whoever was listening, would you think twice before you spoke? I have a feeling you would. When a leader speaks, there is a ripple effect. Your words have a way of not only getting amplified in the mind of whoever's listening, but also repeated, far and wide, throughout your organization and beyond.

That takes some getting used to, and a lot of leaders seem to either ignore that reality or simply forget it. Sometimes, given the workload you face, the constraints on your time, the importance of the decisions you have to make every hour of every day, you can't always taper your tone. You can't always pause to make sure your amplified voice isn't too loud or too harsh. But most of the time? It's your duty as a leader to be aware of your amplification, to use it wisely, to use it sensitively, and to choose not to abuse it.

If you're aware that your words have greater impact because of your position, you can choose to use your words to get results. If you know that your workers are listening when you speak, because you truly care about them (as I've explained earlier, just as you would your own children), and knowing that they might even be a little afraid to cross you for fear of being yelled at (even if you never yell!), you can speak with a certain amount of confidence that whatever you say is going to get done.

Throughout my career, I've held counseling sessions with my subordinates on a regular basis. I'll talk more about that in the next section of this book, but they were similar to what you might call an "employee review" in the corporate world. It's where I would have someone come in to go over their work, their progress, see how they're doing, and talk about their strengths and maybe the areas where they could use some improvement. And because I was doing that from a senior position, what I often found in the course of counseling is that, when the people who were working for me truly believed that I cared, they would always feel bad if they let me down. My subordinates, countless times over the years, would modify their performance, improve what they were doing, and work harder because they didn't want to let me down.

When handled with care, that is the net effect of voice amplification. Your workforce does a better job because they know it matters to you, and they can hear you loud and clear.

Unfortunately, being in a position of power and having that amplified voice can also leave your workforce feeling like they're struggling to be heard. Sometimes they're left feeling like they're in the seventy-fifth row at that Garth Brooks concert, and they're trying to read Garth a private love note over the booming bass of the loudspeakers and the roar of the crowd. Your impact as a leader can be so great that sometimes your workforce feels like an audience. And frankly, I'm embarrassed by that. I want my subordinates to feel important—because they are. And this is another one of those areas where I struggle. It's not an intentional thing, of course, but it's something I'm conscious of and would like to improve in myself.

I do command-climate surveys all the time. That's basically a survey you use to ask the workforce, "What's on your mind? How's it going?" I'll walk into a group of people and give them all a blank three-by-five card, and I'll say, "On the front side, write the three things you like most about this division, and, on the back, write the three things you like the least." It's anonymous, so I get good feedback that way.

In my last posting before I retired from the Army, one area of concern came out loud and clear: My subordinates thought I was just too busy.

I really had three jobs during my final years in the Army: I was the assistant chief of staff for installation management in the Pentagon, which was a full-time job; I was the commanding general of the Installation Management Command (IMCOM), which was another full-time job (and by the way, their headquarters were physically separated: IMCOM had a San Antonio headquarters, so I had to split my office time between Washington, DC, and San Antonio); and then the chief of staff of the Army had me run this thing called the Services and Infrastructure Core Enterprise. If you're going to run a large organization like IMCOM, overseeing business on 163 Army bases around the world, with 120,000 people, you've got to run it like an enterprise, not like a series of silos. So routinely I'd have to get the medical community, service providers, and engineers together to say, "Okay, what are we going to do on our installations to be able to accomplish what is needed at a reduced cost?" That, as you can imagine, was yet another full-time job.

With so much on my plate and so much to oversee, I didn't have any time to waste. As a result, I found myself being very curt with people. That's what came across loud and clear in those surveys: "Lynch doesn't seem to have any time for us because he's always got something else going on."

That embarrassed me. In reality, I had time for what mattered, but I didn't have time to waste. There was a communication breakdown between what I perceived to be giving the time I needed to give and the time my workforce thought they needed to have in order to be heard. That's not an easy thing to overcome, but here's how that breakdown happened and why that perception existed.

When I walk into a meeting, I'm the most prepared person in the room. The meeting's going to start on time, and it's going to end on time. There's going to be an agenda. There have been countless books on this, but hardly anyone seems to follow those guidelines. Ever.

I followed the guidelines. I walked the walk. My meetings would never last more than an hour, so I was going to be prepared. In order to do that, if you were set to give a presentation at that meeting, I insisted on seeing the slides you were going to show or any narrative you were going to read ahead of time. I would generally use my early-morning time period, that 4:00 to 6:30 a.m. block in my schedule, to go over those slides and those notes to prepare for the meetings. That worked well for me, and it meant there wouldn't be any wasted time in those meetings.

The problem is, all these people worked so hard on their presentations, and they'd come into the meeting and want to work their way through the slides. Well, I don't need you to read the slides to me; I already read 'em! So I'd go into the meeting and say, "Get to slide twelve, and tell me more about the third bullet point, because that's what I'm interested in." And frankly, that offended a lot of people. They put time into preparing the slide presentation and sought the opportunity to shine in front of the general. They felt let down or even angry if I didn't give them that opportunity to shine. I knew I had to get through the meeting because I had something else to do in the next block of time, and the next block after that. My days were scheduled from minute to minute most of the time.

That was a problem for me.

I tried really hard at the beginning of the meeting *not* to jump to the point I was most interested in. But when they'd get up there and start talking about stuff that I didn't want or need to hear, I'd have to jump in—"Okay, go to slide twenty-three . . ."—and I could tell that I had taken the wind out of their sails.

To say I regret that is probably too strong. It was what I needed to do. But it was something I was conscious of because I had an impact on people's lives. They didn't leave that meeting feeling good about what they had done. I felt good about the meeting because I got out of it what I wanted or needed, but I'm sure they didn't go home that night and tell their spouse and kids how much they enjoyed being able to present to the general.

As I've spent more time in corporate America as a consultant since leaving the Army, I see that happening in boardrooms all over this country. That's what corporate leadership is doing to their workforces right now: They're taking the wind out of people's sails. They're so busy that they're not taking the time to listen when they already have what they need. And perhaps there needs to be some better balance here.

I don't have a pat answer for fixing this—other than making sure our leaders and managers aren't overburdened with too many jobs at once. But it is something I hope we can become more aware of and work on together.

Even when we don't have three full-time jobs, do any of us really have time for BOGSAT (the acronym for a Bunch Of Guys Sitting Around a Table) in the workplace? I sure don't. That's quadrant 3 activity—going to a meeting just to plan the next meeting. The fact is, a slide show shouldn't be about the act of the slide show. It should be about the content and important points in that slide show. And maybe that's the answer right there. Maybe PowerPoint is just an instrument of the devil!

I like people to leave a conversation with me feeling enriched, feeling like they were listened to, feeling like I truly cared—but sometimes I got so busy that I didn't do that very well. Of course, I was setting a good example by showing that I was going to do the work efficiently and get home to my family at six—so that they could get home to their families by six, too. But I occasionally did it at the expense of some people's feelings. And I think there's something to learn from that.

AMPLIFYING THE POSITIVE

Throughout my career, I've made it a point to go out of my way to make people feel good. And that's an area where the voice amplification of my position would not only have a booming effect but get broadcast far and wide with just the simplest acknowledgment. If some young soldier was doing particularly great on any particular day, I'd stop and call his or her mom or dad: "Hi, this is General Lynch. I just wanted to let you know that your daughter's doing extraordinary work here in the Army; you should be really proud of her."

Other times, especially when we were overseas, I wrote letters home. I sent personal notes to family members, just thanking them for their service. Letting a wife know that her husband's service was appreciated, as was her sacrifice. I can't tell you how much a note like that is appreciated by a wife who hasn't seen her husband in months and has been left behind to tend to the household on her own. I sent notes to veterans, too, thanking them for all they had done—letting them know that their efforts would never be forgotten. I still do it. It takes only a few moments of my time, and I know those letters have an impact that lasts for years. Sometimes lifetimes.

Whether it's coming from a general, a CEO, a president, or any other type of leader, those types of notes inspire pride. They get hung up on the fridge or maybe tacked up on the church bulletin board. Sometimes they get framed and hung up in a special place in the home, maybe passed on to someone's children after they're gone. The effect of that simple acknowledgment is powerful because it's coming from a leader—a leader who's reaching out and touching people's lives.

I sometimes get resistance to these sorts of things in the corporate world. I'll have people stand up in the middle of a presentation and flat-out ask me, "Can you do that if you're the CEO of a private business?"

The answer is, "Yes! Why not?"

"Well, *should* you do it?" they'll wonder. "Isn't that crossing some sort of line?"

My answer is, "Of course, you should do it."

What is leadership about, anyway? Who is it you're leading if not your people? We're all people. There is no "us" and "them." We're all in this together. There is no line. Your impact on the lives of your people is powerful, whether you want to believe it or not. Why not indulge it in the best way possible?

Leading from a disconnected place, leading from on high, leading from afar, as if your people are just numbers or just cogs in the wheel, isn't the kind of leadership we need. What we need is engaged leadership, in every organization, in every company, and in every facet of American life. The more engaged we are in each other's lives, the stronger our organizations and, frankly, the stronger our country will be.

As I continue to do my best to walk the walk when it comes to my beliefs and principles, I find myself more and more engaged as a leader with each and every step. I'm thankful for that. I'm grateful for that. And I'm a better leader because of it.

As you read the next section of this book, I hope you'll understand why.

Part Three

ENGAGED LEADERSHIP

Do nothing out of selfish ambition or vain conceit.
Rather, in humility value others above yourselves.
– PHILIPPIANS 2:3

I f there's one subject I'm particularly motivated to share about, it's engaged leadership. I'm known for and love that phrase. It's a phrase that I hope will inspire leaders everywhere to step out of their corner offices, get down from their pedestals, and lead where it counts: among their people.

Manage by Walking Around (MBWA) isn't a new concept. If you want to know what's happening in your company, you need to get out and walk around. Talk to your people. They know what's going on, and chances are, if they see you and see that you care, they'll be ready and willing to tell you all the information you need to know—and then some.

Of course, it is my belief that leading is about much more than just "managing," so engaged leadership takes that MBWA concept one giant leap further. In my view, it's not enough just to see your workers in the workplace. You need to engage them in their lives. Get to know them. Get to understand them. Let them know you care not just about their output in the office or out on the battlefield, but that you truly care about them as people. Once that's established, you'll find that your people are not only working for you, they're working *with* you.

And believe me, there is simply no stronger place a leader can lead from.

− 16 −

LEADING WHERE IT COUNTS

I often think about the phrase "What would Jesus do?"

Whether it's strangers on the street, people I know, members of my family, or my superiors, co-workers, and subordinates in the workplace, I always do my best to treat people with kindness, compassion, and caring.

Sarah and I have a general rule that we won't walk by anybody without addressing them, and if possible, addressing them by their first name. If we're at the grocery store or Starbucks and someone has a name tag on, we'll look at that name and address them by it: "Thank you, Mary, for your service."

On the one hand, it's just a nice thing to do. On the other? It's a shrewd thing to do. Let me explain.

In Colin Powell's latest book, *It Worked for Me*, Colin talks about the importance of addressing others by name. When he was Secretary of State, he did what I do now, which is manage by walking around. Spend more time walking around and talking to people than being in your office.

One time Colin wandered down to the underground parking garage at the State Department—the first time anybody down there had ever seen a Secretary of State. He just wanted to meet all of the people who worked in the building, and, while he was down there, he asked the parking attendants some questions. It was a very condensed parking garage—the cars parked in rows. At the end of the day, the car that was parked three cars back wouldn't be able to leave until the car in front had left. So he asked the guys, "How do you determine who gets parked in front?"

And the parking attendant answered (and I'm paraphrasing here), "That's easy. It's the people who address us by our name, who care about us, who ask how we're doing and listen for the answer."

The people who drive in with their heads down, toss the attendants the keys without eye contact, and treat them as lesser human beings get parked in the third row—and wind up losing an hour leaving at the end of every day.

I like that story, and it makes a whole lot of sense to me because I've encountered that sort of thing in my own life. Haven't you?

Studies have shown that you can improve service by 80 percent if you address people by their first name. Why would anyone want to miss that opportunity, in work or in life? To not do that is the opposite of shrewd, not to mention the opposite of how we should be treating our fellow human beings. As a leader, addressing people in the workplace, personalizing your communication with them in the hallways, even down in the parking garage, that's just the tip of the iceberg when it comes to caring for your people.

Why should you care? When people are treated better, when people feel better, when morale is better, you get better results.

I have always said, in reference to subordinates, "Take care of them, and they will take care of you." As a leader, it's important to "look down, not up"—to focus on your subordinates. Every day your staff has a decision to make: Do they simply do their job, or do they do their job to the absolute best of their abilities? When people know that their leaders (and managers) have their best interests in mind, they will work harder—every time.

So the question then becomes: How do I take care of my subordinates, especially in tough times?

SHOW 'EM THAT YOU CARE

Morale is improved pretty easily with increased resources. Time off, pay raises, increased benefits, perks, you name it—the more you dole them out, the happier your workers will be. Some of the most successful companies have the highest productivity and most loyal workforces.

Morale is also improved by putting policies into place that put your subordinates and their families at the forefront. I proved this at Fort Hood when I significantly reduced the hours our soldiers were putting in and outright eliminated weekend work. I didn't see one iota of decline in our ability to accomplish missions as a military. We proved it over and over again, when, in the midst of those reduced hours and the increased family time allotted for soldiers and their families, we saw improved safety and other quality-of-life factors across that installation.

But one big key to improving morale—and by default, improving productivity and getting better results from your organization as a whole—is simply increasing communication. It starts with addressing your subordinates by name. That's step one. Show them that respect. Do them that courtesy. And then, quite simply, talk to them!

"People don't care how much you know until they know how much you care." This is something Sarah taught me, and I refer to this truth often. If you demonstrate to your staff that you truly care, then they're going to be more receptive to your ideas, your thoughts, your directions. Just like the story of Colin Powell and the parking attendants, when you demonstrate that you care—like calling an individual by name and saying, "Thank you for what you're doing.

How's your family?"—they treat you better. How do they treat a leader better? By doing better work, showing dedication, and stepping up when it matters.

Of course, stepping up when it matters goes both ways. Once you become a leader, or even a senior manager, there is no such thing as a casual conversation. It just doesn't exist. When you ask somebody, "How are you doing?" and they give you an answer, they expect you to do something with it.

If you work for me and I say, "Hey, how are things going?" and you say, "I'm struggling with my finances" or "I'm struggling with my health," you're going to expect me to do something about it. As a leader, you've got to truly care, truly listen to the answer, and do something. Maybe you need to give that person some more time, or help get them into counseling. Whatever it is, they're going to expect that you do something—or, at the very least, have someone else follow up and check in on them.

If I were just a manager, I might not care as much. I might think, "As long as you're on time and you get your work done, I don't care what happens after you go home."

But I don't want to be "just a manager." I want to be a *leader.* And I think it's important for you to make that distinction in your own mind.

I believe that leaders should love their subordinates the way they love their own children. I've practiced that from the time I left West Point through today. And the root of that belief goes back to the biblical message that to lead is also to serve; that in order to lead in a meaningful way, you have to have a servant's heart. To put it bluntly: You've got to care about people to be a leader.

You can't be a true leader without care, compassion, and concern.

I find myself around a lot of managers when I'm out in corporate America. They want to manage the operation, but when it's quitting time, they don't want to have to worry about the people; they don't want to think about them until the next day when they come in and start work again. Management is pure business. That's all it is. It's profit and loss, trying to meet the bottom line—timecards, pay schedules. A leader has to be a good manager, of course. But I don't think being a good manager automatically makes you a leader. Certainly not a *good* leader.

So, assuming you want to be a leader and that you do care about people, how do you let your people *know* that you care—beyond the one-on-one interactions you have with them from day to day?

You take your message to them in person.

Getting in front of your people and advocating for your beliefs and expectations is part of engaged leadership. The act of being seen, in and of itself, is powerful. And getting in front of your people to tell them how you plan to use your position as a leader to advocate for a better life for *them*? That's just plain good business. Because, and I repeat this often, when people are treated better, when people feel better, when morale is better, you get better results.

Of course, it isn't always easy to increase morale, and I found this out the hard way in my career after I left Fort Hood.

When I first arrived at the Pentagon, it was a miserable workplace environment. Almost everybody seemed to be looking down all the time. Almost everyone I encountered in that massive building seemed angry or irritable. Almost nobody made eye contact as they walked the halls. The overriding daily sentiment was, "I had a terrible commute to get here, I've got a terrible job, I have a terrible commute to get home, and it ain't gettin' any better than this!" There were any number of people who had two-hour commutes in each direction on a daily basis. No wonder everybody's basic mood was, "My life sucks."

I had 500 people assigned to me when I first arrived, and I said, "We're just not going to continue with this misery."

I decided to implement the same sort of life-changing time-management principles I had put into place at Fort Hood. It didn't matter to me that this was a completely different environment, with a completely different sort of workforce. People deserve a life. They deserve to be home with their families for dinnertime. I wanted to communicate that message to my staff, so I did something I had done with our soldiers on base all the time: I called a town-hall meeting.

"Here's the deal," I said as I stood in front of all 500 workers. "I want everybody home for dinner by six." I was naïve about Washington commutes and Washington traffic, so some people came to me afterward and said, "Well, General, here's the deal: We can leave at five like you want us to and be home at seven, or we can leave at six and be home by eight. What do you want us to do?"

Upon analysis, I realized they were right. The commute around DC is one of the worst anywhere in the nation, and rush hour peaks between 3 and 6 p.m. So I relented and said, "Okay, you can leave at six, but you've got to be home by seven for dinner with your families."

Even after that, I got resistance. It was amazing to me. At Fort Hood, that policy was embraced with open arms. The families said, "Thank you, General! We finally have our spouses back, our husbands back, our moms and dads back." But at the Pentagon? They were so locked into the way they'd been doing business, they didn't want to believe that this policy could improve their lives. They somehow thought that if they didn't stay later, they'd have more work to do! But I tried to apply the same mandates I applied at Fort Hood, and, eventually, we got some results. I held monthly town-hall meetings to talk about this issue, along with lots of other issues, so my workforce could see me and understand that these things truly did matter to me. To prove to them that *they* mattered to me. Still, the results were never great. I think it would take years of massive changes and follow-through to make a dent in the culture of despair at the Pentagon. But

I think it's fair to say that at least some of my employees were happier as a result of my policies, and any result that yields happier employees without a decrease in productivity is a major win in my opinion.

The thing that mattered even more than the policies I put into place was the message I was trying to send. As I've said, I believe that constant communication is critical to strong leadership. You've got to talk to your workforce as often as possible. And not just by email. When you type and send an email, you have no way of knowing if the person on the other end understood the email, or understood the passion and tone that you were trying to convey in that email. You just don't know—unless you talk about it. And when you're sending missives and directives to large numbers of workers, or to your entire workforce at once, you have to have forums in which you talk to them in person to follow up. It gives a your workers a chance to see and hear and feel your passion for whatever message it is you're trying to send.

I put that notion into practice in a major way at Installation Management Command (IMCOM), which I ran simultaneously as I worked at the Pentagon. Now, IMCOM is 163 installations worldwide. It's 120,000 people, 118,000 of which are civilian employees. So it's about as much of a real-world an example as you can find anywhere in the military. That IMCOM commander job was headquartered in San Antonio. Splitting my time between Washington and Texas was not easy. It left me rushed most of the time, as I spoke about earlier. Regardless, I made the time to get out and talk to that workforce, my people, in person.

Sarah and I visited 82 out of those 163 installations during the two years I was in command. We'd land. We'd get a tour. Then Sarah would go off and meet with families who had lost a loved one, families who had exceptional family members (children with medical issues), and service providers. I would spend time meeting with installation leadership, focusing on infrastructure issues, security issues, and more. And then I'd hold a town-hall meeting so everyone could see me—their commanding general—standing alongside my wife, so they'd get a feel for what kind of a leader I was.

Up on those stages, I spent a lot of time advocating for work-life balance.

"You've got to be able to get your work done during the day so you can be home at nighttime" was my message, which always elicited applause. I established the 6 p.m. dinnertime rule, and it was well-received with the IMCOM workforce. Again, it was an almost entirely civilian workforce. But the message was bigger than that. It was at one of these town-hall meetings, in Fort Leavenworth, Kansas, where that mother and her thirty-two-year-old daughter decided to spend more time together after hearing me speak. It was only one week later that the daughter passed away. My message got through and yielded results, which, in the case of that mother and daughter, was a life-altering experience. I can't tell you how many times even hard-nosed managers hear that story, get a tear in their eye, and then tell me, "I have to do something about this." If they care one iota about people, they agree that the consequence of working people too hard and too long for no reason, especially when the same results could easily be achieved during a more efficient workday, is ludicrous.

I also spent time on those stages explaining to them why things were the way they were—why certain cuts were being made, why certain decisions had been made, and what I was going to do as a leader to make their lives better while we went through some tough times as an organization.

I cannot stress to you enough just how important that was. My talks had a visible effect on the morale of the IMCOM workforce. And as a result, across all 163 installations, all indicators of performance showed marked improvement during my tenure because the workforce was happier, better adjusted, and felt that they were truly being cared for.

As a leader, standing up for what you believe in and sharing that message with the people you're leading—whether one-on-one or as a massive group—makes a difference. A real difference.

Communication means everything. Especially when one of the things you believe in most is the very audience you're talking to.

REMINDER

Look down, not up.

★ ★ ★

"People don't care how much you know
until they know how much you care."

★ ★ ★

– 17 –

MENTORSHIP

Learning is something that should never stop. We need parents, teachers, guidance counselors, preachers, and others in our lives to help guide and teach us when we're young. I think that's obvious. And as we grow into adulthood and grow into our careers, it is my firm belief that we need something more: We need mentors.

I aggressively sought out mentors at every step of my career, whenever I had a promotion coming up. It didn't matter whether I was moving up to division commander or battalion commander or three-star general, I sought out mentors who currently held or had previously held those positions—individuals who had "been there and done that" who might be able to offer me some cogent advice and counsel. As a "mentee," I knew these individuals had learned lessons by experience that I wanted access to, so I put in the time to track them down, to get through their gatekeepers (if they had them), to make contact, to introduce myself, and to glean whatever knowledge I could from them.

I went searching for advice and counsel from some pretty well-known individuals at times, like George Casey, who had commanded the First Armored Division, and Marty Dempsey, who had also commanded the First Armored Division. You've got to aggressively seek out those types of mentors in whatever field you're in. It's not always easy to reach them, and you can't let the gatekeepers deter you. The same goes for someone who's becoming a COO or a CEO for the first time. Everyone goes into a job relatively cold, so it only makes sense to learn from people who've done it.

In almost every case, I found that those people were receptive to my seeking them out and answering the questions I wanted to ask. Some people were so busy they didn't want to take the time to talk to anybody, but, in most cases, I found the mentors I needed, even if they were short-term mentors.

If you want to learn about something in life, go ask an expert—someone who's living it, who's actually doing it—and, 90 percent of the time, those people will give you answers. People like to talk about what they do. They like to share information about what they've accomplished. In general, people who are good at what they do *like* to be mentors. If you aspire to do new things in your career, go and talk to people who've already done it, see how it went, and see what the issues are.

I do not think my career would have been nearly as successful had I not done that, and I'm always surprised when people tell me they're not doing that in their own careers.

In order for organizations to perform smoothly, I believe organizational leaders need to assign mentors—to tag someone to "pick up the new guy" and show him the ropes. It doesn't necessarily have to be someone in the new guy's chain of command, either. Just someone who's been in the organization long enough, and is dependable enough, to share some expertise and get the new guy through the water. I've never understood the corporate mentality of "sink or swim." If a new guy jumps in and winds up sinking, doesn't that drag everyone else down with him? Or, at the very least, slow everyone down? Of course, it does. Assign a mentor, and that problem is solved.

Organizational mentorship needs to extend beyond the "new guys" as well. Let me share a stark example of this that we discovered in the Army. Prior to 9/11, we had a mass exodus of captains from the United States Army. They were leaving in droves. The Army's chief of staff at the time formed a blue-ribbon panel to investigate why these captains were leaving the Army, and I was a part of that panel.

Guess what one of the primary reasons was for the exodus? You guessed it: a lack of mentors.

The captains we interviewed said, "We're leaving because nobody's talking to us." They were referring to all of us senior leaders.

"Sure, we get emails from you about this and that, but nobody's taking time to counsel us. Nobody's taking any interest in our careers."

Nobody was counseling them or advising them on what they needed to do to advance their careers in the Army. Nobody was talking to them about what to expect should they be promoted. Nobody was working with them to foster their careers, so they simply chose to seek careers outside of the Army once they had the chance.

We asked these exiting captains, "How many of you had a mentor at any time during your time in the Army?" and approximately 25 percent said they had. But when we asked the senior leaders how many of them had acted as mentors to their captains, 75 percent said they had been mentors! A big disconnect.

I think the problem lies in the definition of *mentor*. A mentor isn't just a higher-up. A mentor isn't just a supervisor or a manager. And the mentor-mentee relationship is not something idle. In the Army at that time, our senior officers were not aggressively seeking out captains to mentor. But on the flip side, those captains were not aggressively looking for mentors themselves. So the relationships just never developed.

In my mind, in addition to being someone with knowledge and expertise, a mentor is somebody who is accessible, who listens, and who truly cares. And the most powerful mentor-mentee relationships are not something mandated by an organization but are voluntary relationships between two people. Relationships based on caring.

I've had six primary mentor relationships in my life—with six guys who have a tremendous amount of wisdom to share, and who I know I can always reach out to and say, "I've got this question." When I do that, I'm absolutely convinced that they're going to take the time to listen to me, that they're going to care, and that they're going to give the best counsel they can.

The first mentor to me in the Army was Walt Ulmer, whom, you may recall, I met when he was commandant of cadets at West Point. He was the one who put me on the panel to investigate the cheating scandal, and whom I reported to directly in that extremely difficult time at the Academy. When he retired from III Corps at Fort Hood (the corps that I took over upon my return from the surge in Iraq), he went on to be the CEO of the Center for Creative Leadership in Greensboro, North Carolina. He took that national organization and made it into an international organization, and he continues to be actively involved in leader development. So he's still a great mentor to me, and he has lots of experience transitioning out of the Army in much the same way I have. But I still have lots to learn from Walt.

The second mentor is the guy who gave me the opportunity to command two companies early in my career: the great Doc Bahnsen, who was awarded a Distinguished Service Cross and five Silver Stars in Vietnam. He's a bona fide war hero. Doc showed me what it looked like to take care of soldiers, and how to be a leader—not just in title but in actions. He's still actively involved in leadership development in his retirement in West Virginia.

Major General Tom Tait is another important mentor of mine. Tom Tait was the commanding general of Fort Knox who asked me if I wanted to transfer to armor branch, and to whom I said, "Sir, I've been trying to be an armor officer for nine years!" Tom is the man who called armor branch the moment we landed and said, "Make Lynch an armor officer, or you're fired!" He carried a big stick everywhere he went. He was the epitome of a commander who was out and about all the time. He's retired now and actively involved in activities at the Virginia Military Institute.

A guy named Butch Funk is my fourth mentor. He was the corps commander when I was a battalion commander at Fort Hood. He taught me what commanders do outside of headquarters. It was impossible for me to take my battalion out for training and not be visited by Butch, no matter where we went or when. Butch Funk spent zero time in his headquarters going through long, laborious staff meetings; he spent all of his time out and about.

My fifth mentor is Fred Franks, who retired as a four-star general out of the Army's Training and Doctrine Command, and commanded the VII Corps in Operations Desert Shield and Desert Storm. Fred taught me a lot about being a more senior leader, including the notion that you should never ask questions that you don't want to hear the answer to. He's also responsible for instilling that lesson about taking time to think: "Decide when to decide." In a tough situation, the first decision you make is, "When do I have to decide?" You want to give yourself as much time as possible to weigh options and get answers, but you need to know when it's time to make a decision and get on with it. That's so important. Freddy Franks taught me that.

Finally I want to mention Ben Griffin, another four-star general, who served as the commanding general, United States Army Materiel Command, before his retirement in 2008. Ben was my division commander when I was an assistant division commander (ADC), and he taught me an important lesson on experiential learning, a topic I'll discuss later. When we first met, Ben had a choice to make me either the ADC for maneuver or the ADC for support. As you know by now, I've never had much interest in being the support guy, but he intentionally chose to make me the ADC for support so I could learn about that side of division operations *before* I became a division commander myself. He made it clear that he cared about my career from the outset. He wanted me to learn, so he put me in an environment where I was uncomfortable—but I sure learned a lot. In fact, looking back on it now, I know for certain that had he not put me in charge of support, I'd have been a much less effective division commander later on. Ben's mentorship through the years has been invaluable.

Those are six people I've been blessed to call mentors over the course of my career, and I'm in routine contact with them to this day.

But it's also important to remember that mentoring is a two-way street. As you move up in your career, if people come seeking your advice, it's important to take the time to get to know them a bit and share whatever advice or knowledge you can. In some ways, that's the very definition of "engaged leadership." In order for people to have mentors, we leaders need to be mentors to others. And believe me, you'll learn from the experience, too. The process of teaching and sharing what you know is always enlightening. Ask any teacher, and they'll tell you!

I've personally mentored a great number of people through the years. Even after leaving the Army, today I mentor many, many folks who either worked for me in the past, work for me now, or who have sought me out for mentorship outside of their chain of command.

YOU'RE NEVER TOO IMPORTANT TO CARE

If you want to be an engaged leader, you've got to be a purposeful mentor—not just for the people who currently work for you, but to the people who work around you, the people who *have* worked for you, and the people who may work for you in the future in your particular area of expertise.

The first step is to open your door. In the military, just like in corporate America, the biggest problem with finding a mentor is the gatekeepers. Potential mentors aren't available or accessible, because there is a gatekeeper who gets in the way. That's why I routinely pass out my personal email and cell phone number, so that people know they can get in touch with me. Even to this day, as I'm trying to develop relationships with leaders across the business world, it's hard for *me*—Lieutenant General Rick Lynch—to get through the gatekeepers. They are paid to block access, and they do a great job of it!

So if you're the CEO of a corporation, you've got to figure out how to do this. You can't sit down with your gatekeeper and simply say, "Okay, open the gates." That's not what you want to do. You need to figure out how you can be accessible in a healthy way both for you and for those who can benefit from your mentorship. Your organization (and you) will be better for it.

Then, once you have that accessibility, you have to do the really tough thing: You have to actively listen. That's not always easy. The hardest thing I do is active listening. In general terms, I believe most of us are lousy listeners. You see it all the time as you're talking to people, when whomever you're talking to is looking over your shoulder, seeing what else they could be doing. It's hard to focus on the matter at hand and make the person who's speaking feel like they're the most important person in your world at that time.

I've spent a lot of time trying to learn how to be a better listener. It's one of my weaknesses. I've got to consciously make the effort, because my mind is racing all the time. That's the way I am. I'm always thinking about other things, thinking about what I should say, thinking about what's next on my agenda, as opposed to *being in the moment*. But I've worked on it. And over time, I think I've learned to be pretty good at it.

Then that last piece of mentorship, the way I define it, is to truly care. To demonstrate that you're not only listening, but that you also truly care—and not just about the person's role in your organization or his or her career, but about what's best for the individual person.

Let me give you an example of what I mean.

I'm a mentor to someone who was a one-star general. When the promotion board began meeting to decide who to promote to two-star, major general, he found out he was in the running. He called me, as his mentor, and said, "As I look into the future, I'm not particularly excited about being a major general. I like what I'm doing now, but I can't see doing something that I don't like." He knew I had been a two-star general, and he wanted to pick my brain so he could make an informed decision.

To understand where he's coming from, I have to tell you a little bit about his life. Some time ago, his wife died of cancer. I was at her bedside with him when she died.

A lot of men might have been knocked down for good after something like that. In time, he wasn't. He got remarried. He's got a five-year-old son. And you can bet he doesn't want to miss any time he doesn't have to miss with that wife and son of his. He knows firsthand just how precious and unexpectedly short life can be.

When you're a general officer in the United States Army, you're busy. You're not spending as much time with your family as you'd like, even if you concentrate on it and spend quality time, as I have always tried to do. Couple that knowledge with the knowledge I have about where his priorities lie, and I'm in a pretty good position to give him advice.

He knew he could get ahold of me, he knew I would listen, and I listened hard. He asked me this question: "Do you think I should opt out of consideration for becoming a major general?"

If you've paid any attention to anything I've said in this book so far, you can probably guess my answer. I said, "Yeah, I think you should opt out. You've gone far enough. You're always going to be 'the general,' because you're going to retire as a general. But if you're going to do the right thing for yourself and for your family, you should opt out."

That was my advice.

He was going to do what he wanted to do. A mentor is not a dictator. Not even close. He asked for my advice, and I gave it to him. And I did not give him advice based on what was necessarily best for the Army. Being a mentor isn't the same as being a coach. I wasn't pushing him to go further in the sport, to go for the promotion, to get over the hurdle and win, win, win. That's something different.

As a mentor, I'm looking out for *him*.

If he said, "Thanks for that, but I'm going to go be a major general," and if he wound up being unhappy with that decision, I wasn't going to say, "I told you so. Why didn't you listen to me?" The decision wasn't up to me. It was up to him. And I would respect whatever he chose.

He and I have a three-decade relationship. He and I cried in each other's arms when his wife died. So I based my advice on what I thought was best for him. If he leaves the Army, frankly, that's bad for the Army, because he's a superstar. But somebody else will step up and be a major general, and the Army will go on. When I left as a three-star, I didn't leave thinking, *I let the Army down*. I knew that somebody else would step up and be the four-star and do as well or better than I could have done.

I'll reiterate this point: The way I define it, a mentor isn't just someone who teaches you the ropes or pushes you to the next promotion like a coach. It's different. It's someone who can really listen and help you to figure out what's best for *you*. And you need to be both a mentor and a mentee in your career to be effective in that capacity.

Diversity is a big part of developing effective mentor-mentee relationships as well. People are different. And people who are different want to look up to people like them and aspire to be like them, whether it's a race issue, a gender issue, or something else. So if you mentor people, a lot of times you mentor people who aspire to be like you. That's the natural gravitation of the mentor-mentee relationship. But having diverse opinions and points of view in mentor-mentee relationships is a good thing.

Also, when you're the one asking for advice, it doesn't mean you have to copy what someone else did. It just gives you a chance to learn. Think of it as something that will inform your decisions, but know that you still need to make your own decisions.

That's exactly what that one-star general mentee of mine did: He took my advice, considered it thoroughly, but made the decision to stay in the Army and become a two-star general. I'm not hurt by that. I'm proud of him for making the decision that was right for him. And I'm happy for the Army because they get to hold on to one of their superstars.

Back when I decided to branch-transfer, one of my mentors told me not to do it. "You've already established yourself as an engineer. You're going to struggle as an armor officer." But I did it anyway. I went with my gut. And none of my mentors were thin-skinned about it. Their counsel was extraordinarily important. They let me know the risks. They made me think long and hard about following through before I did it. And when I did go ahead and do it, and I turned that transfer into a massive success, perhaps it gave those mentors a different perspective on the matter.

Having mentors and being a mentor are two of the greatest ways to keep learning—not only while you're on the road to becoming a leader, but once you've established yourself as the type of leader that others aspire to become.

REMEMBER

Be a mentor.

★ ★ ★

"You must be accessible, you must listen, and you must truly care!"

★ ★ ★

– 18 –

ASKING INTRUSIVE QUESTIONS

In school, we got counseling all the time to let us know how we were doing and how we could improve. Think back to your high-school education: Your teachers talked to you, your guidance counselors sat you down now and then, you got report cards, and you most likely had parents or caretakers looking out for those report cards and doling out some level of praise or punishment each quarter or semester.

I'm here to advocate that a grown-up version of that process is important in any work environment, and it's up to leaders to make it happen.

I wasn't counseled nearly enough in my early years in the Army. (Come to think of it, I wasn't counseled enough in *any* of my years in the Army.) When I was, I listened intently, made adjustments to what I was doing and how I was behaving, and moved forward with confidence, knowing that I wanted to please whomever it was I was working for so I could get to the next promotion on my way to becoming a battalion commander. But I was very aware that I wanted and needed more counseling along the way.

Once I became a lieutenant and had a sizable team to manage, I made counseling a high priority and got started right away. I found that the best approach was to sit down with my subordinates on a monthly basis, look them in the eye, and say, "Here are the strengths that I've observed in the last thirty days. Here are some areas for improvement that I think we ought to work on. And here are our objectives for the next thirty days."

I carried that basic approach throughout the rest of my career, including counseling to civilian workers at Installation Management Command (IMCOM) and even now at the university level. As I got more senior and had a bigger span of control, it ended up being once a quarter instead of once a month, but it was still part of my routine.

In general, my counseling sessions took an hour. I had a blank sheet of paper with three blocks of space: Strengths, Areas for Improvement, and Objectives. The reason I phrased it "Areas for Improvement" was because if you say "Weaknesses," people take that personally. In the military, if you tell somebody you "got counseled," the first thing they asked was, "What did you do wrong?" So it's important to find ways to move counseling out of this negative connotation.

Once the basics about work were finished, I always used those counseling sessions as an opportunity to ask what I call "intrusive questions." They were human questions.

"How's the family?"

"How are your parents?"

"How's your home life?"

"Is there anything I need to know about that might be affecting your performance?"

"Is there anything going on in your family that we should be a part of?"

"Are your kids doing particularly well in school? Perhaps I could send them a note of congratulations?"

Engaged leaders ask intrusive questions. People don't care how much you know until they know how much you care. And I always found that to be a powerful time at the end of those sessions.

Don't get me wrong: I got my points across. If I wasn't satisfied with how someone was performing, in the course of the counseling, they got that point. But it wasn't negative. It wasn't, "If you don't straighten up, I'm gonna fire you!"

I would finesse it so that, when the counseling was done, they knew their performance had to improve. But at the same time, they knew that I cared just because I was taking the time to talk to them.

As a three-star general I was counseling two-star generals and senior-level civilians—guys who had been in or around the military for thirty-five years. And I realized one day that, in my thirty-five-year career, I had been counseled like that on maybe only five occasions! Only five times in thirty-five years did one of my leaders sit me down and say, "How are we doing? What can we improve on? What are our objectives for the next thirty days?" And notice the use of pronouns: "we" and "our."

It's important not to make the person you're counseling feel like you're on the attack or putting the entire burden on them. You want to make it known that you're in this together. Asking the intrusive or personal questions definitely helps smooth that over.

I've found that some leaders and managers are uncomfortable asking intrusive questions—as if somehow we're violating privacy or asking stuff that's none of our business. The thing about asking questions is that they don't necessarily have to get answered. In the course of the counseling conversation, anyone has a right to say, "That's none of your business, General." But at least they could tell that I cared, simply because I was asking. That makes it a worthwhile endeavor.

Of course, as I've mentioned before, once you're a senior leader, there's no such thing as a casual conversation. If you ask the question and get the answer, there is an expectation that you're going to do something about it—otherwise you lose credibility as a leader. I saw that example in some of the poor leaders I worked under through the years, and I vowed not to follow their example.

When you open the door and ask the question, you need to be prepared for unexpected answers. As you well know, when people go home at night, there are strange things that go on behind closed doors. People have unfortunate circumstances. As hard as this is to believe, I have had two workers who, on two separate occasions, went home to find their wives had committed suicide. One of the workers has proceeded on in his life, remarried, and seems to be doing okay. The other is having a much harder time moving on. You occasionally get answers that are quite troubling, and you have to figure out how to help, what to do, and what to watch for.

In the military, we get trained on suicide prevention, and you learn that sometimes you have to ask the hard question—you have to look a person right in the eye and ask, "Are you contemplating killing yourself?"

If the answer is "Yes," you have to get them help. So I'm well aware of that reality, and I know how to get someone additional counseling if they need or want it. Leaders have to be prepared to take action for their subordinates' health, the same way a parent would for their children.

So you do get answers that sometimes make you say, "Man, oh man, I wish I'd never asked that question."

But you did. And now you've got it. And you've got to do something with it.

It's all part of being an engaged leader. It's all a part of loving your subordinates the way you love your own children.

Think about this: You ask your kids intrusive questions all the time.

Where'd you go last night?

Who's that friend?

What are you doing on the Internet?

You ought to be doing the same sort of thing for your subordinates. Not for the purposes of spying on them, or to dig for negative information. Rather, to connect with them, human being to human being. Get to know your employees. I also found ways to get to know my subordinates better without asking intrusive questions of them directly, yet simultaneously making them and their families feel good about their enlistment in the Army. From the time I was a lieutenant until the time I retired, I called somebody's mom or dad on a daily basis.

The process would go something like this: I'd meet some youngster, a new arrival, or someone doing a good job, and I'd ask, "Who do you love the most? Who's the most important person to you?"

I'm aware, of course, that we have a dysfunctional society because we have dysfunctional families. I apologize to my kids all the time for raising them with such a boring existence: they've got one mom, one dad, and they're stuck with us. But most people you come across have stepmoms or stepdads, stepbrothers and sisters. I tell Sarah sometimes I need a scorecard because I can't keep track of who's who! My own parents were both married and divorced, and I grew up with stepbrothers, so I knew enough to ask that question: "Who do you love the most?" Once I got that information, I'd ask for that person's phone number, and then I'd call them. I did this stateside as often as I did it from a satellite phone in the desert in Iraq. If the subordinate said the person they loved the most was their mom, I'd immediately pick up the phone in their presence and dial up Mom.

"This is Lieutenant Colonel Rick Lynch, and I just want to share some good news with you." I immediately let them know it was good news, because when people get a phone call from the Army, they automatically assume that it's bad news. So I'd get that out right away. And then I would say, "I'm here with your son right now, and I'm very impressed with his work. I'm glad he's a part of our team. You've trusted us with your most precious resource, your son, and I'm going to commit to you that we're going to take care of him."

You can imagine how surprised and pleased a mom or dad or sister or granddad would be to get a phone call like that. But it was also a great feeling for me as a leader to share some good news and to let that soldier know I truly cared about him. That goes a long way, especially down the line, should things ever get tough.

I would also use those phone calls to gather a little information. I would ask Mom, "Is there anything I should know about your son?"

And she would tell me every time!

"Did you know that my son had an anger-management problem when he was in high school?"

No, I didn't know that, but thanks for the info.

"Did you know he had a drinking problem?"

"Did you know he had suicidal ideations in his first unit?"

It's amazing how moms will open up to you when they know you care about their child. Instantly, as an engaged leader, I would know more about that soldier than I might have learned any other way. And I repeat, it was not because I was trying to spy on him, but because I wanted better knowledge of that soldier. Do you think he would've come into my office and told me he has an anger-management problem, a drinking problem, and suicidal thoughts? No way! But you can get to those problems through asking intrusive questions. Making phone calls home was a powerful way I did that.

This is another one of those areas that seems to bring massive resistance in the corporate world. *Why?* Why are we separating our humanity from our jobs? It doesn't make sense. We're all in this together. Do you think your employees don't have parents, siblings, and spouses? Of course, they do. Do you think they don't talk about work at home? Do you think their life in the workplace doesn't affect their home life, and vice-versa? Making those phone calls gave me more information about the individuals who worked for me so I could be a better, more caring leader. It gave the people back home a good feeling, knowing that a senior leader actually cared about their loved one and wanted to share some good news with their family. Is there anyone in that equation who isn't better for the experience? No!

Look, everybody's got problems. Have you come across a human being who doesn't have a problem? They might pretend they have no problems: "Everything's great, General. Everything's great! Having a great day."

By asking intrusive questions, you find out more about your people, and, as a result of that, you can help them better; as a result of that, they know their leaders care; as a result of that, they improve their performance. *Ipso facto.*

If you take care of your subordinates, they will take care of you. Simple.

Just make sure you're ready to actually take care of them before you get started down this road. Be prepared to follow through. If you say, "I'm going to take care of you," but you don't? Then you lose all credibility.

Take care of your people, and they will take care of you. Neglect your people, hurt your people, overlook your people, leave your people in the lurch? Buddy, beware. Because when the chips are down, there will be mutiny.

If you need a more bottom-line argument for "asking intrusive questions" of your subordinates, think about this: Things go wrong. In any organization, there will be problems. There will be obstacles. There will be mistakes. A lot of times things went wrong in outfits I commanded. But the people who fixed those things were my subordinates. I didn't fix those things—my subordinates did, without my even having to ask.

Because I had asked intrusive questions, because I showed them that I cared, their going the extra mile to overcome problems was simply a matter of fact. They would take care of it because they didn't want to let me down.

Why didn't they want to let me down? Because I hadn't let *them* down.

Can you imagine how smoothly just about every outfit in America would work if we all went to work with that mentality?

REMEMBER

Engaged leadership is important.

★ ★ ★

"Love your subordinates like you love your own children!"

★ ★ ★

– 19 –

DEMANDING, NOT DEMEANING

I demand that people do their job. I've always demanded that people do their job. Being a caring leader has nothing to do with being soft or being weak. And a leader has good reason to demand that people work to the best of their abilities.

I'll use my position at IMCOM as a primary example here. The mission of IMCOM is to provide our soldiers, civilians, and their families with a quality of life commensurate with the quality of their service. That's a big task. An important task. A vital task. So I was incredibly demanding of the 120,000 employees at our 163 Army installations around the world, and I had every right to be.

First off, those employees were getting a paycheck. More important, they were taking care of our soldiers and their families, our nation's most precious resource. So I wouldn't tolerate substandard performance. When I talked to people in counseling sessions or otherwise, I would be very demanding.

"This is your job. We agree? My expectation is that you're going to do your job. And if you don't do your job, then we're going to talk about what actions we have to take because you didn't do your job."

I didn't yell or scream. I was never demeaning. That makes a big difference. A leader needs to make sure he or she is demanding, not demeaning. Why? Because you're the one setting the example. You're the one setting the bar—and, hopefully, raising the bar—for your subordinates. As a leader and as a human being, you're not supposed to be demeaning; instead, you're supposed to follow the Golden Rule: Treat people the way you want to be treated.

My wife always put it another way when she spoke to soldiers: "Do what your mothers taught you."

The Golden Rule is about dignity and respect. You cannot stand up as a leader and say you care about your subordinates, and then fail to show them dignity and respect—no matter how angry they might make you. To do so only sends a message to your subordinates that you do not mean what you say.

In all of my time as a senior leader, you couldn't find one human being who would tell you that I raised my voice at them or cursed at them or demeaned them in public. I don't do that. That's not my style. What you will find is people who will tell you that I was hard to work for because I was demanding. And if they were not performing, I did make it known that they were not performing, and sometimes that would happen in an open forum.

The first example that jumps to mind was out on the battlefield in Iraq. I had an intelligence officer in combat who didn't always live up to my expectations. That's putting it mildly, because, oh, by the way, in combat, without intelligence, people die. *People die.* So there were times in an open forum when that intelligence officer would clearly not be performing, and I'd make it a point to make sure he knew that I didn't think he was doing his job. I had every right to yell at him. I had every right to curse and swear and call him all sorts of names if I wanted to. His lack of performance was costing lives. But I didn't do that. I didn't say, "What the hell are you doing?" I didn't demean him. I simply let him know where he was failing and what he needed to improve upon—with great urgency. Lives were on the line. He needed to do better.

Yelling, screaming, cursing—none of that would have made him work any harder. It only would have put him down and, in fact, might have had an effect opposite of what I desired. He might have lost respect for me and then performed even more poorly than he already had. As leaders, we have to be aware of the impact of not only our words, but our demeanor and candor. It's just the right thing to do. The Bible talks about this in Colossians 3:5-12 (see appendix 2).

At Fort Hood, my demanding that folks release their soldiers in time to be home for dinner at 6 p.m., not work on weekends without my personal approval, and release them at 3 p.m. on Thursdays for family time was difficult. On many occasions, I had to get "up close and personal" with leaders who couldn't understand the importance of this, or who chose to ignore it.

There was one time a private called me and asked whether enforcement of family time was a policy or a recommendation, because in his company, it wasn't being enforced. Boy, did that make me mad! Here I was, a lieutenant general, having to take the time to place a phone call to a company commander, a captain, to explain to him that he didn't have an option. He needed to follow my orders! Even then, this captain had the audacity to try to explain to me that he didn't have a family, so my order shouldn't apply. "So why do I have to go home at three on Thursdays?" he said. I just about blew my top. This was the Army. In the Army, you follow orders. Plain and simple. But I kept my anger in check and explained to him—relatively calmly—the importance of leading by example. I could have yelled and screamed. I had every right to yell and scream, but I didn't.

The fact is, yelling, screaming, and demeaning in any way can get you into all sorts of trouble. There was a piece in the news just recently about a leader who's been accused by his subordinates of being demeaning. They claimed that he had a pattern of cursing at them and calling them names—and it got so bad it hit the news! Talk about terrible PR. Unfortunately, these days a lot of leaders are scared to be demanding because they think they're going to be mislabeled as "demeaning." There's a line there. I've always tried to stay on the left side of that line, and so should you. But, as leaders, we cannot let go of our demands.

If you want to have a high-performing organization, individuals in your organization need to be high performers. That's not rocket science, right? If you've got a headquarters of a thousand people, like I did at IMCOM, and those thousand people are high-performing people, you're going to have a high-performing organization. But if you accept marginal performance or poor performance, it's going to drag everything down, and the unit itself is going to be less effective.

So I demanded adherence to standards. I demanded that people do their job, and if they didn't do their job, then I took appropriate action, which included additional counseling, moving them to a different position, or firing them.

The danger of all of that—and it's happened in the military lately—is that people who are not performing want to file false accusations about their leaders for harassment. An equal-opportunity complaint. Some marginal performers, rather than perform, will go out of their way to find (or make up) reasons why their bosses are giving them a hard time.

So I find a lot of leaders who won't be demanding because they don't want to subject themselves to that possibility. That's troubling. As we all know, there is a good portion of our population who doesn't want to perform to standards. They want to get the paycheck. They want the job. But they want to come in and do nothing all day long.

I tell people all the time, "You can choose to be part of the solution or part of the problem." And there are some people, no kidding, who *choose* to be part of the problem. They get great joy out of coming in and causing problems.

You can't let that deter you. As a leader, you've got a job to do. Just do it.

Don't lower yourself or your standards to meet the needs of the naysayers and the poor performers. Instead, go in strong, and do just the opposite.

It is imperative that you establish high standards. There are people who have worked for me in the past who've said, "The problem with Lynch is that he always raises the bar higher!" Yes, I do! *How is that a problem?* Especially when it came to taking care of our soldiers and their families, as we were at IMCOM. As far as I'm concerned, our performance was never good enough. We, as a nation, don't pay them enough.

TAKE A GOOD LOOK AT YOURSELF

I think society has it wrong. I believe that the two most important groups of people are our service members, who protect our freedoms, and our educators, who guarantee our future. But as a society, we've got them at the bottom of the pecking order in terms of pay and compensation. We pay actors and athletes an enormous amount of money, but we don't pay service members and educators even what they deserve. In order to give the service members compensation, rather than give them additional pay, it was my job to give them a better quality of life. So I always raised the bar. If we accomplished a goal at IMCOM, I didn't say, "Okay, that's good enough." I'd say, "Okay, now let's raise the bar higher. Let's raise the standard. Let's take it to the next level." That's how you create a high-performing organization—to never be satisfied. Never sit on your laurels, as they say. As a result, your people have to continually try to improve. That's a *good* thing!

Of course, you've got to walk the walk in order to instill that desire for improvement in your workers, and I constantly tried to instill that desire by showing improvements in my own areas of responsibility.

I often tell my people that the most important piece of furniture in your entire house is your mirror. Every day when you look in that mirror, the reflection back has to be somebody who's making a difference, who's sacrificing himself for the greater good, who's trying to do the best he can on that particular day. I do that every morning when I'm shaving. I ask myself in the mirror: *What do I need to work on? What do I need to do to improve? How can I be better?*

Leaders need to do that every day. When you do, your subordinates will see that effort, and, without you even saying a word, they will naturally want to emulate your improvements. It's an inspiring thing.

Just always remember that to lead is also to serve. If you reflect a servant's heart, your subordinates will understand that you don't feel you're pompous because you're the leader or because you're continually raising the bar. If you're an engaged leader, they're going to realize on some level that you're their servant. That's empowering to them and empowering to you, too. It raises your whole organization.

How do you develop that servant's heart? How do you realize that, even when you're the guy in charge, your job is really to serve all of these people who work for you?

"Hey, I'm the leader. They're serving me!" That's a more typical attitude—and it's exactly wrong. The managers are the guys who say, "Okay, seeing how I'm the guy who's signing your paycheck, you're working for me." I don't think a leader takes that attitude.

Instead, a leader looks down, not up.

A leader looks at and listens to the people he's leading. He's not just looking out for himself and his cronies, or trying to serve yet another leader he's trying to please or perhaps usurp.

A leader thinks, *I care about my subordinates at all levels. It's really important to me that they have meaningful and fruitful work and that they have opportunities to take care of their families.*

As a leader, I'm serving them to help them accomplish what they want.

To show them this, I spend a lot of time talking to my people about their personal goals. I ask, "What do you want to accomplish? As you project yourself mentally into your future, where do you want to be?"

And then my job as a leader is to help them get there. That's a servant's approach. That's important. To lead is also to serve. Jesus talked about this.

We, as a nation, need to advocate to people in all walks of life how important it is to be a giver, not a taker. The best way to do that is to walk the walk: To be a leader who is a giver, too. A leader who wants and needs to do the right thing for his or her subordinates. Whether it's giving them the time off they need, or monetary bonuses, or benefits that allow them to live their lives with less stress and worry, or simply allowing space for your employees to express themselves and their ideas, you need to find ways to give. You need to serve the people you're leading in order to serve the organization as a whole.

I'll repeat these two principles, because you should never forget 'em:

Leaders should be demanding, not demeaning.

And leaders should look down, not up.

REMEMBER

Be demanding but not demeaning.

★ ★ ★

"Everyone must perform to his or her full potential."

★ ★ ★

– 20 –

MAKE IT PERSONAL

When I took over IMCOM, I quickly realized that the organization had taken to spending a lot of time in quadrant 3: doing reports for the sake of doing reports, going to meetings just to plan the next meeting. With massive budget cuts looming and an imperative to clean up IMCOM's act, I launched a campaign called Stamp Out Stupid, in which I solicited ideas from my staff on how we could "do less better"—how we could improve our operations, cut out redundancies, improve efficiencies, and of course maintain (and, hopefully, greatly *improve* upon) issues of work-life balance.

How did I solicit these ideas? I gave out my personal email address. To everybody.

I said, "Give me your ideas."

In the first six months, I got more than 500 recommendations on how we could Stamp Out Stupid.

They weren't all great recommendations, but I would say a good 20 percent of 'em were solid. That's 100 ideas that helped me modify how we were doing business, right from the minds of the people who were in the thick of the work and had the best knowledge of the situation. The other emails were filled with diatribes from people complaining about their lot in life, or comments like, "They're making me work too hard." But in general, I got a slew of good ideas that were then up to me to act upon.

That personalized communication—opening up a direct line to me that the workforce could tap into—did something else as well: It gave them a sense of empowerment. It gave them a voice they didn't have before. And that's powerful. Suddenly it wasn't just me dictating ideas. It was them suggesting ideas, being heard, and seeing action taken because of it.

That brings up another important point: It's important to listen to ideas from people who aren't like you. We often surround ourselves with people of similar values, similar opinions, similar backgrounds, even similar points of view. As leaders, we need to be celebrating diversity and opening ourselves up to a variety of points of view that might be different from our own. Believe it or not, you don't have all the answers! There are a lot of very smart people out there. The best thing you can do for yourself is to find them and listen to what they have to say. I accomplished some of that with this one simple program, by opening the doors to so many opinions from across the workforce.

Some people thought I was crazy to give out my personal email address. "Why would you do that? You'll be inundated! You'll never see the end of it!"

I disagreed. I care about the people who work for me, and I want them to know that I care about their ideas. Sometimes the only way to hear from people in a large organization is to open up a line of communication that didn't exist before. And in a time of steep budget cuts (which I'll talk more about in Part 4 of this book), I truly needed those ideas. I needed the employees who were on the ground, in the thick of this organization, to clue me in to the bottlenecks and road bumps that existed in the organization's infrastructure. Handing out my personal email address just made the receiving of that critical information that much faster than any other system I could think of.

You can go too far, of course. When I was the corps commander at Fort Hood, I was aggressively trying to tell the Army's story. We are America's military, and after all of my work in Iraq, having served as the spokesman for the force, I knew how important it was to let the American public know what we were up to. It's all about strategic communication, so I set up a weekly televised interview on the local television stations as well as a weekly radio interview with one of the largest radio stations in the state of Texas: WACO 100. The station's range extends from Dallas to San Antonio, and every Thursday at 8 a.m., they'd allow me to get on the air for thirty minutes to talk about America's Army. They called it "The Fort Hood Report."

One day I got so excited about asking for input on how we could do things smarter, I gave out my personal cell-phone number on the air. Now remember, this was Dallas to San Antonio! I realized about three hours into it that I'd made a significant mistake. Everybody and their brother wanted to call and tell me their views on how I should run the corps. I eventually had to change my number. Pretty stupid. When I got home, my wife reminded me that a little bit of restraint might have been in order. But my intention was good!

Constant communication is critical if you really want to improve your efficiencies. If you want to find out what they're doing out there that really makes no sense, you've got to ask your workforce—because they're the ones who know. (Remember: Look down, not up!) And you've got to create an environment in which they'll feel comfortable sharing their ideas.

There are still people out there who think, *If I raise my hand and say I've got a recommendation, I'll be persecuted.* No one wants to be Tom Cruise in *Jerry Maguire*, writing a brilliant memo about change and then losing your job just because you're passionate about it. And companies shouldn't be looking to let someone go just because they're passionate about wanting to make the organization better—even if they're talking about standing the organization on its head a little bit. After all, remember this: Jerry Maguire wound up the big winner in that movie. He never should have been let go from that agency. His views were the right views. We need that kind of passion in the workforce. Leaders need to recognize and listen to those voices.

That's not always easy to do, of course. There are a couple of difficult dynamics that you're working through. One is a general resistance to change. It's called institutional and organizational inertia: "This is the way it is because this is the way it's always been." You have to work hard to break through that if you want to create a dynamic and adaptable work environment.

The second dynamic is that the people of the workforce feel too paranoid to raise their hand: *If I raise my hand, they're gonna beat me down, so I'm just going to accept this. I know that it's wrong, but it's just the way we do business here. If I raise my hand, then I'm gonna get persecuted.* That's a major problem you'll have to work through if you want to be an engaged leader.

The best way to address these dynamics is to give your people a sense of pride and ownership in the organization.

In the Army, I tell soldiers all the time that I'm humbled to be in their presence. Think about what we're doing now as a nation. We've been at war for twenty years. Most of the men and women who are in the Army today volunteered to join the army after 9/11—*after* we went to war. They were sitting at home, watching the most recent explosion, reading about the most recent horrific act in the newspaper, and then went out and enlisted in the Army. So I tell these youngsters that I'm humbled to be in their presence. They are proud to be in the Army. They have a pride in our mission—defending our freedoms and our way of life.

In the corporate world, it's important to try to instill that same pride in the organization. If people are proud of the organization, proud to be part of the workforce, if they feel vested in the organization, they're going to be more willing to do things to try to improve productivity, efficiency, and so forth. But you, as a leader, really have to be the one to instill that sense of ownership and pride. At IMCOM, as I did this "traveling road show" of sorts and held town halls to talk to our people, I would always tell the story of the impact of what they're doing on the lives of soldiers and their families.

Our job was to provide soldiers, civilians, and their families with a quality of life commensurate with their quality of service. What I tried to get my staff to believe is that they were not just making a paycheck—they were making a difference in the lives of people. I'd often say: "You've got a choice in life. You can read history, or you can make history."

What I tried to do with the IMCOM staff is to make sure they knew they were *making* history. They were working hard so that these soldiers could go back for multiple deployments and not break the family. They'd come home knowing their family was still well taken care of. And it worked. We did such a good job that, before I left, when we polled the military spouses and asked how many of them would like their soldier-spouse to continue their career in the military, 70 percent said "Yes." Seventy percent! And this was *after* we had been at war for ten years!

Pride and communication are a powerful combination. And the personalization of communication means more than just using your words. This is definitely a case of walking the walk—where being a lifestyle evangelist is important.

As I traveled to our Army installations around the world, talking about the importance of work-life balance and the importance of family, I would always travel with my wife. People would see me, and they'd see her: The video matches the audio. If I said, "My family is important," but my family wasn't with me, that would have been an indication that maybe my family wasn't so important after all. But to say my family is important when my family is there, right up in front of them, standing with me—that's lifestyle evangelism in action. That's a level of personal communication that is seen, heard, and felt by the audience, which, in this case, was my staff.

Empowering the workforce, making sure they feel like they're part of the organization, that they have a vested interest in working hard and doing the right thing, is important. And it's important to corporate America as well. In fact, we all know there are corporations out there that are known especially for treating their employees well, giving them perks, stressing flexible schedules to encourage work-life balance, and so forth. Some of those companies are among the top companies in all of America, and you have to be in some sort of denial not to think that empowering their workforce isn't one of the core reasons those companies have done well.

I consult for H-E-B, a grocery-store chain in Texas, which was started in 1916 by Herman E. Butt (hence, the initials). His son Charles Butt runs the company now, and even though they're only in Texas and have a couple of stores across the border in the country of Mexico, they are the twelfth-largest privately owned company in the nation right now. *Twelfth largest.* They hired me as a consultant for military outreach, and I spent a lot of time with their corporate leadership talking about how they're running their operation. Here's how they make it personal: They refer to everybody in their organization as a "partner." Not an employee, but a partner. And you get a sense as you walk around that these partners really feel that they're a part of the organization and that the organization cares for them. It doesn't matter if they're a top-tier manager, a lifelong cashier, or a high-school kid snagging carts out in the parking lot. They know the company cares for them because they see it not only in bonuses and compensation, but also through education and health benefits—the kinds of things that make workers and their families both proud and secure. That's a good feeling.

They're the twelfth-largest company in America, and they have grocery stores only in the state of Texas. What does that tell you? Do you think it's a coincidence? I don't. If you want to have arguments about the chicken and the egg, I will argue every time that your people come first. When you take care of your people, they will take care of your company. Every time.

It can be done. It *must* be done.

People sometimes stand up when I'm giving talks to corporate America and ask, "How does what you did in the military apply to what we're doing in corporate America today?" The answer is simple: Leadership is leadership.

They ask, "How can we personalize the experience with our workforce when our HR department is telling us not to make our decisions personal?"

The human-resources dynamic in corporate America is just amazing to me. There are people out there who believe that, in the HR world, you can't ask your employees complicated questions or the personal "intrusive" questions I mentioned earlier like, "Tell me about your family" or "How's your dad doing?" There's a belief that there's a line that says you can't ask your staff questions outside of what they do for you day to day. I hear that all the time. Where did those lines come from? Those lines make no sense. We're all people. We're all connected. We're all in this together. And the more together we are, the better our work is going to be. It's not that difficult. But leaders have to be the ones who define where the lines are—not the HR department!

Leaders have to be involved. We have to take care of our people.

I do see improvements from the way things were in past decades, especially in some areas of manufacturing and blue-collar work. I think about my dad. My dad operated a paper cutter. That's what he did for thirty years at Champion International, eight hours a day. He pushed a green button to start the cutter, and, at the end of eight hours, he pushed a red button to stop the cutter; then he went home. He didn't care about Champion International. He didn't care how the company did. He never once believed that the company really cared about him. All he knew was that he had to go for eight hours a day and that, at the end of the week, he'd get a paycheck. There was no personal tie to the corporation. None whatsoever.

I think things are a little different in many companies today. Especially top-tier companies.

I had a chance recently to tour a factory at the second-largest office-furniture manufacturer in the world, HON. They are located in Muscatine, Iowa. I didn't even know Muscatine, Iowa, existed! And I went up there in the middle of winter, no less. But you could tell at that factory that the workers were engaged and felt like they were a part of the organization. I hope that's a reflection of our learning more, of our understanding more and caring more as the years have gone by. Our people deserve a better quality of life than my dad had, and part of improved quality of life involves having a workplace that people want to be a part of.

As I spend more time in corporate America, it just so happens that everywhere I find happy employees, connected employees, and engaged employees, I also find incredibly strong and profitable companies.

In my mind, this is no coincidence; there is a direct correlation between the two. And in every case, the engagement, the connectivity, and even the happiness started with the precedent of the personal level of attention set by leadership.

– 21 –

ACCEPTING RESPONSIBILITY

If common sense were truly common, more people would have it.

When you step back and look at a lot of the decisions I've made and actions I've taken as a leader, the average person might say, "Well, that makes sense. That was just pure common sense. Why didn't somebody do that sooner?"

The reason nobody else did it is because common sense is not that common.

If we want leaders to get things done, we have to empower them with the authority to make bold decisions and stand by the decisions they've made—regardless of broader perceptions, prevailing winds, or office politics.

I can't remember a time in the United States military when I took a poll to determine what decision I ought to make. I saw other leaders trying to lead by consensus and figure out what the most politically digestible option might be. The way I see it, that's leading from a position of fear—fear of repercussions, fear of reprisal, fear of getting yelled at, or just plain fear of looking bad in someone else's eyes. Part of the reason for all of that fear is that we've become a society full of blamers and doubters, full of television pundits who yell and shout about what everyone did wrong when they've never actually done anything good themselves. Look at the political ads. It's striking to me how many political ads focus all of their attention on what the other guy's done wrong, and yet say nothing about what the candidate who's running is actually going to do right. That's not what leaders do. That's not what leadership looks like. Leaders take action. Leaders make the hard choices and accept the responsibility for those actions.

I think we're demoralizing our leaders and our valued workers by not supporting them when they make difficult decisions. This applies to leaders at all levels. In the Army, we call it "top cover" when your leaders stand by your decision. If you don't have that top cover, then, every time you make a decision, you'll look over your shoulder and think, *What's going to happen if I get in trouble?*

I tried to provide top cover to all of my subordinates so they knew that, if they made a decision because they thought it was the right thing to do, I was going to support them in that decision. I don't see a lot of that in the corporate world. Instead, I see a lot of CYOB (Cover Your Own Behind).

Look, not everyone is going to make the right decision all the time. But if we're leading and working from a place of fear, no decisions are ever going to get made efficiently or wisely. Leaders cannot feel constrained by somebody constantly looking over their shoulder, and neither can workers. That's one reason why it's important for leaders to surround themselves with competent subordinates before they delegate. You simply can't suffer incompetence, because that sets you up to fail. If you know you've put competent subordinates in place, then you should give them the authority and freedom they need to get the job done right. You just have to be there to back them up.

The act of accepting responsibility and being responsible for your subordinates comes in many forms. If you truly care about your subordinates the way you would care for your own children, you'll accept the fact that you're responsible for looking after their safety and well-being. Corporate America is pretty aware of this in the workplace when it comes to issues of safety, workers' compensation, and so forth. But I'm here to argue that leaders need to take that responsibility one step further.

TAKE RESPONSIBILITY, OR NO ONE WILL

When I returned to Fort Hood after the surge in Iraq, I realized I had spent about sixteen years at that installation over the course of my career. I wasn't taking command of a place I didn't know; I knew the place pretty well—or so I thought.

Let me tell you that walking through the door as a leader gives you a whole new perspective. Even if you think you know a place, it's important to get to know your workforce all over again—how they're working and living their lives. Never assume. (You know what they say about assuming!)

I've always loved being with soldiers. I like their energy. I like their enthusiasm. In the evenings, I loved going into the barracks, because that's where the soldiers lived, and I continued that tradition the moment I returned to Fort Hood. I'd always take Maggie, my Labrador retriever, with me. It was amusing because some of the soldiers thought Maggie was a drug dog. They got nervous that I was running some kind of inspection, when all Maggie was trying to do was be social. She couldn't tell marijuana from a cigarette if she wanted to. Anyway, I went through that first weekend, and I was shocked. The barracks, and especially the behavior in those barracks, was nothing like it was the last time I had lived on that base. First of all, the most senior person I could find in any barracks was a specialist. That's an E-4 pay grade who's been in the Army just a couple of years. I couldn't find any non-commissioned officers or any commissioned officers.

There was no leadership presence in those barracks.

Well, you can imagine what kind of trouble a bunch of young guys—many of them living away from home for the first time—might get into with no supervision. Now multiply that a few times because we're on an Army base and in the middle of fighting two wars.

There was one barracks complex that made even police officers nervous. Before the police would go in there, they would put on their body armor. They knew that the barracks was so rowdy that the soldiers would throw stuff at them. These are police officers at Fort Hood, Texas! So I got my corps leaders together the following Monday to talk about engaged leadership and to encourage them to go into the barracks in the evenings.

I wanted to know how it got this way, so I asked them, "Where is everybody?"

And the recurring theme was, "General, we're just so busy. We have so much going on, we don't have time to go back into the barracks in the evening. That's not our job. We're leaders from eight to five, and, after five o'clock, it's somebody else's problem."

Typical manager-speak. In my opinion, that's just not true.

Here's what else I discovered: We in the Army, for efficiency's sake, had decided to turn over management of the barracks to a civilian corporation. The management was intended to take care of maintenance—issuing keys and fixing things. Property maintenance, not people maintenance.

But leaders across the corps had decided, "Oh, we turned barracks over to this civilian management, so it's no longer our problem."

I explained to them that they were wrong; it *was* their problem. So, the next week, we got back to having staff-duty officers go through the barracks routinely at night.

It didn't take much. Just the presence of leadership in those barracks turned things around. The police stopped wearing their body armor.

The blotter report—a record of action and discipline reports kept by the military police—was wiped nearly clean practically overnight. Why do you think that was? Leader presence. Leader engagement. People walking through the barracks. It was an amazing thing to me. The leaders weren't cracking down or doing anything to strong-arm our soldiers into behaving better. All they did was show up.

I also spoke directly to our soldiers. I asked them, "Who do you think these barracks belong to?"

And they replied, "Well, they belong to us."

"No, they don't! Those are United States government facilities. They belong to me," I told them with no room for doubt. "You just happen to be occupying that space, so you've got to treat it like it belongs to me, not to you."

That got through to them. It didn't take long, and it didn't take all that much effort—just a little engaged leadership.

Fort Hood was basically a large city. There were a lot of moving parts. I couldn't be everywhere at once, and I had to find ways to develop partnerships with people who could help our soldiers and their families in all aspects of their lives. One easy way to do that was to get to know people in leadership positions throughout the organization. Sarah and I would entertain at our home sometimes two or three nights a week. One night it would be the school super- intendents. The next night it would be the police chiefs. Fort Hood was so big that there were seven different school districts, so getting to know leaders in each area was a big step forward, and their getting to know me helped improve communication on a person-to-person level. I wasn't some anonymous leader dictating policy changes. I was a partner who clearly wanted their lives to go more smoothly and wanted to see this Army base become the best base it could be. It's amazing what happens when everyone feels like they're a part of the same team.

I spoke earlier about the improved conditions that came in the wake of the decisions I made to send everyone home for dinner with their families at 6 p.m. and to mandate family time and weekend time off. Along with lower divorce rates, lower rates of domestic violence, and lower suicide rates, the actions I took sparked a markedly improved traffic-safety record.

In the past, in the large city that Fort Hood really was, we had a record of experiencing a traffic fatality about once every three weeks. It was dismal. Whenever you drove through the gates, you would see this sign marking the number of days we had gone fatality free. It never got higher than thirty.

When I took command of the corps, I took responsibility for that number. And that number climbed, day after day, to the point where we went 245 days without a fatality. A huge improvement. A noticeable improvement. An improvement that meant the world to our soldiers and our families. And I attribute that directly to this focus on the family that I put into action. Families are committed and concerned for the safety of their loved ones, so if you give them the time to focus on safety issues and do the right thing, they're going to be more involved.

There was one more piece of the puzzle that led to the improved safety record, though: I demanded that leaders be held accountable for the safety of their subordinates—not only in the workplace but also beyond the workplace.

For example, if one of our soldiers left the gate and got stopped in the civilian world with an expired license or expired insurance card, that soldier would face disciplinary action. That's a no-brainer. But that soldier wasn't the only one to get in trouble; the soldier's leader also got in trouble.

If you love your subordinates like you love your own children, you've got to worry about them the way you'd worry about your children. You wouldn't let your son or daughter get behind a wheel without having a license or proper insurance. You wouldn't let your kid get on a motorcycle that he or she hadn't been trained to operate. So why would you let your subordinates do those things?

Under my watch, leaders were doing safety checks.

Does that seem unreasonable? Corporate America is concerned about lost workdays, lost productivity, and more. So think about this: If you can take some responsibility to help make sure your workers are maintaining basic safety standards both in and out of the workplace, saving them the time and hassle and possibly dire consequences of ignoring those standards, you're going to save yourself tremendous headaches and lost productivity that can come as a result of their ignoring the basic rules.

An Army base is a little different from the rest of the world, of course, and I could take additional measures to make sure our soldiers were on their best behavior day and night. For example, I put ranks on the windshields of our cars.

Before I got to Fort Hood, there was a basic understanding that there would be no markings to designate rank on the windshields of vehicles because they didn't want terrorists to know where a general or a sergeant was.

I said, "No way." I wasn't afraid of terrorists in Texas. I was much more afraid of our servicemen thinking there wasn't any leadership present as they moved around the base. I wanted my people to know, whether they were on- or off-post, that somebody was watching them—and that person was a leader. You could identify a leader under my watch simply by looking at their car because, on their windshield, right underneath the rear-view mirror, we put a sticker that showed their rank. If you were coming out of a restaurant and fixin' to do something stupid, like get on your motorcycle without putting on your helmet, and you glanced up and saw a windshield with a colonel's insignia, what would you do? You were a lot less likely to do something stupid, because you knew you were being watched.

Then I enforced general order number one, which was basically this: "Everything you do on base, you have to do off base, regardless of the state laws." This was especially important when it came to motorcycles—the vehicles that seemed to lead to a higher incident rate of traffic fatalities. I'm a motorcycle guy myself. I've ridden a Harley-Davidson for thirty years, and I've never had an accident because I drive defensively. I assume that the other guy is going to do something stupid when I'm riding a motorcycle. I make that assumption. I'm properly trained, and I wear protective gear, so that if something does happen, I'll survive the crash. But in the state of Texas, there is no law stating that you have to wear a helmet. You could leave the base (where helmets are required), take off your helmet, crash, and die. So I said that helmets were mandatory whether or you're on base or off. I had the authority to do that. So these kids knew that if they went off base and didn't have their helmet on and got stopped, they'd be in big trouble. They also knew that, if they went off base and got in a wreck, it was going to be a line-of-duty "No" determination. A line-of-duty determination is whether we're going to use the resources of the United States government to cover your medical expenses. If it's line-of-duty "No," you're on your own.

Taking responsibility for their safety—and putting measures into place that would make sure they took extra responsibility for taking care of themselves—had great results. These youngsters knew they had to wear their protective gear, they had to be properly trained, and they had to be properly equipped. The leaders knew that if something happened to their subordinate, too bad for the subordinate, but also too bad for the leader.

When I'd get all the new arrivals together every Wednesday at three o'clock—a group that would often number around 500 because

Fort Hood is so big—I'd have the leaders stand up, and I'd say, "Welcome to this great place. Let me tell you what I expect of you as a leader," and I'd emphasize this leader accountability in the area of safety. If corporate America did that, there would be much less concern about lost workdays and workers' compensation—because engaged leaders need to have a role in the safety of their workers.

On a factory floor, these youngsters working at the furniture factory or the paper factory are required to wear protective eye gear and protective gloves to operate the machinery. And if they choose not to do that and they get injured, it's my feeling that it should be bad not only for them but also for their leader—the supervisor who's supposed to be right there and who's clearly been observing the unsafe behavior without enforcing the rules. If he's observing that behavior and he tolerates it, then he's an ineffective leader, and there needs to be consequences for that.

Safety is paramount, and leaders need to be held accountable. We had a couple of fatalities across IMCOM in which civilian workers were doing the wrong thing around heavy equipment and got crushed. But it could have been avoided. A leader was watching the whole thing and should have been held accountable for someone not using the right jack stands or the right protective equipment or whatever it might have been. In those cases, I could hold the leader accountable for what the subordinate did by docking wages, fining them, and even removing them.

You can't stop all stupid behavior, of course, no matter what safety measures and consequences you put into place. We have incidents in the military of accidental discharge. In combat, we go through detailed weapon-clearing procedures, so before a soldier comes back into an operating base, he's got to physically clear his weapon, and his leaders have to check it—knowing that if there's an accidental discharge on base, somebody could get hurt. Unfortunately, we had a lot of problems with accidental discharges at home, because people would go home and start drinking or goofing around, and they'd pull their weapon out and shoot themselves or their loved ones unintentionally. I didn't hold the leaders accountable for that. Leaders cannot be everywhere at once. Your subordinates have to take some responsibility for themselves and their actions, of course, and there are certain things you just don't have any control over. But with things like driver's licenses, insurance cards, bald tires on cars, motorcycle training—the leaders working under my command *could* have control and influence in those areas. So I made sure they did.

Whenever possible, I also encouraged my leaders to go and visit our subordinates in their homes. Again, this might cross a line in the corporate world that some people see as invasion of privacy, but I just don't see it that way. We all need to get to know one another. It's important for everyone's safety and well-being that we're watching out for each another.

It is my belief that, if you're a leader, you're responsible for your subordinates and their families seven days a week. I've made that my passion ever since I became a commissioned officer. When I was in charge of a platoon of thirty-five people, I made it a point to visit my thirty-five people in their homes at least once a month. Not as some sort of inspection or invasion, but just to see how the families were doing, maybe take some flowers to the wife, bring some hamburgers over and cook up dinner on the grill. For one thing, it was fun. But it also allowed me to see how they were living.

How can you care about your people if you don't know how they're living? Only 40 percent of United States military families live on military installations. So if you care about how they're doing, you need to go visit and see how they're living. If there was a time when I was in charge of too many people to go about that myself, I had our officers go and visit the soldiers at home. Most of the time, it's just a friendly thing that leads to our soldiers and officers connecting on a deeper level, so they're more comfortable working with each other and communicating. It's amazing how many personal-communication goals can be reached very quickly around a backyard barbecue. But there are other times when you find something unexpected and can really help turn somebody's life around before it's too late. At one point, we found that one of our off-base soldiers was in such financial straits, his kids were living in a plywood extension off the side of his mobile home. This soldier was too prideful to bring those troubles into work with him. If one of us hadn't gone out there, we might never have known. And what would have happened as that financial pressure continued to build? We all know how serious financial pressure can get. It affects everything you do. It affects your life, your kids, your health (both physical and mental), and it certainly affects your work. The long and short of it is that we were able to help that soldier get control of his finances, get back on his feet, and get his kids into proper shelter befitting an American soldier and his family.

In corporate America, the idea of a civilian manager knocking on a subordinate's door is really difficult to digest—I realize this. But the concept is still important. You've got to know about your people. You need to check on how they're doing, show interest in their lives. Ask the intrusive questions that get to those answers, at the very least. You can get to a lot of issues without physically going out to their house, and I'm absolutely convinced that, if you do that, you'll be a much more effective leader.

As a leader, I take responsibility for every single subordinate in my care. And the only way to do that is to get leadership on all levels to take that responsibility as well.

That's just common sense, isn't it?

★ ★ ★

Part Four

THE ART OF ADAPTATION

*I have fought the good fight, I have finished
the race, I have kept the faith.*
– 2 Timothy 4:7

When the chips are down, when everything's on the line, when the whole team's looking to you for answers in the face of challenges bigger than anyone saw coming, will you be able to adapt and persevere? More importantly, have you led in a way that will allow your people to adapt and persevere along with you?

The art of adaptation comes down to much more than a simple set of rules or guidelines. It comes down to the very roots of who you are, the foundation you've built, the confidence and trust you've inspired, and your ability to truly lead your workforce, team, or troops with their best interests in mind. Throughout my own life and career, I've personally adapted to new jobs, new scenarios, new bosses, new technologies, and new challenges every step of the way. I've done it with strength. I've done it with positivity, seeing opportunities in every obstacle. And I've done it by staying true to my character and beliefs. Can an entire organization adapt in similar fashion? You bet. Adapting as a leader and leading through adaptation takes much of the same fortitude and positive attitude—only there's a whole lot more on the line. This isn't just about you. This is about everything you've done and everything your people have done. This is about success vs. failure. This is about your company, your school, your organization, your country—and whether it'll live to see another day.

Adaptation is the key to survival. And leadership is the key to adaptation.

− 22 −

UNDER FIRE

Sometimes bad news comes in the dark of night.

It was 4:44 a.m. on the morning of May 12, 2007, when a group of al-Qaeda operatives staged a guerilla-style attack against one of my platoons in Iraq.

The army's Third Infantry Division and Task Force Marne, which comprised the 25,000 soldiers I was in charge of leading through the surge, had barely been there a month. We were engaged in heavy combat from the start, but the thing that was knocking us down time and time again, costing losses of vehicles, progress, and lives, was the scourge of IEDs.

Improvised Explosive Devices, or IEDs, were the enemy's weapon of choice. Planted on roadsides. Buried in the dirt. Silent, invisible killers. Our platoon had set up guard in a critical stretch of important road alongside the Euphrates River called Route Malibu, which the enemy had repeatedly booby-trapped with IEDs. Our enemies were so determined to take out this route (which the coalition forces needed), that they had taken to sneaking up to the craters left by previous IED explosions, planting new IEDs, and refilling the holes. We had to stop this. Thus, the reason for our platoon's presence.

We stood guard with trip wires around the perimeter, night-vision goggles utilized, and more. But the enemy was stealthier than anyone realized. They snipped the wires. They snuck up to the Humvees. They tossed percussion grenades into the darkness to disorient our team. In the chaos, they shot and killed four United States soldiers and an Iraqi interpreter—and they dragged three of my men, alive, into the darkness. Kidnapped.

There hadn't been such a disturbing incident since Jessica Lynch had been kidnapped back in 2003. And the thought that three of my men were being held, possibly tortured, and God knows what else by these al-Qaeda thugs, left me fuming. The first thing I did was drop to my knees and ask God for help. I'm the one who says you have to love your subordinates like you love your own children, so when something happened, I took it very personally. I wouldn't have made it through without God's help.

I immediately put every resource we had into finding those men. We offered a $200,000 reward for information. We wanted our men alive, and we wanted their kidnappers—those killers—brought to justice. The pressure was immense. And despite all of our power, our equipment, and our motivation, we made little to no progress in the days that immediately followed.

On May 23, Iraqi police found the body of one of those soldiers floating in the Euphrates. With the other men still nowhere to be found, hopes were fading. Morale was down. But I refused to give up. I reaffirmed my dedication to the search at the end of that month. I assured their fellow soldiers, their commanders, and their families that they would have all the resources they needed to keep searching, even if that meant taking resources away from some of the other tasks at hand. It was the right and only thing to do, as far as I was concerned. Those were my soldiers. My children. We owed it to their families.

Meanwhile, the surge pressed on. For six straight months, we would be engaged in combat operations in this complex environment of an insurgency, fighting not only the Sunni insurgents but the ideological and organizational influences of the terrorist cells of al-Qaeda, who were backed by monetary and weapons support from Iran. Our situational and operational awareness was strong, thanks to the work we'd done long ago in the deserts of California to ramp up the technology to fight this kind of war. We finally had the soldiers and resources on the ground to accomplish what we needed to accomplish, but the ups and downs of that sort of daily combat are enough to tax even the most resilient person's strength and will.

No sooner would we have good news than it would be pushed aside by something terrible. There was one day that June when two of my men used their keen eye and good instincts to stop a suicide bomber who was ambling toward one of our outposts in an innocent-looking farming truck—filled with 14,000 pounds of explosives. That intervention deserved celebrating. The American public needed to hear of that sort of bravery and action on the part of our soldiers. Yet on that very same day, another suicide bomber detonated his vehicle on a bridge we used to bring supplies up from Kuwait, killing three of my men and wounding six others in the process. The celebration quickly turned to tears, prayers, and damaging headlines.

As the months passed, the scourge of IEDs grew more frequent and severe. Roadside bombs were ripping apart our convoys and killing our men. We went out on foot looking for the insurgents who were planting these things, sometimes moving door-to-door. Routine patrols in supposedly secure areas would suddenly erupt. Men fell. The enemy's forces grew smaller with each step of our progress, but they also grew smarter. They would set up obvious IED-looking devices, forcing our vehicles to steer around them, only to hit a true IED buried down the other path of the fork in the road. On August 11, 2007, a sniper opened fire on one of our platoons along the West Bank of the Tigris River. One of the men was wounded and evacuated as the rest of the platoon rushed to the building where the sniper was hiding. Turns out the sniper was only a ruse. As the soldiers busted in, spreading through the house with weapons ready, searching room-to-room, a huge explosion ripped through the building, collapsing walls and burning some of those men alive. The entire house had been turned into one massive IED.

I lost five soldiers in a single moment.

It was the worst one-day casualty count since the surge began.

Again, I took it personally. I fell to my knees. I asked God for help.

We were making progress, but at what cost?

The Triangle of Death was living up to its name. The slaughter we witnessed, not only to coalition forces but to the Iraqi civilian population because of this insurgency, was unbearable. For six months we endured, we pushed on, we won, we suffered setbacks, we charged ahead through the intensity of battle in 110-degree heat, and pressed against the relentlessness of the insurgency, not knowing where the enemy might rear its ugly head, where it may have left its hungry weapons buried just beneath the sand or just behind an unopened door.

There had to be a better way. There had to be hidden opportunities in the midst of all this hardship.

We had the "means"—our resources during the surge were immense. We could see the "ends"—the rebuilding of Iraq as a free democracy. What we needed to find was a different way to get there.

Leaders see opportunities, not obstacles, right?

As the months went on, I saw an opportunity in the unlikeliest place of all. I saw opportunity in the eyes of my enemy.

Just as I would never lead a business sitting in some corner office, I didn't lead from the safety of a hidden bunker somewhere in Iraq. I followed the basic tenets of Manage by Walking Around. I treated my role as commander in this war the same way I treated any other leadership position: as an engaged leader. That meant I engaged with our soldiers and officers—getting to know them, throwing a ball around with them when we could find moments to relax, picking up a satellite phone and calling their mom or dad from the field just to say hello and to let them know that their loved one was safe. It also meant that I spent time with the people we were fighting for.

The more time I spent with the Iraqi people, the more I enjoyed being around them. What I realized is they were just like us: They wanted freedom from fear, they wanted to be able to send their kids to school, they wanted a functioning government, they wanted to be able to provide for their families. Just like us. And they're educated. If Saddam Hussein did anything right, he invested in the education of the Iraqi people. Why he chose to do that, I don't know, but he did. The more I hung around these Sunnis, the more I realized that they could be a part of the solution instead of part of the problem.

Back when I was first negotiating with the Sunni insurgents in 2005 and 2006, there were multiple occasions where I sat down across the table from fifteen or sixteen of these guys, all of them armed, and they blatantly told me, "We hate you." I was able to calm things down a bit in those days just by sticking to my principles and talking to them as people, trying to diffuse the hatred by letting them know our true purpose. Letting them know that we weren't there to stay, that we wanted to help them by helping all of Iraq become peaceful and free of the oppression they had faced for so long. I was alone in those negotiations, except for an interpreter, and yet my presence represented all of America and the entire coalition force. Any one of them could have pulled a gun and blown me away just for the power trip of it, from the sheer anger they felt—especially at that point in the war, when tensions between the Shia and Sunni populations were about as high as they could get. But by talking to them like the human beings they are, by looking them in the eye, by taking responsibility for what we had done and were doing, and being honest with them about our intentions, I was able to break through.

In fact, it was at those negotiating tables where I learned an incredibly valuable bit of information about the Sunni insurgents. "We hate you," they said. "But we hate al-Qaeda worse, and we hate the Persians (that's what they called the Iranians) even more." So in terms of a hierarchy of hatred, we were number three. That seemed like an opportunity to me, and, eventually, as I proved in action, it was.

Even as we were engaged in combat throughout 2007, I looked around and realized that these Sunnis were no longer a united front entrenched against us. Something had changed. The majority of these people, on any given day, were fence sitters. On any given day, they were waking up and making the decision, "Am I going to attack the coalition or not?"

DO SOMETHING DIFFERENT

The tide had slowly turned against al-Qaeda in a big way, because, in their desperation to hold on to what little power they had, they had turned to brutal tactics to get their way. Terrible, barbaric, terrorist tactics like slaughtering children and parading the bodies in front of their mothers. Not exactly the kind of behavior that puts you in the good graces of the population you supposedly want on your side. It was supposed to be a show of strength, instilling fear in the Sunni population so they would join al-Qaeda in the fight against the Americans. The problem is, leading by fear always fails in the end. It never lasts. Eventually, the population that's been fearful will rise up against you. I knew that. I saw that happening. And I decided to try something new.

Turns out, a lot of that daily "Should I attack the coalition or not?" decision was purely financial. After asking around, I realized that, if a Sunni planted an IED, the insurgency would pay him two hundred dollars! The only reason the Sunnis would do that is because they had no other source of income, and they had to find a way to provide for their families. And, oh, by the way, they didn't like the fact that we were there. We were occupiers. People think we were there as liberators, and that's true. But after about a week, no matter what your original intentions were, you're viewed as occupiers. Think about it: If you had somebody bouncing around your town in tanks and Bradleys, you'd feel the same way. I could understand their reasoning.

What I realized we had to do was take these potential obstacles, these fence sitters who were planting IEDs, and turn them into opportunities. What I tried to figure out was how to subsidize them so they wouldn't choose to shoot at us or plant bombs.

I had this asset called the Commanders Emergency Resources Program, the CERP program, which gave me a relatively unencumbered chunk of money to do whatever needed to be done on the ground to help our efforts. It could have been used for building *things*. Instead, I used it to build a *movement*: the Concerned Local Citizens program.

Basically, we went around and asked the Sunnis to join in our efforts to stop the violence, and we paid these "volunteers" eight dollars a day for their efforts. That was a pretty significant chunk of change, to both them and to us—especially as dozens, and eventually hundreds, of Sunnis started to volunteer for the program. But it was certainly money well spent. It worked. As a result of that eight dollars a day, these Sunnis had a source of income, which meant they didn't have to plant the IEDs anymore. As a result of the removal of that financial stress in their lives, they were less likely to be hostile toward the coalition forces. They stayed on the right side of the fence.

By January of 2008, this program blossomed into what became known as the Sons of Iraq program. Once these Sunni volunteers stayed on the right side of the fence, they started to get interested in securing themselves rather than relying on us to provide all the security for their towns. Every day, I'd spend all day walking the streets of Iraq, meeting with leaders in the local areas who had been empowered by the Sons of Iraq program. They were the first to tell us about insurgents. They would tell us, "That guy doesn't belong here. We don't know where he's from," or "Even though this guy's my cousin, he tends to do some bad things." Heck, there was one old man who started personally guarding who came into or out of his town—sitting at his self-created roadblock with nothing but a knife in his hand.

It didn't take long before the effects were felt all over the region. By the spring of 2008, we had 25,000 Iraqis enrolled in the Sons of Iraq program. The number of IED attacks fell significantly, almost by default. And that changed everything.

It changed the course of the war.

This all sounds logical and good and reasoned now, with 20/20 hindsight, but I've got to tell you: Turning this obstacle into an opportunity was one of the scariest things we could've done. It couldn't have been riskier. Lots of these "volunteers" had American blood on their hands. In the town of Jurf as Sakhr (pronounced "Jervisucker"), there was a guy leading the insurgency who was trying to kill me as I was trying to kill him. Suddenly, he decided he wanted to become part of the Sons of Iraq program. So there I was, giving this man—who was an insurgent not twenty-four hours earlier—a hug on the streets of Jurf as Sakhr! He was going to become my friend, not my enemy, under this program.

Talk about risky business! These guys were wearing those loose, traditional one-piece garments, so you had no idea if they were armed as you went to shake their hands. They knew we were armed, obviously, but talk about calculated risk.

How did I know we could pull this off?

First of all, I had faith on my side. I prayed every day, and I knew we were doing the right thing. That's powerful. "What, then, shall we say in response to these things? If God is for us, who can be against us?" (Romans 8:31).

Second, I took this thing one step at a time. I was pragmatic. I didn't do this in one big sweeping move. It was locality by locality, over the course of many months. You could just get a sense from talking to the people when they'd reached that point where they'd had enough. It went all the way back to talking to the Sunni insurgents in 2006, when they told me, "We hate you. But we hate al-Qaeda worse, and we hate the Persians even more." I saw that hierarchy of hatred as an opportunity then, and here it was, a year and a half later, as an opportunity realized and a turning point in the war.

Of course, the biggest theme here is really just that we tried something new. As a leader, you can't be afraid to try new things. The definition of insanity is to do the same thing over and over again and expect a different outcome. In this particular case, in Iraq, we were just trying something new—with a large amount of calculated risk. We were extending partnership and trust to perceived friends who could have turned out to be enemies with access to stab us in the back. But we understood the risk, built in safeguards, and found success. I had five brigade-level commanders who worked for me across the battle space. We would sit down with a cigar and say, "Where are we at? Are we ready?"

There were sixty-two patrol bases, and the young captains and soldiers who ran those bases knew the Iraqi people nearby each base. If you had those lines of communication open with them, you could get a good sense of what was happening and how ready those people were to stop being our enemy and start being a part of the solution.

But make no mistake: The call had to be made at my level because of the risk involved. If a young captain said, "Now's the time," and it wasn't the time, and he lost soldiers, his head was on the chopping block. So I had to give them that "top cover" I've spoken about. I had to take the responsibility for saying, "Now's the time."

I had to take that responsibility because I knew we had to try this.

I'll say it again: If something's not working, try something different.

Sure, it was a big risk. On any given day, I could have lost a whole company of people. They could've easily walked into an ambush. People got aggravated with me because I got to the point where I would be on the streets, in the markets, and in the houses, and I'd actually remove my body armor and my helmet. I was trying to have this relationship with the Sunni people, and when you're looking at them through ballistic sunglasses and you've got your helmet and your body armor on, it's not exactly conducive to productive conversation. They're out there in their traditional garb and you're in body armor? It just didn't work. I had to walk among them the same way I would walk among the troops back home or in the barracks at Fort Hood.

Of course, there were some cultural issues to overcome, too. For instance, the Iraqi people do communal meals. And as Americans who were now working with the Sunnis rather than against them, we all experienced "goat grabs." That's when they'll kill a goat, roast it, put it on a big bed of rice, and put it on a table. Then everybody just reaches in and grabs their goat meat. This guy you're now working with will reach in with his hand—no plastic gloves, but bare hands (and you don't know where those hands have been)—and grab some of that goat and hand it to you. If you didn't take it and eat it, they were offended. These are the same guys we were trying to kill the day before. Now I'm literally eating out of their hands! So, at any point, it could have become a disaster.

All of it was a calculated risk, and it really was "adapt or die." We had to change. We had to adapt. We had to find new opportunities. And we had to do it despite lingering feelings of hatred that existed on both sides.

Despite the resources I had thrown into the search, nearly a year had gone by since that 4:44 a.m. platoon attack when three of my men were dragged off into the darkness—and two of them were still unaccounted for. No amount of progress or reconciliation could alleviate that horror. The mother of one of those missing men slept with a cell phone under her pillow every night just in case someone called with any news. I was aware of that the whole time. The horrors of war, and the horror of a mother not having answers about the whereabouts of her boy for that long, haunted me.

May of 2007 is when that platoon was ambushed. In August of that year, the house-borne IED took out five of my men in one fell swoop. Now here we were four months later, walking into Iraqi houses every day under this Sons of Iraq program. If we relaxed our guard, that sort of disaster could have hit us all over again. But we had to do it. We had to shift the equation. We did. And it worked. It changed the course of the war in Iraq, and it was time for yet another adaptation.

Almost overnight, I had to shift gears from combat operations to capacity building.

★ ★ ★

– 23 –

REBUILDING

The Sons of Iraq program brought some assurances of peace, but we needed one more big round of force to lay it to rest. On January 10, under my command, we dropped 47,000 pounds of bombs on military targets south of Baghdad. The strikes were remarkably effective, and no civilian casualties were reported whatsoever. Then on January 20, ten days later, just in case anyone was thinking we were through, we did it again: 34,500 pounds dropped on forty known enemy targets—most of them in a matter of minutes. We were through fooling around, and we wanted the enemy to know it.

Backed by the Sunnis in the Sons of Iraq program, who wanted to stem the violence themselves, and our soldiers on the ground, who never let up despite so many months of intense fighting and suffering the scourge of IEDs, the plan worked.

The tide of violence turned. And now it was time to get to work in a whole new way: rebuilding Iraq's economic, governmental, and social capacity. The Sons of Iraq program wasn't enough to sustain a healthy economy. Plus, we were spending nearly $10 million a month to employ those Sunnis and keep them on our side of the fence. That wasn't sustainable. That wasn't our job beyond the short-term fix it was meant to be. The Iraqis needed to get their country and economy back, and to start making a good life for themselves.

So I had to change my focus.

As a leader, I had to ask myself: *How am I going to get the economy up? How am I going to get the government established? How am I going to get the road networks working? How am I going to get the clinics built, the schools going?*

Frankly, those are skill sets I didn't have. No one on my staff had those skill sets, either. We're the Army. We weren't trained in capacity building—but that was the situation we were in.

Look down, not up. I lived by that principle. It was no different in Iraq. When looking for answers, I went to the people. I learned that the area we referred to as the Triangle of Death had been teeming with life before the war started. There were a thousand fish farms and probably as many chicken farms located in that one region south of Baghdad. If we wanted to give the Iraqi people what they needed, we needed to bring those livelihoods back.

So as we headed into the spring of 2008, this two-star general, who'd spent most of his adult life living in Texas, had to become an expert chicken and fish farmer.

We had to figure out how to help the Iraqi people take these baby fish, these fingerlings, to their fish farms, grow them to some level of vibrancy, and then transport them to market in 110-degree heat.

This is what we, a heavy combat division of the Army, had to do in order to start to win this war—in order to continue the turn of the tide that would eventually get our soldiers out of there in 2011. I tapped my soldiers for whatever expertise they might have, I solicited ideas, and, in putting our heads together, we actually designed and built refrigerated trucks to transport fish to market. We figured out how to put the right facilities and infrastructure together so the fish could grow in their local farms and get sold and wind up on dinner tables.

In the chicken-farming business, we sent a team to Holland to buy 50,000 fertilized eggs. We brought these eggs down into the battle space and set them up in incubators—a giant version of the little cage with a light bulb you might set up in a second-grade classroom. I learned more about growing chickens and growing fish than I ever wanted to know or thought I'd need to know, but that was what we needed to do.

The essence of an Iraqi is a sense of identity within the family. They're people of honor—and if we could figure out how to help them with their livelihood so they could take care of the family, they wouldn't need to shoot at us or shoot at each other any longer.

That's how you turn the tide in a war-strewn country hit by insurgency: by building capacity.

I realize it's funny to picture this hard-nosed American general becoming an expert poultry farmer and fish farmer. It's probably difficult to think of me touring a truck factory that we got back on its feet for manufacturing after all those months spent trying to kill the very people who might be working in that factory.

But adaptation is the key to survival. It's the key to winning. And I hope you can take some lessons from that, no matter what kind of organization it is you're trying to lead. If I could repurpose my team from killing people to poultry farming and fish farming overnight, you can certainly adapt your workforce to an ever-changing marketplace.

We could have maintained the status quo with the Iraqis, continued to kill them, continued to persecute 'em, continued to walk the streets of Iraq with our weapons ready—but where would that have gotten us? We had to adapt. We had to say, "No. It's time to stop doing what we've been doing. It's time." It was one region, one town at a time. But even so, it was time.

I was the one to make that call and to take that risk for my men because I knew it had to be done.

Incrementally, the Third Infantry Division and Task Force Marne began building police stations, laying water pipes, and bringing radio stations back online, in addition to reviving the fish and poultry farms. And by June, our mission was complete. There was still plenty of building to do, and there were still al-Qaeda forces to be dealt with here and there, but those tasks would be passed along to new divisions, under new leadership.

If there was a deep regret among my men, one pain that was still pulling at my heart, it was that we hadn't located those two soldiers who were still missing. We had good reason to believe they had been killed. But the fact that we hadn't found them, hadn't been able to give their parents or any of us that closure, was tough. Fortunately we got some fresh leads before we left, and by July the bodies of both of those soldiers were found. Their remains were flown back to the United States, and their parents were able to finally let go of the aching hope and painful wondering that kept them awake for so many nights. They were finally able to grieve.

I was able to grieve, too.

In the course of those 15 months in Iraq, we lost 153 of my men and women. That's 153 sons and daughters who lost their lives based on where I put them on the battlefield—because I took responsibility for the actions of every leader and every soldier under my command. I carried laminated pictures of each of those soldiers with me wherever I went in Iraq. And I carried those pictures home with me. I placed them on my desk, where I could see them each and every day as a reminder of what we had done, what we had accomplished, and the sacrifices it took for us to complete our mission. And I sought solace in Scripture, especially John 15:13: "Greater love has no one than this: to lay down one's life for one's friends."

Those laminated pictures were a reminder of just how important it was for me to make decisions as a leader, knowing that every decision I made affected the life of someone under my command. In Iraq my decisions affected lives in the gravest manner possible. Back home? Well, however we affect the lives of our subordinates is just as important, isn't it? After all, we need to love our subordinates as we love our own children. I will never let go of that belief. Ever.

The Army gave me my third star when I returned home from the surge. They put me in command of Fort Hood. And I knew I would do everything I could in that position to help our soldiers and their families live the best lives they could.

That was my job. That was my new mission. Fighting in Iraq, and winning—through all of the sacrifices and the lives that were taken—inspired me to want to do more. As a leader. As a husband. As a father. As a servant of God. After all, I had been gone fifteen months. I had missed a lot. I had missed two of Sarah's birthdays. I had a lot of time to make up. And as the leader of Fort Hood, I had a lot of people to look after.

I would do whatever it took to adapt to that new role, and to see to it that the people under my command were given the tools they needed to adapt to the challenges we would all be facing together moving forward. And I would do it without sacrificing my family. I would do it while enriching my life and the lives of those around me.

I came back from Iraq fired up to continue the mission of leadership I had embarked on decades ago. Only now I had all of the tools and experience to get the job done.

★ ★ ★

– 24 –

BUILDING RESILIENCY

Charles Darwin said, "It is not the strongest of the species that survives, nor the most intelligent that survives. It is the one that is most adaptable to change."

I think that premise applies equally to people—in the workforce, in school, in government, in sports, and especially in life. I also think that premise applies to corporations and organizations of all stripes. It's not the strongest corporations that survive. It's not the most intelligent organizations that make it. It is the corporations and organizations that are most adaptable to change.

So, as a leader, you have to ask yourself: "Are my troops the strongest of the species? Are my subordinates the most adaptable to change of any subordinates out there? Is my staff able to weather the storm of competition and rapid technological change? Or are my competitors breeding a workforce that's going to adapt faster, stronger, and more capably while simply leaving us out here to die?"

Then you have to ask yourself, "How do I develop subordinates who are the most adaptable to change? How do I develop a team that's capable of surviving, well, just about anything?"

Chances are if you've made it this far, if you've become a leader, if you've weathered the changes and obstacles in your own life with aplomb, you're probably what I would call a resilient person. And that's a good thing, because that's what you're going to need your people to be, too.

The key to adapting to change is resiliency.

Webster's has two closely related definitions for *resiliency*. The first is "capable of withstanding shock without permanent deformation or rupture," and the second is "tending to recover from or adjust easily to misfortune or change."

Many strong examples of resilient individuals can be found in the Army. Think about it: Not every soldier who deploys to combat operations comes back devastated. Many of them come back enriched.

I am one of those people.

I fought in Desert Shield and Desert Storm, spent a year in Kosovo, had two other deployments to Iraq, and then had a third period of time when I was in and out of Iraq from Naples, Italy, as part of my NATO command. When I went into combat, I saw some horrible things. I felt life-and-death pressures unlike anything I ever imagined I could survive. Yet when I came back from combat? I wasn't devastated. I was enriched! I had been challenged. I had been forced to work through difficulties, and I found that, through all of that, I had grown in wisdom, strength, and fortitude. Those experiences, as difficult as they were, shaped me into a better leader. I didn't wither under the pressure. I didn't fade. I got stronger. I got smarter.

That is the essence of resiliency.

The question is whether resiliency is something inherent in certain individuals or something that can be fostered and instilled in individuals. I believe it's both. There are some people who are born capable of weathering almost any storm. It's just in their DNA. But I've also witnessed firsthand and been a part and parcel to what we've done in the Army to help build resiliency in our soldiers.

We need resilient soldiers and officers up and down the entire chain of command in the Army. We know that. We want that. We fight for that. So, as the Army, we studied what makes a person resilient, and we found there are five key components: spiritual fitness, physical fitness, emotional fitness, societal fitness, and familial fitness.

SPIRITUAL FITNESS

Spiritual fitness is not about any particular religion. It's about acknowledging some greater power that will help you through difficult times and on which you can rely for strength. At Fort Hood, Texas, we built a resiliency campus. I took the chapel that Sarah and I were married in and turned it into a "spiritual fitness center." Where a chapel is a place of worship, this center was a place of growth. It wasn't tied to any denomination. All were welcome. It was a place intended for folks grappling with problems to go and seek help from the higher power they believed in. It was full of literature, music, refreshments—everything welcoming and inviting. What I was trying to do was give these youngsters in the Army a place to go in the middle of the night if they needed a source of strength, to be able to get that source of strength.

We'd also use this facility to gather our soldiers and share stories. I told them the story of what happened the day our platoon was attacked and three soldiers were dragged away—and how I dropped to my knees and prayed for guidance. I told them the story of the house-borne IED that took five of my men, and how we worked through that—how spiritual fitness gave me the strength to keep going. I told them how I prayed for strength, courage, and wisdom every morning, and how I say the prayer of Jabez every morning, too.

For those who don't know, the prayer of Jabez is in the book of First Chronicles. The prayer is dropped in among a long genealogy that is virtually unreadable. However, the prayer itself is a hidden gem. It says, "Jabez cried out to the God of Israel, 'Oh, that you would bless me and enlarge my territory! Let your hand be with me, and keep me from harm so that I will be free from pain.' And God granted his request," (1 Chronicles 4:10).

Considering the experiences I've had down through the years, evidently, God is in the business of enlarging territory. I sometimes joke that I need to stop saying this prayer, because God just keeps on granting me bigger and bigger responsibilities as a leader!

But jokes and light conversation aside, the thing I really like about that prayer is the part about God's hand being with me and keeping me from harm. And the last line is the key: "God granted his request." That's the key to spiritual fitness right there. If you believe that, if you believe that there is some higher power that will always be there for you and will keep you from harm, then you're free. Free to live. Free to move through whatever trouble you're facing. Free to face down life's fears and obstacles, from the day-to-day struggles to life-or-death challenges as big and scary as the ones I faced in Kuwait or Iraq.

Whether it's the prayer of Jabez or some other meaningful prayer, I believe prayer is part of a healthy spiritual-fitness regimen. I also believe prayer can yield some pretty amazing results.

In addition to the policies I put in place at Fort Hood, I attribute much of the improved safety record we developed under my command to the power of prayer. Routinely at dinners, functions, and banquets, we paused to ask God to be with our soldiers and our families. I believe he answered that prayer. (Truth be told, I believe God answers all prayers—even if sometimes His answer is "No.")

That belief is powerful. Taking a few moments to put spirituality into practice is powerful. Reading the Bible is powerful. The combination of all of that gives me peace. But it also helps me as a leader and as a human being to share that peace with others.

There were several occasions when one of my soldiers was hurt in training, and when I visited them in the hospital, I'd pray to God for healing. There were many times when God granted that request, and with the help of our great medical professionals, we would see soldiers recover "miraculously." When I was a battalion commander at Fort Hood, Sarah and I, along with our chaplain, went to inform a young Army wife that her husband had been killed in a vehicle roll-over. When she met us at the door, she was holding her baby in her arms. And she collapsed when she heard the news. Luckily, we caught the child before she hit the ground. We prayed to God for strength, courage, and wisdom to get us through that. We reached out to her parents, who were on a cruise when it happened, and, miraculously, they made it to their daughter's side by nightfall.

It's stories like these that I'd share with our soldiers, to make them ask themselves what it is they believe in. Do they believe in a higher power? How do they stay in touch with that higher power? Are they spiritually fit and prepared to deal with crisis and loss in their lives—because like it or not, we're all going to face heartache and pain at some point. I know that I couldn't have made it through my time in Iraq, or just about any of the difficulties I've faced in life, without my belief in God and the devoted attention I've paid to my own spiritual fitness. So I used that space to talk about it—to talk about how I set my priorities in life, putting God first, family second, and career third. Giving your workforce the time and place to worship as they see fit truly matters. People need belief in something they can hold on to when everything seems to be falling apart. It's important for leaders to provide an environment that allows that to happen—and then it's up to each individual to find those answers for him- or herself.

PHYSICAL FITNESS

I think it's fairly obvious why physical fitness is important in the Army. In combat, in 120-degree heat, wearing seventy pounds of body armor while people are shooting at you, you've got to be physically fit. But physical fitness is about much more than muscles, so I made sure my forces had what they needed in order to train their bodies to handle the pressure. I took one of the many gymnasiums at Fort Hood and turned it into a broad-spectrum physical-fitness resiliency center. We focused on CrossFit training, yoga, meditation, Pilates, even aromatherapy, to help folks control their nervous systems and learn to stay calm under pressure. We encouraged everyone to focus on all aspects of their physical well-being.

There's a book I like called *Younger Next Year*, and it stresses the importance of constant movement. Don't be sedentary. I've talked about incorporating two hours of physical fitness training into my daily routines, even in the heat of combat in Iraq, and how I insisted my subordinates follow the same routine. If we could do that in the desert while taking fire, you can do it where you live and work. There is simply no excuse for not getting the exercise and physical-fitness training you need. As a leader, you can find ways to encourage your subordinates to get fit and stay fit. Build a gym at your headquarters. Can't build a gym? Start a lunchtime running program or an on-site yoga class, or make a deal with a local gym to drum up business by offering a discount for your employees. If your staff is physically fit, they will be more resilient—in their lives as well as their workplace. It literally takes strength, as the old song goes, to pick yourself up, dust yourself off, and start all over again.

EMOTIONAL FITNESS

The third component of resiliency is emotional fitness.

The book *Emotional Intelligence* talks about having an EQ, just like we have an IQ. Your people need to be emotionally stable in order to face pressure and change when necessary. As a leader, you can help them by creating work environments that support emotional stability, offering counseling services through your health plan or some other arrangement, providing support services or referral services when necessary, and simply by treating your subordinates as the human beings they are.

A lot of this comes back to treating your subordinates the way you would treat your own children, doesn't it? You want—no, *need*—your children to be emotionally healthy and fit, the same way you need them to be physically fit and healthy.

SOCIETAL FITNESS

A fourth component is societal fitness. It's important that your team members have commitments to their community, so that the community is there for them and they are there for their community. It's important that your team members answer this question well: "Is it bigger than just you?" Looking outside yourself—seeing the big picture—is an essential part of life. Encouraging and rewarding your employees for volunteer work, supporting community outreach from within your organization, and making sure that your teammates are engaged in philanthropic efforts on a local level and that your community engages on a personal level with your team—all of it can help create those powerful connections that make your people feel like the community has their back.

FAMILIAL FITNESS

The final component of resiliency is familial fitness.

This one came easy to me. Putting family as a priority, making sure my workers and soldiers got home for dinner and spent nights and weekends with the people they love—that's key. Your relationship with your immediate family—no matter who it is you call "family"—is a key to happiness, stability, and strength.

A subset of the family-fitness component is finances: Are you established financially? We would ask soldiers, "Before and after you deploy and come back, will you be financially fit? Do you have financial stability?"

If the answer was "No," we'd work with them. Courses in budgeting, accounting, saving for retirement, and more are easy things for most leaders to set up for their people. Making sure salaries are in line with the cost of living and that benefits are covering important pieces from medical insurance to tuition reimbursements to emergency funds when possible, can give your subordinates and their families a peace of mind that will better allow them to focus on the tasks at hand when the chips are down.

Again, most of this falls in line pretty easily when you love your subordinates as you would love your own children. You wouldn't want to see any of these components missing in people you truly care about, and the steps required to offer guidance and assistance in these areas are not difficult to take. If you truly care, you can indeed set a structure in place in corporate America and elsewhere to build resilient employees—so that, when confronted with difficult times, they will come out of them enriched, not devastated.

Go ahead and let your managers complain all they want about the costs of these things. As leaders, we have to stand up and let it be known that the cost of not taking care of our people is much greater. The cost of not building a resilient workforce could well mean that your company will not survive as your competition and the world around you continues to evolve. Plain and simple.

After all, Darwin's lessons aren't the only the place you'll find words about the power of resiliency and adaptation. The Bible has something to say about the subject, too: "Not only so, but we also glory in our sufferings, because we know that suffering produces perseverance; perseverance, character; and character, hope" (Romans 5:3-4).

Look at the five components of resiliency that we uncovered in our research in the Army. Then think about how they apply to your own organization and what you can do to foster the growth of each of those areas in your subordinates. The payoff will be immense.

– 25 –

EXPERIENTIAL LEARNING

In looking back at my own career—and almost any Army career—I think there's another clear key to building resilient, adaptable soldiers: giving them plenty of experiential-learning opportunities.

Experiential learning is just what it sounds like: Learning from experience.

In general terms, a member of the United States Army has opportunities to learn from institutional learning, organizational learning, and self-learning. That's generally the way it works in corporate America as well. Whether it's the Army or an international conglomerate, we have an expectation that you, as a professional, are going to develop yourself professionally. While we expect that, you can expect that we'll help you grow professionally, and you can also expect that we'll put you in an organization where you'll learn on the job. You'll learn by doing. We call that "experiential learning."

The key here is to put your people through a variety of different on-the-job experiences as a way to make them as adaptable and resilient as possible.

In the Army, especially with general officers, we intentionally pull people out of their comfort zone and throw them into something else whenever we have the chance. In fact, I would say I spent six out of my ten years as a general officer out of my comfort zone. When I was the chief of staff at Kosovo Force (KFOR), I was out of my comfort zone. When I was the operations officer for Southern Europe in Naples, Italy, I was out of my comfort zone. When I was the spokesman for the force in Iraq, I was *way* out of my comfort zone.

When I had a chance to become an assistant division commander, my superior, Division Commander Ben Griffin, said, "Hey, Rick, I can make you the assistant division commander for maneuver and you'd learn nothing because you already know all that stuff, so, instead, I'm going to make you the assistant division commander for support."

That type of career maneuvering in the Army was purposeful. The point was that keeping me in one position, even one that I was good at, wouldn't give me a breadth of experience. The thought was that, by causing me to move to a side of the division that I'd never been in before—to force me to move outside my comfort zone and experience something new—would make me a better division commander when I got my next promotion.

Later on, when I went to IMCOM and took over all the Army installations worldwide, I was once again out of my comfort zone. It was 120,000 employees, of whom only 2,000 were soldiers—the rest were dedicated civilians. That was a significant point of adaptation. I had to ask myself (and my mentors), "How do you take the mannerisms and techniques you used when you led soldiers and apply that to leading a civilian organization?" The answer was that I had to adapt. I had to learn on the job.

Now that I'm out of the Army, I'm doing it again. I'm in an environment where I'm dealing with university personnel—a faculty—which is very different from what I did in the Army with the Department of Army Civilians. It's a different focus, a different temperament, a different prioritization. Getting through it and working within a new expectation structure—military vs. civilian vs. university faculty—is pure adaptation. And because of the experiential learning I've encountered along the way in my career, I've learned how to discern ways to effectively lead all three of these very different groups of people.

In the military, soldiers respond to orders. You tell 'em to go left, they go left. They don't argue the point. (At least that's the way it's supposed to work!)

When you're dealing with civilians, they'll listen to the order and then make a determination about whether they're going to do it. Even though they acknowledge that you're the guy in charge, a lot of times they're going to listen and make up their own mind. So you have to be conscious of that, and, as a result of that, you have to tell your people not just what to do but *why they're doing it*. That's a major point of adaptation.

Soldiers want to be told what to do, and then they'll do it. Then they'll say, "If you get around to it, General, please tell us why we did it." But civilians? They want to know up front why they're doing it. They want it to make sense. They want to know that this isn't an exercise in futility before they get started. A lot of managers forget that—to their own peril. Then they're left wondering why their people aren't doing what they were told to do! Making this important adaptation when I got to IMCOM was a primary reason for going out on the road and visiting as many installations as I could during my two-year run. I had to get in front of those 120,000 workers and let them know the "whys" behind all of the changes and budget cuts the organization was going through.

In the academic world, on the other hand, I find myself dealing with a big "What's in it for me?" attitude. First of all, the academic-research world has a major problem with silos: Every college, every department is doing its own thing, and none of them are communicating with one another. It's a problem the United States military faces, and plenty of big corporations face it as well.

Think about it this way: The Army is a 1.1 million-person, $245 billion enterprise—just like Coca-Cola's an enterprise and Procter & Gamble is an enterprise. If you run your enterprise as a silo—every group doing its own thing—you're going to be much less efficient than if you cooperate across divisions and brands. The essence of an enterprise is: "Quit worrying about what's best for me, and start thinking about what's good for all of us."

When I ran the Services and Infrastructure Core Enterprise, an organization that was attempting to bridge the gaps between various services at our Army installations, it wasn't about the three-star who ran the medical community, or the three-star who ran the corps of engineers, or the three-star who ran all the services. It was about, collectively, how do we approach our end-state in an efficient fashion using the enterprise approach? I've spent a lot of time talking to corporations about that, and they struggle with it. I've spent a lot of time talking with university presidents about it, too, saying, "We've got departments that aren't talking with one another and are concerned only with their departments and not what's best for the university as a whole, and we need to address that—because it's a cultural change."

The second problem I see in academia is the unbelievably inordinate use of the first-person pronoun. Among the staff at universities, everything is about "me." "I did this, this is mine, I'm not going to tell you about what I'm doing because I'm going to protect my intellectual property."

How, as a leader, can you get over a hurdle that big? Once again, my experiential learning has come into play. I've had to figure out that my role as a leader at a university isn't just to tell the faculty what we're doing and why we're doing it, but to tell them what's in it *for them*. What's the incentive for them to want to cooperate? That's especially true with tenured faculty. Even the president of a university will tell you that you can't tell tenured faculty what to do. I mean, the system says that if you've got tenure, you're safe. There's a tenure-review process every six years or so, but I don't think anybody in the history of any university has ever been removed! So there couldn't be a more dysfunctional system, and a leader has to figure out how to work within that system—a system in which there's no real incentive to do anything different, where the attitude is, "This is what I'm going to do because I've been doing it this way so far, and the job pays pretty well, so why should I worry about doing anything different?"

Figuring out how to lead through any of those sorts of frameworks involves adaptation. It takes an ability to stand back, look at a population, and try to figure out, "How can I lead and manage these folks?"

The point I want to make here is that, if you have a wide breadth of experiential learning behind you, you can adapt. If I could get what I wanted from our soldiers in the Army and the Sunni population in Iraq, chances are I can get what I need in the university system. And if you've laid a foundation of adaptation and resiliency brought on by a broad range of experience, chances are you can get it done in whatever corporation or organization you're leading.

So ask yourself: Have you been in your comfort zone for too long? Is there something you can do to shake things up? Is there a move you could make that would challenge you in some way you've never been challenged before? Because every time you do that, you're going to grow stronger, and your ability to lead will grow stronger, too.

– 26 –

DO LESS BETTER

Dealing with budget cuts is a lot like going to war.

Let me explain what I mean.

Carl von Clausewitz wrote a book called *On War*—a book that all military leaders have to read. It's required reading to this day despite the fact that Clausewitz was a Prussian soldier and philosopher who died back in 1831. I've probably read it twenty times over the course of my military career. Everywhere you go, they make you read that book because its thoughts and lessons apply to so much of what we still aspire to today.

One of the things Clausewitz talks about in *On War* is ends, ways, and means.

The "ends" refers to the end-state, or what you're trying to accomplish; the "means" are the resources you have to accomplish it; the "ways" are the methods by which you're going to get it done.

When I took over IMCOM in my last two years in the Army, the powers that be made one thing very clear: The ends were going to remain the same. We had 163 Army installations worldwide, and it was our job at Installation Management Command—make that *my* job as the head of IMCOM—to provide our soldiers and their families with a quality of life commensurate with their quality of service. That's what we were tasked to accomplish, and that's what I *had* to do. No ifs, ands, or buts.

There was just one problem. We had a $20-billion-a-year budget at our disposal when I started my command, but as soon as I walked in the door, I was told that by the end of those two years, our proposed budget would be cut back to $15 billion per year.

Can you imagine? "Don't change what you're doing. You need to deliver the same services you've been delivering. You just need to do it with potentially $5 billion less."

If that's not just about as daunting as going to war, I don't know what is. And if Clausewitz's words ever applied to a situation outside of war more directly than they did to this, I can't imagine what it would be.

To break it down in *On War* terms, ask yourself this question: If your ends are constant and your means are reduced, what do you have to do? The answer is: You have to modify your ways. Just as we did in Iraq in initiating the Sons of Iraq program, you have to change the way you're doing business. How? You can look for increases in effectiveness, increases in efficiency, different approaches—but whatever it is, you have to do it smartly so you'll still accomplish the same ends, even with significantly reduced means. That's what Clausewitz argues. And that's what we did at IMCOM. We worked to maintain that end-state with billions in reduced resources—a reduction of 25 percent—and because of who I am and what I stand for, I saw to it that we didn't sacrifice our people to do it. I don't mean that we didn't trim the workforce. We did. In the end, there was no choice. But we did even that in the most humane way possible, while giving those who would be forced to leave the means necessary to move on successfully. I'll talk more about how I did that momentarily, but what I'm saying here is that we accomplished our trims without overburdening the workforce.

We accomplished our goals while still getting everybody home to their families for dinnertime.

If you know anything about me by now, you understand how important that was to me. Hopefully you're beginning to recognize how important it is to everything I hold dear, and to everything we should hold dear as Americans. Because budget cuts are happening. Everywhere. And I believe too many of those cuts are being made carelessly, sometimes recklessly, with only short-term gains at the heart of each panicked decision. That needs to stop. There's more than one way to skin a cat, folks, and I know for a fact that there's more than one way to trim the fat—no matter how much fat you've got to trim.

Five *billion* dollars is a lot of fat! Someone else could've come through the door slashing and burning everything in sight when faced with the cuts that were coming. Someone else might have taken resources away from everyone and told everyone to just "ruck up." Another leader could have fired big chunks of the workforce and told everyone else to make up for the work by working three times as hard—and if you've spent any time in corporate America, I'm sure you've seen that scenario time and time again. It seems to be the standard practice these days: Just make sure everyone works longer hours for less pay and reduced benefits, and tell them to suck it up!

I refused to do that.

Figuring out how to adapt the organization to those massive cuts without compromising my personal values and beliefs was absolutely critical. And that meant making those cuts while taking care of our most important resource: Our people.

MAKING EFFICIENCY EFFICIENT

I hate the phrase "Do more with less." That's code for "abusing your workforce." "Do more with less" implies, "I'm going to give you fewer resources, so you've just got to work harder." That, my friends, is absurd.

It's the polar opposite of how we should be treating our people, and the antithesis of good business practice, as far as I'm concerned.

I say, "Do less better."

"Do less better" means focus on what's important. Prioritize your tasks. Allocate your time and your resources. Resources are generally in three categories: people, time, and money. When companies get into a situation where they're facing reduced resources, what management automatically seems to fall back on is a position of making people work harder. And I think that is exactly wrong.

It's yet another case of "what managers do—not what *leaders* do." And we need more leaders.

Going back and forth between IMCOM's San Antonio headquarters and the Pentagon during this process, I picked up on a few things—mostly things that made me grateful that San Antonio is a long way from Washington.

The first thing I noticed was that, when you talk about millions at the Pentagon, nobody cares. But talk about billions? I can guarantee you people will listen. Inside the Pentagon, there were continual budget cuts. Every time you turned around, you were losing some money. If you made a decision not to go to a meeting when budget was being discussed, you were going to lose part of your budget. In fact, there was a phrase in the Pentagon to describe this phenomenon: "If you're not at the table, you're on the menu."

Whenever you have budget cuts inside the Department of Defense, rather than looking at which program to cut or what headquarters we could do without, we would salami-slice everything. The so-called "easy way" was to just take 10 percent away from everybody rather than close something down.

That, candidly, is the wrong way to do business. All you're left with after making across-the-board cuts is no one having enough money to do what they need to do. Instead, why not make smart cuts and give certain areas of your organization—the right areas—the money they need to do what they do even better? Too often, that thought fell on deaf ears.

Combine that with the fact that most people throughout the organization had no idea what cuts were coming, how deep those cuts would be, or how their departments would be affected each time a new set of cuts came down, and the whole thing just created waves of uneasiness and a workforce that never knew where it stood. There's no better way to create an unstable organization than to keep your people in the dark.

My job, the way I saw it, was to eliminate any such nonsense at IMCOM.

My approach from day one was to communicate with subordinates all the time so they knew where I was coming from—and so they would know what was coming. As I described previously, I traveled to my staff and talked to them directly. In person. I sent written communiqués all the time to tell my people what was happening and *why*. Remember, IMCOM had 120,000 employees when I started, of which only about 2,000 were military personnel. This was a predominantly civilian workforce, the size of a Fortune 100 company. Civilians don't just follow orders. They need to understand those orders. They need to know where they stand. They want to feel connected to the decisions. So telling people about the situation was paramount.

My next step was to engage the staff in the decision-making process. I made the final decisions. Don't get me wrong: I wasn't about to turn IMCOM into some feel-good commune where decisions were made by raising hands around a fire while we all sang "Kumbaya." But I did appeal to the workforce to share their ideas on how we could make cuts, given the hard, cold fact that cuts were going to happen.

IMCOM itself had become extremely bloated over the years. Think about this: The Army had an $80 billion budget pre-9/11 that grew to $245 billion over 10 years. Headquarters, size of forces, things people were doing that they no longer needed to do—you could see that everywhere. So, my message was, "Okay, we're going to lose this money, and we don't want to have to cut back on staff. You've all got families to feed and house payments to make. I want to make the reduction of the workforce the very last option. With that in mind, help me see where we can do things differently and save a whole lot of time and money in the process."

That was the start of the Stamp Out Stupid campaign, which I described earlier—an effort that yielded about a hundred solid ideas from my staff. Ideas that I was able to turn into action.

The fact is, the Department of Defense had become expert at starting programs, but it was very poor at ending programs that had become unnecessary or redundant. Part of that was due to political pressures. I'd go to the Hill on a regular basis, called over by a member of Congress, and the conversation would always go like this: "General, we understand the budget cuts you're dealing with. We applaud the efficiencies you're pursuing, but we'd appreciate it if you'd pursue those cuts in somebody else's district."

That was all well and good. I'm glad they voiced their concerns. I was happy to listen. But the political concerns were not the most important concern to me. What was most important was protecting our people. So I'd leave the Hill and go back to work—aggressively working to cut through costly redundancies and unnecessary expenses regardless of what "district" they fell in.

One big area where I could make cuts was in our reliance on contractors. By definition, contractors cost a lot more than your old workforce. IMCOM had a thousand people in its headquarters, and 543 of them were contractors. That was one place I immediately said, "Let's do less better. We're going to eliminate our reliance on contractors."

In the first year, they were migrated into other contracts elsewhere. There was a great hue and cry, of course. The contractors felt they were entitled to those jobs and thought I was being the mean guy. We had to work through that, and it wasn't easy, but we ended up having a much smaller headquarters, and the headquarters itself was able to work more efficiently—protecting the Army civilians in the process.

As an engaged leader—Managing by Walking Around rather than dictating any of this from some corner office—I'd see people working on things and I'd ask them, "Why are you doing that?"

"Because we've always done it that way" was a red flag for me. With massively reduced means, there is no excuse for doing things the way they've always been done unless they're the most efficient ways possible. One of the biggest red-flag areas I came across was reports. I was told that our headquarters required a total of 640-some-odd reports to be filed each year. That's 640-plus reports from 163 installations worldwide. That sounded like a lot.

How many of those reports actually make it to my in-box? I wondered.

Turns out only 40 of those 640 reports ever made it to the decision-maker!

"Why are we doing that?" I asked. "What good does it do? If the vast majority of reports result in no action, what's the point?"

You could've heard the crickets.

The fact was, many members of the workforce relied on those reports to justify their existence. They gathered those numbers and made those reports. That was their job.

I decided to eliminate all of the meaningless reports. Reducing reports meant reducing the amount of work and, in some cases, reducing the number of workers where it was truly justified.

Filling out reports for the sake of filling out reports is nothing but hole-digging. What's hole-digging? It's the sort of thing a leader witnesses when he walks by an employee and sees them working hard, breaking a sweat, digging a hole by the side of the road. "Good work," the leader says as he or she walks on by. The following day, the leader walks by and sees that employee hard at work again, only this time the employee is filling the hole back in. The point is, the employee is working hard, but he isn't accomplishing anything. The way I see it, there's a whole lot of hole-digging going on across America, and it simply needs to stop.

In my campaign to Stamp Out Stupid, I asked my staff to find me places where we were hole-digging at IMCOM, and to email me directly with their thoughts. When I went out on the road, visiting eighty-two of those installations during my two years, I would get up in front of our workers and demonstrate the hole-digging story with great theatrics to make it perfectly clear, so they would understand that I was eliminating reports (and, therefore, sometimes jobs) for good reason.

I wanted them to think for themselves, *Why* couldn't *we eliminate those reports? What would be lost?*

I wanted them to ask the question, "Is it good enough to keep doing something simply because everyone who came before did it a certain way?" And I wanted them to know that the answer is, "Absolutely not." In fact, that practice, that policy is the opposite of good. No one in your organization should be working with no progress. No one.

It was clear to me from commanding at Fort Stewart and Fort Hood that IMCOM potentially had too much overhead. Ten years prior to my arrival, there was no IMCOM. It was a new organization. By the time I got there, it was clearly bloated. In addition to IMCOM headquarters and our 163 installations, there were regional headquarters set up as go-betweens for the garrisons and IMCOM headquarters. A senior-executive civilian or a general officer led each of these regional headquarters. And each of those regional headquarters had become bloated with staffs of three hundred to four hundred people.

When I asked our staff to Stamp Out Stupid, almost uniformly, they said, "We need to get rid of regional headquarters." In short, they were pass-through headquarters. Go-betweens. Just bloat smack dab in the middle of the organization.

Gee, I bet you haven't seen any of *that* in corporate America, have you? What about in other government organizations? Schools? Universities? You name it, and it's got bloat in the middle somewhere. It's as if the bloat of our organizations has grown right along with the average waistlines of the American public! It's like a symptom of years of excess. And it's not healthy.

I eliminated one regional headquarters right at the beginning of my command and dropped IMCOM down from seven to four regional headquarters before I was through—with lots of gnashing of teeth in between.

Putting 300 to 400 people out of a job is something that goes against my nature, of course. These are people with families and mortgages and college tuitions to pay for. It was imperative from the very beginning that we work hard to find these people jobs somewhere else. We gave them that latitude.

I learned a lot about downsizing from Reg Brack, chairman emeritus at Time, Inc. (the great magazine conglomerate headquartered in Manhattan). He's another mentor of mine who I've turned to for guidance from time to time, especially when struggling with these sorts of issues—having to let go of so many individuals whom I feel such a strong duty to protect, as I would my own children. His take, which I've come to embrace, is that when it comes to downsizing, you have to depersonalize it—but you also have to do it with compassion.

Even though you love your staff, when your organization no longer needs them, you've got to do away with them, but you've got to do it with compassion. Help them find a different job, get more education, move to a different place, whatever it may be. We tried to make it as painless as possible.

No matter how gently I tried to do it, there was a whole bunch of unhappy people out there because they'd always had these regional headquarters, and the idea that you could do away with those regions was unthinkable to them. But when all was said and done, when we went from seven headquarters to four, you couldn't tell the difference. The organization ran just as smoothly—if not more smoothly—despite millions in cuts and the absence of all of those people. So it needed to be done. And making those hard decisions—that's what leaders have to do.

STAND UP FOR YOUR DECISIONS

The problem I see in many organizations is that nobody today wants to accept responsibility for tough decisions. I went to those regions and personally stood up in front of those 300 or so people and said, "I'm going to deactivate this headquarters, here's the timeline, and here's what we're going to do to help you."

We found many of those employees work in other installations. We helped with job searches elsewhere. We provided every bit of assistance we could. And even so, people were mad at me.

The thing I found out the hard way is that generals are almost continuously under investigation for one thing or another. Unhappy employees make anonymous allegations against generals all the time. I suffered lots of that, even though I was trying to do all of this in a kind and gentle fashion. We went above and beyond to help with moving people into new positions and new areas, but we still had a lot of unhappy people because they lost the job they had. It just comes with the territory, and I tried not to take it personally.

While all of this was going on, I was working to make the work-life balance better for every single employee in that 120,000-person-strong organization. "Do less better" was my never-ending mantra, as I refused to pile more work onto employees' plates to make up for any employees that we let go. In fact, I worked to take things off of their plates all the time. I refuse to abuse a workforce, and when it comes right down to it, the only person who can determine what to take off anyone's plate is the leader. No one else is going to touch it because they don't want the leader getting mad about something not being done the way it's always been done. That's true no matter how many times you tell your staff otherwise. The leader has to be the one to step up and say, "We don't need to do that anymore. Focus on all of that other good work you're doing, and let's let that one thing go."

When you run a large business, half of your money is tied up in payroll, health insurance, and so forth, and it's up to you to trim from programs or services that won't harm those all-important areas. For IMCOM, that meant cutting some long-established programs. The Army had billions invested in programs that had outlived their usefulness. It seemed like common sense to just about everyone to go ahead and cut those programs, but once again, politics came into play. If I tried to cut a long-standing program, chances are there was a government contract involved or a constituent of some member of Congress who was going to be affected. Suddenly I'd get called over the Hill to justify cutting a program in their district.

Escorted over to an office by a congressional liaison, I'd sit down and face a roomful of people who knew I was speaking the truth: "We have a deficit, and we *have* to do this."

But at the end of the day, they need votes. They need happy constituents. So they tried, even though I was resolute. Nothing ever changed in those offices other than the fact that they might be able to say to someone important to them, "I talked to the general in charge, and he heard me."

But I didn't change any decision based on trips to the Hill. I couldn't. Those outdated, no-longer-useful programs had to go.

Remember, I had $5 billion to trim! And I wasn't going to trim anything that would affect the services that were important to our soldiers and their families. They were the people I was charged with caring for, not some congressman's constituents.

Of course, some people, no matter what you tell them, take it personally, and that's hard. The hardest thing I had to do during my two years at IMCOM was draw down the workforce. In the end, we cut about 3,000 positions under my watch. I did everything I could to do right by those people, given the unbelievably difficult circumstances. But I know a lot of those people resent me for it, and, for a leader who cares, that's not easy.

I have to live with my decisions. I stand by my decisions. And I certainly have plenty of decisions that have weighed on my heart. As a leader, that's just inevitable.

Looking back at my time at IMCOM, I'm reminded that taking care of our soldiers and their families is the primary goal of that massive organization. Seeing to it that IMCOM operated efficiently and effectively in delivering on that mission no matter how much the budget was slashed was actually a way for me to honor those men and women in my work—along with every man and woman in uniform across all of our Army installations around the globe.

So as tough as it was, I'm proud of what we were able to accomplish in those two years. I'm proud of the workforce that helped me to Stamp Out Stupid. I'm proud of all of those employees who embraced the notion of "Do less better" while also embracing my desire to see them manage their time better and get home for dinner. And I'm proud of all of those men and women who moved on and made way for leaner times that were unavoidable. As much as they were the "casualties" or the "wounded" of this war in the form of budget cuts, I hope they know that they, too, made a difference—an important difference—in the lives of our soldiers and their families.

★ ★ ★

– 27 –

TRANSITIONING

In the United States military, about two years prior to retirement, they ask general officers to take what's called a General Officer Transition Course. Like it or not, it really gets you thinking about the issues you're gonna face in retirement. You do that even before you have a definitive retirement date, when everyone knows you're long enough in the tooth that you *will* have to retire sometime. Then, once you have a definitive retirement date, they ask you to go through the course all over again. So we've got a pretty rigid approach about how to prepare generals to transition out of the military.

I embraced those courses for one very important reason: Going through them early gave Sarah and me lots of time to think about what we wanted to do after we got out of the army. (And make no mistake about it: A military spouse is very much *in* the military. It affects their lives just as deeply, if not more, than any soldier's or officer's.)

Pretty early on, she and I came up with the idea that we weren't ever going to use the word *retire*. We were simply going to use the word *transition* to mark our move from one form of service into another. The more I thought about it, the more I made up my mind that, whatever I did once I left the army, it was going to be meaningful and substantive work around people with shared values.

I have to say, it's nice to have that kind of freedom: To truly choose what it is you want to do. We all have that choice. Everything in life is a choice, isn't it? But we don't always exercise that right to choose, especially when it comes to career. There are just too many pressures on us when we're young and, especially, when we're married with children—pressures that lead us to sometimes make choices that are rushed and, let's face it, aren't always ideal. Preparing to transition out of the military gave me the opportunity and time to properly consider my options and to weigh those options against what truly was most important to me.

They coach you in the military about the four variables in the basic career equation—the job itself, the pay, the location, and the proximity to friends and family—and it's up to you to figure out how you want to weigh those variables. What's most important to you? In Sarah's and my transition, what was most important to us was to remain in the Texas area, to be close to our family and friends, and then to have meaningful, substantive work. We didn't spend a whole lot of time talking about how much money I wanted to make; that just wasn't at the top of either of our priority lists.

On November 17, 2011, I changed command, and, on the first of January 2012, I officially entered the retired rolls of the United States military.

My first command decision in "transition" was to take four months and do nothing but spend time with Sarah and my family. We spent time with my son, Lucas, who's an entrepreneur now right in our home state of Texas, and we traveled to California to see my daughter, Susan, who's an actress now, and we traveled to Ohio to see my dad, and so forth. It was a wonderful gift not to have to truncate our vacation time to hurry back for some pressing matter or, God forbid, another deployment. It felt good to operate on *my* time instead of military time.

Leaving the army as a three-star lieutenant general, I found plenty of doors open to me in the civilian world. About twelve companies wanted me to consult for them. I had pro bono opportunities at a good number of nonprofits that wanted my help. And I had a few companies that wanted me to work for them full time, running parts of their organizations.

In the end, I boiled it down to what made the most sense for me and my family and what best lined up with my goals for the future. I would consult with three companies. I would make speeches around the world about leadership. I would write this book. And I would take advantage of the chance to run the University of Texas at Arlington Research Institute, with a goal of using advanced technology to help humanity. That desire can be traced all the way back to my time at MIT, later endorsed by my desire to be in charge of something and bolstered by my experiences on the battlefield. After all, I still keep that stack of laminated pictures on my desk, commemorating those men who died on my watch in Iraq. Many of them might have lived had we used unmanned vehicles and other technology in their place on the battlefield.

All of it is meaningful and substantive work around people with shared values.

I used that desire as my lens for what I wanted to pursue, and that is exactly what I am pursuing.

I began "working" again on April 2, 2012.

After thirty-five years in the military, it seems like it would be hard to adjust to civilian life, right? Wrong! It actually couldn't be better. The only problem is that Sarah and I have a serious facial affliction: We can't stop smiling!

I loved being in the Army, but I love being out of the Army, too. It's worked out well. Perhaps if I had devoted my life only to my profession, I'd have had unbelievable fears and worries that I'd walk out of the military and have nothing. But I prioritized my life way back in the 1980s: My relationship with God came first, my relationship with my family came second, and my profession always, always came third.

Think about this: In the military, when you assume command, there's a big parade. You stand on a platform, and people give speeches, and when the parade is over, this giant group of soldiers do what's called a "pass and review": they turn right face and then left face; then they pass in front of the reviewing stand so the new commander can observe this fine group he'll be leading for the next two years. When all of those soldiers finally walk away, the new commander walks away with them. It's a wonderful ceremony, full of symbolism and honor and tradition.

Two years later, there's an identical parade—only this time with a new commander. The speeches are all about saying goodbye to you and welcoming this new commander. The pass and review is for this new commander. And when the soldiers walk away, that new commander walks away with them, and you're left standing there on the podium with your family.

If you sacrificed spending time with your family during those two years of command, guess what? You're standing there all by yourself. And then what?

You were the big man on campus for two years. You commanded that unit. You had hundreds of guys saluting you everywhere you went. But now what? What are you? The fact is, no matter what your position, you are always the husband of your wife and the father of your children, and *that's* what's important. Even the president of the United States is president for only four years—eight, if he's lucky. What happens when those years in the White House are over? He is always the husband and always the father.

At the end of the parade that was my career—which was thirty-five years of active duty—when the Army walked away, I was still standing on that platform with my family. We simply transitioned from Army life into another form of life. When I walked out of the military, I had zero concerns that I would be entering civilian life as a lonely man, because I had dedicated time to Sarah and the kids.

A lot of folks might have fears or worries as they prepare to head into retirement from any profession. But candidly, because I stayed true to my beliefs and priorities, I didn't have any. My identity was never, "I'm the general." My identity was, "I'm Sarah's husband and the father of Susan and Lucas." Staying true to that made this whole transition easy, because I maintained my identity after I took off the uniform.

I won't say I didn't have concerns. One big tangential concern was that I might lose my ability to touch the lives of soldiers, personally, on a daily basis. Over thirty-five years, I had developed this passion for soldiers and their families, and I was worried I might lose the ability to spend time with them and work for their benefit. But I soon found that was an unnecessary concern. I'm still working with soldiers. There's a large ROTC battalion at U.T. Arlington, and I'm involved in training the cadets. I can continue that sort of work for the rest of my life, or at least as long as I can walk, if I so choose. Even out of the military, I can still reach out to soldiers as much as I want to. So it's not a problem.

I think there are always ways to stay involved in something you love.

DO WHAT MAKES YOU HAPPY, AND YOUR LIFE WILL BE FULFILLED

My mantra in my life has been to touch lives and make a difference, so I've devoted a lot of energy since my retirement to leadership development and sharing my experiences of leading in difficult circumstances to bodies large and small, including in corporate America and the nonprofit world. I'm continuously amazed at how the lessons I've learned in my military career apply so aptly to so many organizations and to so many people from so many walks of life.

Sure, I retired as required. But my ability to touch lives and to "lead" remains.

As I've said before, I achieved my highest goal in the Army back in 1993. Everything after that was gravy. So retiring wasn't a letdown. It was just a next step.

People ask me all the time, "After thirty-five years in the Army, what's your favorite memory?" and "Where'd you make the most difference?"

I have to say, my favorite time was just after I accomplished my career goal: becoming a battalion commander and serving as a lieutenant colonel from 1993 to 1995. Why? I think it's because, for the first time, I was really in charge and really had the ability to affect the lives of soldiers and their families on a broad yet still-personal level. There I was heading up the First Battalion of Eighth Cavalry, 450 soldiers and their families, and the Army gave me all the trust and confidence and opportunity I needed to make a difference in those people's lives. I was there every day with those soldiers and their families—not in some office or headquarters somewhere, but right there with them. Day and night. It was a wonderful time. Sarah and I cherished every moment of every day.

As for where I made the biggest difference? That's easy: Leading Task Force Marne in the surge. Taking those 25,000 soldiers into the Triangle of Death and turning it into the Triangle of Life in fifteen months—that truly was the culmination of nearly everything I had worked toward and everything I wanted to be as a leader in the Army. Transitioning that team from combat operations to rebuilding has to be just about the most extreme example of adaptation in action that I can imagine. It was a case of saving lives—countless lives, in fact, on all sides—while changing lives for the better. It was a case of setting an example for our soldiers and the Army as a whole, as to just how broad and adaptable we could be as a force for change in the modern world. And I hope it serves as an example to the world.

I stand back in awe of what we were able to accomplish in that harsh environment, in the middle of that seemingly impossible situation.

Of course, the funny thing is that, now, I don't spend a whole bunch of time sitting around thinking about it. In fact, I don't spend a whole lot of time thinking about the Army, period. I find myself so active in philanthropy, research, and making presentations that I can't remember a single moment in the last few months when I found myself sitting around thinking about the Army except when I've been working on this book. That's pretty amazing, considering it's just about all I thought about for thirty-five years. Heck, thirty-nine years when you count West Point!

The only explanation I have for that ability to let it go and for my ability to move on is that it comes as a direct result of "living my dash." It's a direct result of staying true to my priorities in life. It's a direct result of walking the walk and practicing what I preach. I've been able to adapt to life outside the Army just as easily as I adapted to changes within it because I've always focused on what it takes to be a resilient person and a resilient leader, and I've focused on seeing the opportunities in this career transition rather than the obstacles that might have seemed so daunting to someone else in my position.

It took a lifetime of lessons and a litany of experience to reach this comfort level, of course, and today, I'm making the most of everything I've learned by sharing my passion for leadership wherever I can. It's my great hope that some of these lessons will have an impact on your life and career and that, in time, you'll share the positive results of your own leadership lessons with others, wherever you can.

After all, we're in this together. And it's up to us leaders to help make sure that we all move forward, through whatever obstacles we face—with strength, with grace, with dignity, and with honor.

In the end, it's up to leaders to lead. And it's up to you to decide what kind of a leader you want to be.

It's your choice. It's your decision.

But if you're gonna be a leader, I hope that you always remember: The very future of our businesses, our churches, our schools, our governments, our country, and especially our people depends on one thing: *you.*

I pray that you make the right choices. I pray that you build a solid foundation on which to stand and then stand on that foundation firmly. I pray that you set your priorities in life, and that you always, always put your people first. Because the more of us who do that, the better off we're all going to be.

Part Five

WHAT CRISIS?

"Consider it pure joy, my brothers and sisters, whenever
you face trials of many kinds, because you know that
the testing of your faith produces perseverance."
— James 1:2-3

Well, I hate to say I told you so, but . . . I told you so!

Back when I wrote the first edition of this book, I warned that we live in a volatile world. If you look at the original introduction, you'll see that I warned of "budget cuts and shortfalls, global competition, shifting demographics, loss of morale and of moral direction, and a never-ending series of rapidly changing technological challenges that seem almost too big to bear." But that was just the start of the challenges we face as leaders. As I described in my second book, *Work Hard, Pray Hard*, there's a term we used in the military to describe certain worst-case scenarios on the battlefield: VUCA. It stands for "Volatile, Uncertain, Complex, and Ambiguous." As I said in that book, VUCA is sometimes just the way *life* is: "There have been wars and plagues and immense struggles since the beginning of time. There were problems yesterday, and there will be new problems tomorrow." And it's true.

It does not matter if you're on the battlefield or in the boardroom, at some point or another, *something* is going to come along and throw a major wrench into all the good plans you put into place. And that's exactly what happened in the beginning of 2020, when we first started to hear about a "Novel Coronavirus," which was highly contagious and apparently spread through the air, which had the potential to cause a devastating and potentially fatal illness called COVID-19.

In just three months' time, we went from zero cases in the United States to one case in Washington State to hundreds of thousands of cases all over, which led to a 72 percent decline in airline travel. Airports shut down, businesses closed, schools canceled, we faced toilet-paper shortages, had a hot debate on whether wearing masks is an effective tool to combat the spread, and we made a mad dash as a nation to create a vaccine—all while people tried to figure out how life and work could possibly go on when we weren't allowed to go into our offices anymore.

I don't really need to tell you all of this, other than to remind you that, if you're reading these words, you've been through it. You have personally survived a global pandemic that killed upwards of 3.5 million people. It changed the way we work, the way we communicate, the way we teach, the way we respond, and even the way we treat viruses—and potentially all sorts of other ailments and illnesses. (Talk about a lesson in Opportunities, Not Obstacles: It's thanks to the urgency of the pandemic that pharmaceutical companies were finally able to work together to unlock the positive potential of mRNA vaccines.)

So let me ask you: Before 2020, did you see a pandemic coming? Did you personally prepare for it? Probably not. Hardly anyone did, despite decades of warnings from scientists around the globe and a history of worldwide pandemics that didn't reach the U.S. in significant numbers.

The better question is this: Were you prepared to handle and bounce back from a crisis, whether or not you knew in advance what that crisis might be?

That's why Adaptive Leadership is so important.

The thing we cannot let ourselves forget as this latest pandemic fades is that the world is *still* in a state of VUCA. It's *always been* in a state of VUCA. We have to be prepared for the unexpected.

It was ten years after 9/11—an unforeseen event that changed the world in a matter of *hours*—when I began doing speeches for *Adapt or Die*. Back then, I always reminded my audiences that we were a nation at risk because of external threats from foreign terrorists and ongoing tensions with Russia, North Korea, and Iran; over time, my message evolved, as we faced increased *internal* threats from domestic terrorists, divisive people, and a growing lack of respect for law-enforcement personnel. And not one of those risks has gone away today. We still have those risks on top of an increased awareness that another pandemic or outbreak of some sort could come along and shut everything down again. We can't ignore that. We're international people, increasingly working on an international playing field. Diseases and viruses, whether they show up in South Texas or Colorado or New York City, or in a seemingly far-off place like China, or Africa, or South America, are simply more likely to travel with us the more we travel.

What I'm trying to say is this: Whether we like it or not, it's gonna happen again. Maybe not tomorrow, but at some point. Which is why it's more important than ever for leaders to develop the techniques and tools that are required in order to lead through crisis.

All of us are experiencing a crisis of global proportions. Hopefully you have a pretty good idea what worked for you and what didn't work for you. And if you don't, you might want to sit down for a while and think about it: How did you handle this pandemic? What were your strongest traits under these unprecedented challenges? What were your failures? How can you do better next time?

Adaptive leaders in the business world didn't panic in the face of this crisis. Adaptive leaders, the kind of folks who understood the principles I've shared with you here in this book, took the bull by the horns, stared it down, and figured out how to defeat it. We all saw it happen: those who weren't prepared, those who weren't willing to change, saw their businesses suffer and even wither away in a matter of months. Others adapted, and just made do, or managed to scrape by until things got back to a situation that felt closer to "normal." And while that's a much better approach than just rolling over and dying, some of those businesses are still on the edge and uncertain whether they'll really survive all the changes they've endured.

And then there are the other guys—the businesses that adapted in a way that took advantage of the opportunities the pandemic created.

On a smaller scale, you probably saw examples of this at some of your favorite restaurants. The restaurant industry was hit hard during the pandemic, no matter how you look at it. Lockdowns, government restrictions, public hesitancy around vaccines and mask wearing, workers who (rightfully) questioned whether waiting tables was a job worth risking their lives over—it all took a toll. When you look around today, some of your favorite spots are probably closed for good, and some of them are struggling and barely making ends meet; but a few of them are thriving more than they were before the world shut down. Why? Because they opened up outdoor tables, put in take-out windows, set up delivery services (even if they'd never considered offering delivery in the past). They pared down menus and offered higher-profit items that weren't on the menu before. In some places, they worked with local leaders to allow alcohol "to go" for the first time ever or made other changes that brought in profits and allowed them to keep all of their people on staff. And I guarantee you that, in every one of those cases, the people in charge did everything they could to take care of the people who worked for them—because none of the adaptations could have taken place without a solid staff in the kitchen and out front.

It happened in big businesses too, as some companies simply did nothing, lost all their people, lost all their profits, and folded. Others saw CEOs willing to cut their own pay just so they wouldn't have to furlough any workers and quickly adapting to a new work-from-home paradigm that they might never had been willing to try in the past.

I personally was operating a thriving business before the pandemic hit. I was doing speeches around the country, on average, every other week, hosting leadership tours in Gettysburg, Vicksburg, and Boston for corporate groups multiple times per year, and doing all sorts of leadership-development training for small groups and individuals at nineteen different companies in between. By early 2020, I had speeches and tours booked out all the way into 2021—when suddenly all those in-person opportunities evaporated. My business took a major hit, which meant my personal income took a major hit. That not only affected my plans for the future—it had the potential to disrupt the comfort and financial security of my wife and family. I couldn't roll over and do nothing. So I adapted. I made the best of it. I embraced new technology to get me through it, so I could keep delivering my messages and stay involved with my clients via Zoom and Teams. I changed my routines and schedules to align with staying at home and not traveling anymore. And I started work on the pages you're reading right now, so I could continue to carry my mission forward if and when the pandemic ever subsided.

Adapting was pretty easy, actually, compared to the alternative—because I was already well-prepared to handle unforeseen changes. Putting my own leadership principles into action in this time of crisis *worked*. I not only survived, I came out thriving. My business is profitable, my family is doing great, and my calendar for 2022 and beyond is filling up faster than ever. I'm not saying any of this to be boastful. I'm saying it because I want you to get to this point, too—a point where you can not only handle a crisis, but survive and thrive no matter what life throws at you in the future.

What you're about to read in this brand-new Part 5 addresses not only leadership through crisis—tied in part to lessons learned during the pandemic—but more adaptive leadership lessons that I've learned from my time in corporate America during the decade-plus of my post-Army career. And it all starts with a topic that corporate America seems to struggle with the most, not only in times of crisis, but *all* the time: Communication.

– 28 –

COMMUNICATION IS KEY

Let me say this as simply as I can: Communication is the key to being an effective leader in a difficult situation.

Now I'll say it again, a little differently, for those who didn't catch it the first time around: The key to being an effective leader in a difficult situation is *communication*.

Without communication, you can't accomplish anything, even in the best of times, let alone in the most difficult of times. So I'd like to expand here on the points I made in Chapters 8, 9, 16, and 20, and talk about what it means to "communicate."

First of all, there a couple of quotes I find useful when it comes to communication. The first, a favorite of mine, is from Abraham Lincoln:

"It's better to be quiet and be thought a fool than to speak up and remove all doubt."

I think that one's pretty self-explanatory. And the second is from Plato:

"A wise man speaks because he has something to say; a fool because he has to say something."

Unfortunately, what I've found in working with senior leaders in corporate America is that, often, they're not thinking before they speak. Speaking just to hear the sound of your own voice, speaking because you're supposed to (whether or not you're prepared), and speaking without considering all of the facts just gets people into trouble.

Sarah, the wonderful teacher that she is, likes to share an acronym with leaders, which is the very same acronym she used to share with kids in her classroom. It's a pretty easy one to remember: THINK

What does THINK stand for?

Is it True?
Is it Helpful?
Is it Inspiring?
Is it Necessary?
Is it Kind?

As leaders, before we speak, we want to remember to THINK. Especially when things are already difficult. Rather than make things *more* difficult by saying things that are untrue, not helpful, not inspirational, unnecessary, or unkind, you've got to THINK before you speak. This applies equally in good times and bad, in times of prosperity, in times of struggle, and in times of crisis.

Once you're THINKing, the next thing to consider is how to communicate with your people in the clearest, most-effective way possible.

When the pandemic hit, a lot of leaders made the mistake of throwing the baby out with the bathwater—they stopped communicating just because they couldn't hold their regular in-person morning meetings, or they switched to email, which isn't really "communicating" at all (as I spoke about in Chapter 16).

What Adaptive Leaders quickly discovered during the pandemic is that, in the absence of face-to-face communication, which is always best, the second-best style of communication has now become visual technology, which allows you to see the person you're speaking to.

I remember watching *The Jetsons* cartoons on TV as a kid, where somewhere in a far-off future full of flying cars, George Jetson talked to his boss, Spacely Sprocket, on a TV screen. Back then, none of us ever thought that would come true. But here we are in a post-pandemic world where Zoom and Teams and a variety of other platforms have become readily available to almost everybody in the workforce.

Early in the pandemic, many corporations were hesitant to try anything new, and since they couldn't get together, they were simply having conference calls using voice only. But as everyone knows from years of experience, conference calls aren't exactly an effective use of everyone's time. There are jokes and funny scenes in all sorts of movies and TV shows about people falling asleep or goofing off or making jokes while conference calls are happening, and the boss never knows because he or she can't see the person or people on the other end of the line. Zoom and Teams take care of that, but more importantly, they give everyone on a call the added benefit of picking up on nonverbal communication, which is a big part of what human communication is all about.

As someone who learned about robotics early on in my career and worked on a virtual battlefield, not to mention who ran the Research Institute at the University of Texas at Arlington after my transition from the military, I've learned to not be afraid of technology and to use it to my advantage and the advantage of others whenever practicable. So I coached all of my clients into using the virtual technology that was available to them within weeks of the quarantines and shutdowns in 2020.

"Okay, to get you off our backs, we'll use Microsoft Teams," some of them agreed. But when they did that, nobody turned their cameras on! So it was just another voice meeting or conference call using the computer instead of the phone. They weren't actually using the technology they had at their disposal.

As I learned at IMCOM, and as I see reflected in the corporate world all the time, the hardest thing about getting a new idea *in* is getting the old idea *out*. People were stuck on the way things used to be, so they couldn't see the way it *could* be. Zoom was relatively new at that point, but the basics of teleconferencing and individual platforms like Teams had actually been around for quite a while. We just never had to use it, so most of us didn't. Now? We use it all the time, and I do not think that will go away, even after the pandemic is a distant memory. It's technology that's here to stay. So why not use it to our full advantage?

There are whole documents written about Zoom protocol and how to use the technology, so I'm not going to go through that here. But I do want to mention three things that I remind my clients of all the time.

First, Zoom and Teams and the like are *visual platforms*, which means you've got to use the camera. Turn it on! And insist that everyone who's on a Zoom meeting keep their cameras on, so you can interact with them and command their full attention. From that point, it's up to each of us, and especially us leaders, to acknowledge that the camera is on and stay engaged. Which means you ought not be looking off. Don't be playing with the dog or answering texts mid-meeting. You should be looking into the camera and being part of the conversation.

Second: Show up looking like you're actually showing up for work. Admiral Bill McRaven (U.S. Navy, retired) made a pretty famous speech at the commencement at the University of Texas a while back, in which he said the first thing you ought to do when you get up is make your bed. (He turned that speech into the title of his book, which is well worth reading.) Making your bed matters, he said, because now you've got a completed task at the very start of your day, and that will lead to other completed tasks as well.

In the world of Zoom technology, the same sort of thing applies: If you simply roll out of bed, brush your teeth, keep your pajama bottoms on, and then put something on that looks like a shirt, you might be more comfortable, but that does not translate to you being "at work." You might be logged in, but you're really still at home in your pajamas. What I tried to do throughout the pandemic is exactly what I do now. To demonstrate what right looks like, I'd shave before my Zoom calls, I'd make sure I had a proper shirt on, or in some cases, a jacket—to demonstrate that you ought to dress for work. It's not just about Zoom protocol and being in an outfit, but to prepare yourself to be mentally "at work."

If you're not doing this already, try it. You'll be surprised how effective it is, and as a leader, it'll have a trickle-down effect on your direct reports: If nothing else, they'll show up dressed to please the boss, and that little bit of extra attentiveness will go a long way.

The third thing that needs attention when using this technology is recognizing that you're allowing other co-workers into your home, so your backdrop should be appropriate. There are people who've learned how to put artificial backdrops in. I never bothered with that, but I've seen some people use it in interesting ways. One of my clients recently showed up on a Zoom call looking like he was sitting in Red Square, in Moscow, when I knew for a fact he was talking to me from his ranch in rural Texas. I've seen some people have backdrops where it looks like they're in a conference room, which certainly sets the mood. And I've seen people with backdrops of fancy bookshelves and stylish offices that exude something way beyond what their little apartment looks like in real life. But the main thing is to make sure your real-life backdrop isn't a distraction and isn't inappropriate.

I use my backdrop as a marketing tool. If I'm sitting in my office, you can see my books and some of my West Point paraphernalia on the shelves behind me, and nothing else. If Sarah's on a call with me, I usually take it up in our game room, using a wall full of West Point prints and Army paraphernalia as a backdrop for the two of us. If you don't have room to do that, then a blank wall is better than nothing, and what you don't want is spouses walking in and out, naked toddlers running in, or a dog taking a poop in the corner while you're trying to make your point. You wouldn't let that happen in the workplace, and you shouldn't let it happen while you're trying to communicate on Zoom. (Remember, when you're working from home, your home *is* your workplace—at least during designated work hours.)

Now, recognizing that people are human, we all make mistakes, and not all of us live in dwellings large enough to command the sort of privacy a Zoom or Teams meeting calls for, a little empathy and understanding has to be part of the equation. Everybody has different circumstances, and those circumstances may be greatly affected by something as disruptive as a pandemic. But no matter what, we've all got to be conscious of the fact that, when we're on camera, we ought to be professional.

So: Dress for work, have a backdrop that's not distracting, and please, if you're going to use the technology, turn the cameras on, and actually *use* the technology.

THE MEETING AFTER THE MEETING

Here's the thing about communicating, especially through new technologies: Just because you're talking to people doesn't give you any guarantee that they're hearing what you want them to hear, let alone properly interpreting that information. They may not have any idea how to act upon what you've shared with them once the meeting is over.

I average at least five daily calls a week, with nineteen different clients, which has given me a broad perspective on how they each handle Teams and Zoom calls, and I can tell you that every one of them handles things a little differently from the others. We aren't even close to establishing standard protocols for these technologies yet, which can make things confusing and difficult for everyone involved. But worse? We haven't established any consistency on how to follow up on these meetings—and in my experience, the *meeting after the meeting* has always been one of the most important parts of the process.

Last summer, I was invited to listen in on one of my clients' meetings. There were eight people on that Zoom call, all listening to the same executive speak. We all heard the same meeting. Then I had each of those eight people call me afterwards to say what they thought they heard—and each and every one of them said something different.

That's every leader's nightmare, isn't it?

Here's the lesson: You cannot assume that everybody heard the same thing, just because you held a meeting.

When we're in-place and in-person, there's always a meeting after the meeting. People walk out together, into the hallways, over by the coffee pot or the watercooler, and they talk about what just happened and what they just heard. Sometimes direct reports purposefully gather in somebody's office, among themselves, to come up with a plan to address what they just heard. And that natural process of regrouping to achieve understanding is an important one.

In Iraq, when I was a two-star general, we would meet with our four-star commander on a regular basis, and when our meetings were over, all of us two-star generals would go out into the hallway and ask each other, "What the hell was he saying in that meeting? And what do we do now?"

It sounds funny, I know, but it's just human nature. Even in times of extreme duress, and maybe *especially* in times of crisis, we all listen a little differently, we all hear a little differently, and it takes some effort to get on the same page. There's nothing wrong with that. But having a way to sort it all out *matters*.

That "meeting after the meeting" or some kind of replacement for that valuable step in the process needs to happen in the virtual-meeting world, too.

How serious a problem is this? After studying and surveying this missing piece of the puzzle across all nineteen of the companies I consulted with through the pandemic, I found there was a collective loss of 30 percent of productivity because of the lack of post-meeting meetings to sort things out. It should be noted that I witnessed hardly *any* loss of individual productivity over that same time period, since people were generally on par or better-focused when working from home than they were in the office. But the drop in collective/organizational productivity was massive, and that clearly needs to change. A 30 percent drop is not something any company can live with for long.

So what's the solution?

Instead of just scheduling more virtual meetings to address what's said in virtual meetings (which could easily backfire), there's another way to address this important step in the communication process. And it's sort of an old-fashioned one—but it works. You ready for this? Have a recorder present for every meeting. I'm not talking about a tape recorder or the online video-recording capability that's available on Zoom. I'm talking about an actual human who takes notes and clearly sums up the primary points that were made in that particular meeting.

In Iraq, everywhere I went, every day, for fifteen months straight, I went on patrol. And during patrol meetings with local sheiks and tribal chiefs, I always had a recorder present to write down the key points of our conversations. As soon as we were back, she typed up those notes and disseminated to the whole command a rundown of what had been said. That way, everyone in my charge was on the same page about what was discussed in the field.

That extra step to communicate clearly was invaluable.

In corporate America, you should absolutely do something similar. Notes should be recorded and widely disseminated (unless they're privileged and confidential, of course). And in my experience, you always need to be talking two levels down. If you're the man or woman in charge, chances are your executives already know what you're telling them. So the direct reports to your direct reports are the ones you need to be communicating with if you want to get things done.

Think about this: If you have seven direct reports, and they each have five to seven direct reports to them, that means you need to be communicating with close to 60 people in total. You don't want or need 60 people in the meeting to accomplish what you want, but you *do* need to communicate two levels down, and those 49 people who weren't in the meeting can get the gist of the meeting in five minutes when they look at those notes from your recorder.

There is one pitfall to this, which I've heard leaders complain about in more than a few instances: The dissemination of notes increases the risk of someone breaking an organization's confidentiality. A leader isn't going to share notes on a meeting if they can't trust their people to *not* disseminate the notes to outside agencies. And here's my answer to that concern: If you've got people you don't trust in your organization, that's a much bigger problem! Take care of that. Building and restoring trust is important. (We'll talk about this a lot more a couple of chapters from now.) You need to know with confidence that your people aren't going to tell outsiders any information you don't want them to know.

In Iraq, I made sure all of my leaders knew what I talked about in the field, and I expected all of my senior leaders to do the same thing. It meant that we were all on the same page. Everybody knew what was going on. It was wartime. There were lives in the balance. In the course of any crisis, that same dynamic is in play.

THE IMPORTANCE OF SITUATIONAL UNDERSTANDING

In order to be able to have situational dominance, you need two things: situational awareness and situational understanding. That applies in corporate America just as it did on the battlefield.

Situational awareness means we're all generally seeing the same thing.

Situational understanding means we're not only seeing the same things, but we have the same level of understanding of what to do about what we're seeing.

I learned about this as a Digital Brigade Commander and carried it right over to every corporation I've advised. And what I do is help executives to create a dashboard.

When I was in charge of 120,000 civilian employees at IMCOM, I had to develop a standardized system to allow me and everybody else not only to see the same data but to make sense of that data. Otherwise, it would have been chaos. So from that, I learned to help corporate leaders put together a dashboard that gives everyone the same information in their organizations as well, no matter how big or small. But that dashboard is useful only if it's updated regularly and kept current. It's kind of like a consumer-facing website: Any website that's full of old, outdated information, wrong prices, wrong hours, or broken links ain't useful to anybody. Keeping that website up without updating it can hurt a business more than help it, because it's communicating the wrong information to potential customers—and if they're frustrated, those customers will walk.

The same goes for internal communications. Current and clear is the name of the game. But that's not enough.

Once we're all looking at the same dashboard, then we need to make sure that everybody knows, "What do those numbers mean? What does that metric mean? What does that change in numbers up or down mean?"

It's just like looking at a dashboard in a vehicle. If the oil light comes on, it should be obvious to any driver that you need to pull over and add some oil, pronto, or you run the risk of doing major damage to your engine. But believe it or not, that's not obvious to a lot of people. A lot of people look at the oil light and don't give it any more or less importance than they do the "service due" light (which refers to routine maintenance), or the "door ajar" light. Maybe because they've never been taught, or maybe because they lack firsthand experience, they have no idea that the check-oil light is crucial. They think it's just an optional thing to pay attention to. And next thing you know, they've driven a hundred miles with that light on, seized the engine, and junked the whole car.

As good communicators, we've got to make sure everybody understands what's going on and knows how to judge the information that's right in front of them, so we can then work together to move forward.

For a historical reference, which is part of what I share during leadership retreats when I take corporate executives and teams to battlefields and other historic sites across this nation, the difference between situational awareness and situational understanding becomes crystal clear.

It's especially clear at Gettysburg.

I won't get into the whole three-day battle here, but for those who don't know, Robert E. Lee was the General leading Confederate soldiers from the South on a long march to get new supplies when he unexpectedly ran into a whole bunch of Union soldiers gathered near Gettysburg, Pennsylvania. Lee took one look at the situation, and because he was an experienced and extremely savvy leader, he knew that taking some key terrain surrounding Gettysburg would be critical for his success. His subordinate leaders clearly saw the same terrain. It was all there right in front of them. But Lee's subordinate leaders did *not* understand the importance of what they saw in the same way he did.

One key spot that needed to be taken was an area called Culp's Hill, and he directed a man in his command named Gen. Richard Ewell, "Take this hill if practicable." Lee thought Ewell understood the urgency of the situation and the importance of his order. But Ewell didn't have the same situational understanding, so he basically went back into the field and said, "My soldiers are tired. I'm tired. I've only got one leg—so let me take that hill tomorrow, when I get around to it."

Gen. Ewell's decision to not act immediately was a major factor in every part of Lee's plan falling apart. Some might say that one failed understanding cost Lee the battle, which was the turning point of the Civil War. (In case you hadn't heard: In the final outcome, the South lost.)

Just to summarize: Lee and Ewell had the same situational awareness, but *not* the same understanding, which not only lost the battle but changed the course of the entire Civil War.

Communication matters.

UNDERSTANDING TIMING

The difference between Ewell attacking Culp's Hill when it might have been achievable versus later on, when the Union had taken firm control of that hill, was only a matter of hours. Think about it: A few hours' difference arguably cost the South the entire Civil War. (That's an oversimplification of events, of course, but that statement has some big truth at the heart of it.)

Here's an inarguably true statement: Everything is timing. And in my experience, almost everything takes longer than you think it's going to take. Corporate leaders don't seem understand that. As a commander in the military, and as a corporate executive, I take whatever time estimate I'm given, and I multiply it by two. And when I want things done quickly, I keep that in mind—in reverse.

Back to Gettysburg for a moment: When Lee told one of his other Generals, Gen. Longstreet, "Do this as quick as you can" on the morning of the second day of the battle, Longstreet interpreted that as meaning it was okay to wait until late afternoon. If he had acted in the morning, the Confederates could have had taken Little Round Top, another key high ground in the area. But Lee wasn't clear enough in his urgency, and Longstreet wasn't responsive enough in his execution to get the job done. It was another disastrous turn for the Confederates, which eventually led to Pickett's Charge—an incident in which so many of Lee's soldiers fell, the Confederacy had no choice but to give up and retreat.

This same sort of miscommunication on timing goes on in corporate America all the time, with the additional complication of lots of employees and officers who try to please their bosses by giving overly optimistic assessments of how fast things can happen.

"*Cum grana salis*," I tell executive leaders. Bosses should take everything their direct reports tell them about timing with a grain of salt. Whatever estimates they give you, doubling those estimates for your own planning purposes makes it a whole lot easier, and more realistic, to accomplish necessary tasks without added stress. And hey, if they manage to pull it off on a faster timeline, great! But that Latin saying goes back to Roman times for a reason: Not much has changed. And if you've created an environment where people are always trying to please the boss instead of giving accurate estimates, sometimes your people are going to give you overly ambitious assessments of how quickly things can be accomplished.

So listen and communicate timelines with some healthy skepticism.

On the other side of things, especially in corporate America, if your staff says it's going to take them six days to get something done, and your experience tells you they can do it in three, your experience and expertise as a leader needs to be communicated clearly as well. (Be Demanding, Not Demeaning, as I told you earlier in this book.) When dealing with direct reports, don't let them tell you it's going to take longer than *you* know it should take. Say, "No. Here's your goal," and state it clearly.

Of course, that's when people start labeling. Everybody who worked for me says, "Lynch was never satisfied," and I take that as a compliment, not a criticism. As a leader, it's okay to say, "That's good, but not good enough. What else can we do with the available resources? How quickly can we do this? How efficiently? How effectively can we get it done?"

The goal is not to get by. It's to keep getting better.

STATE YOUR GOALS

By the way: Corporate leaders have to establish the goals in the first place. It's up to leaders to say, "What's the purpose of what we're doing?"

In the pharmaceutical world, I've encountered some leaders who firmly believe that the purpose of what they're doing is helping humanity, and we saw that on display during the accelerated development of a COVID vaccine, which was done in partnership across corporations that normally acted as rivals. I've also encountered some leaders who believe their sole purpose (despite the business they're in) is making money.

Guess which ones are more successful? Guess which ones survived the pandemic better than others? (We'll talk more about the bottom-line importance of Taking Care of People in the last chapter.)

Making money, pleasing the Board, which is put in place to ensure you're a profitable company with fiduciary responsibility to the shareholders, is of prime importance to any corporation. It has to be. The thing is, a company's mission doesn't have to please just one or the other. It should please both! But it's up to leadership to define that and to communicate that—so the people in your company can actually make it happen.

Corporate leaders need to establish: What is our *raison d'etre*, what is our purpose, what is our mission and goal?—and do so clearly and consistently. It only gets more important in times of crisis because people are scared, they're uneasy, they feel like the rug's being ripped out from under them in all sorts of ways. They want to know where you stand, so that *they* can be sure they're standing on solid ground.

Take that to heart: In times of trouble, you, as a leader, can provide the solid ground that people need, simply by communicating clearly with your people.

They *need* that. Just as you need it from *your* leaders.

THE SEVEN PRINCIPLES OF COMMUNICATION

Just to review for a moment, to be an effective leader in times of crisis, you have to THINK before you speak, use available technology properly, and more. But the most important part of any communication involves actually learning how to communicate, and that takes some skills.

After working with corporate leaders for all these years, I've narrowed the skills needed to be an effective communicator down to seven tasks (which are based on learnable and improvable skills):

1. Listen
2. Be Aware of Nonverbal Communication
3. Be Confident

4. Be Empathetic
5. Be Open-Minded
6. Be Clear and Concise
7. Give and Get Feedback

All communication starts with listening. I know that's the opposite of what many leaders think, and the opposite of what many leaders have been taught and put into practice, but it's true. Fully 70 percent of communication is in the hands of the listener—because without a listener listening, nothing is actually ever communicated. If you're talking or you're typing, and you're transmitting, but you're not getting through to anyone because they're not listening, then you're not communicating at all.

But it's more than that. As leaders, we *have* to listen to our people. We have to be open to learning from them, to hearing their concerns, to listening to their ideas—otherwise, rarely, if ever, will they wind up listening to *us*.

As a general rule, it's better to listen than to talk. Always. And, as a leader, it's immeasurable how important that trait is. I talked about this a little bit in this book already, and I talk about it extensively in my second book, *Work Hard, Pray Hard*. On just about any battlefield in history, it was the leaders who listened to their people in the field, who paid attention to the insights, observations, and recommendations of their trusted subordinates who prevailed. And it's the leaders who acted on high, who ignored sound advice, and who liked to listen to themselves talk who lost.

What does it mean to listen? For one thing, if somebody's talking to you, and you're messing around, looking over your shoulder, not paying attention, or just hoping they shut up so you can make your point, that's not good listening. I confessed back in Chapter 17 that I can be a lousy listener. Ten years later, I'll say it again: I still am.

But I *am* working on that. It's a critical skill that you've gotta have. So I'm always talking to and, more importantly, *listening* to people about ways to be a better active listener.

Part of actively listening comes from nonverbal communication, because we're supposed to be attuned enough in communication to hear what the people are telling us, even if they're not talking to us. And if we wanna be an effective communicator, we've gotta avoid all those traps ourselves. Look people in the eye, avoid any kind of external distractions, provide nonverbal feedback in response to what they're saying, and make sure that what we heard them say is what they intended to say.

That's harder to do when you're not in-person, which is why it's so important to use technology effectively. On Zoom and Teams, as I've already mentioned, turn the cameras on, and use them. And if Zoom or Teams isn't available, then pick up your phone. It seems like people forget that these iPhones we're walking around with are called i-*Phones* for a reason. Talk to people! The inflections in your voice are far superior than anything that can ever be conveyed in an email or text, and, very often, the verbal communication is much more concise (because it's more understandable and nuanced) than any amount of texting could ever be.

Part of nonverbal communication is also just being friendly. The fact is, people respond better to a friendly speaker (or listener) than to a stern one, an angry one, or a seemingly uninterested one.

My daughter nailed me one recent Friday because I was in a bad mood for whatever reason, so I wasn't being an effective communicator. She pulled out her phone and took a picture of my face when I was trying to communicate. She showed me a picture of my face. Then I realized how mean I looked while I was staring at her. There was no communication taking place because I wasn't being friendly.

Now, it's probably not a good idea to take a picture of your boss's face while he or she is talking to you. But don't you wish you could? Imagine what would happen if we did that to all the "lousy leader" types of bosses, like the ones I spoke about back in Chapter 7. It sure would be funny to see a collection of photos of those faces in action, all failing to communicate in dozens of different ways.

But that wouldn't be very empathetic of us, now, would it? And another part of communicating effectively is displaying empathy. We need to show those we're speaking to that we understand their situation—especially in times of crisis, when their worlds may be turned upside down—and conversely, we need to listen and actually care about what our listeners are telling us. We have to stay open-minded and ready to respond, which shouldn't be hard to do if we're actively listening.

Remember: There's no such thing as a casual conversation when you're a senior leader. If you're listening with empathy and open-mindedness, you'll be prepared to act if what you hear is something that needs to be acted upon.

Once all of that is in place, and practiced, and once those skills become a part of your routine in every bit of communication you're involved in, then and only then can you turn to the most important aspects of communication besides listening, and that is being clear and concise.

If you're going to be an effective communicator during difficult times, you must think about what you're going to say before you say it, and you've gotta say it in such a manner that you get your point across even in a proverbial elevator speech.

No matter what it is you have to say, you should be able to get your main points across in the amount of time it takes to go from the first floor to the tenth floor in an elevator ride. Whatever it might be—verbal communication, written communication, text—it seems the number-one issue I'm having to cover in my leadership training for executives is their boss is concerned about their inability to be clear and concise. In the chapter on Voice Amplification (Chapter 15), I mentioned how frustrated I get when somebody puts together a fifty-page PowerPoint presentation and expects me to listen to fifty pages of material, when I just want to hear what's on page twenty-three. Well, that urgency became even more paramount during the pandemic. Just remember, even though you've got a lot of time to write a long email at your desk at home, the person who's reading the email doesn't have time to read that long email.

My rule? If you absolutely must get your points across in an email (as opposed to a phone call or Zoom meeting), then get your points across in the first three lines. If you want to write a three-page email because you're bored, go ahead—but make sure you get the points across in the first three lines.

That should always happen if you're gonna be an effective communicator. *Always.* And in the middle of the pandemic, when people were isolated in their houses, wondering what the hell was going on since they couldn't get any sense from the usual casual conversations around the watercooler at headquarters, clear and concise communications from leaders made all the difference in putting the workforce at ease.

And finally, at the end of every communication, there should be room for feedback. Remember the Zoom call with eight different people who heard eight different things at one meeting? Always have a recorder there at the session, and send out notes on the session; then give people a chance to share their feedback on the notes, to make sure they're accurate, within 24 hours or so after the notes are disseminated.

In smaller, one-on-one conversations, the feedback can be immediate. In the military, we use "back briefs and brief backs." Back briefs are the first step. Let's say you and I are talking. When you're done talking, I say, "Here's what I heard you say," and I repeat the key points back to you—just to make sure what I heard you say is what you wanted me to hear. If something is off, you then have a chance to correct what I heard. That's called a back brief. It's instantaneous—it happens before the meeting is over with. Now, that really works only if it's a one-on-one. If it's a Zoom call with nine attendees, you could accomplish this by making it a point to call the nine attendees right afterwards and ask, "How's it going? What'd you think of the meeting? What did you hear me say?" Those are back briefs.

Then, in the military, about three days later, we were required to come back and do a "brief back," which is the listener's opportunity to tell you how they're gonna execute what you told them to do. Back briefs and brief backs. That's how you get structure in your communication. And I guarantee that adding some structure will add to the overall clarity of your communication.

Try it out. It's pretty straightforward: Have a recorder capture the meeting notes, build in a back-brief mechanism and a brief-back mechanism, and you'll wind up with better results.

By the way: Those back-brief and brief-back methods of communication work pretty well in personal relationships, too. Try actively listening to your significant other, responding in a way that makes it absolutely clear that you heard what they wanted you to hear, and then come back later with more feedback and a plan to act on whatever they told you. Chances are you'll see some smiles and appreciation come your way.

Sarah and I try to put these types of communication skills into practice every day. They make a difference, even though they don't take up very much of our time.

Way back in 1993, Sarah and I went to a course on how to be a battalion-level commander and his spouse. There were 500 people there, and one of the things they told us during that week-long course was, "You gotta carve out 15 minutes for each other, every day." We all looked at the instructor, thinking, "What the hell is he talking about? Only 15 minutes? You can't get anything done in 15 minutes." But since 1993, Sarah and I have carved out 15 minutes every day just to talk. I catch up on what she's doing, she catches up on what I'm doing, and we share 15 minutes of effective communication for that short period of time.

Honestly, just that short amount of effective communication each day has helped us to get through every challenge we've faced in now-almost-forty years of marriage and counting.

It's funny, but that age-old marriage issue of what's more important, Quantity Time versus Quality Time, seemed to reach a peak with a lot of couples during the pandemic. And it's an important topic to think about in our professional lives as well.

Which leads me to another topic that deserves a closer look: Prioritization and Time Management.

– 29 –

MAKE THE TIME

Prioritization and time management are always important, but in order to be a leader during times of crisis, it's critical. You have *got* to set clear priorities and boundaries, and you've *got* to manage your time correctly to avoid burnout—*and* avoid burning out your people.

Most leaders I work with are Type A people, and most Type A people tend to wake up with a ready-made list of things they're gonna do that day. The A-plus type folks have got a plan not only for the day, but for the week, as well as a plan for the next six weeks, and a plan for next six months. So they're managing a weekly calendar, a six-week calendar, and a six-month calendar.

What I find when I look those task lists over is that 60 percent of the tasks they list could be delegated, deferred, or deleted. Sixty percent! And this is uniform now, as I train people in all different fields. They say, "I'm too busy. I can't allocate time to do this or that thing that I want to do."

"Really?" I say. "Let's look at how you're prioritizing your time."

I mentioned the Franklin Covey productivity box back in Chapter 13, but that box is actually based on The Eisenhower Box, which deals more particularly with prioritization than productivity. (As its name suggests, the Eisenhower Box is based on methods used by Dwight

D. Eisenhower, our 34th President—and, I might add, the former five-star Army general who planned the invasion of Normandy during World War II. Impressive guy.)

The Eisenhower method, like the Covey Method, involves breaking tasks down into four categories, or boxes: Urgent and Important; Urgent and Less Important; *Not* Urgent but Important; and *Not* Urgent and *Not* Important.

When you categorize what needs to be done into these four boxes, it becomes clear that what's *Not* Urgent and *Not* Important should be treated as such, put on the back burner, or maybe even eliminated from consideration entirely. On the other hand, tasks that are Urgent and Important need to be dealt with right away and with the utmost care and attention. The Urgent and Less Important require quick action, but they shouldn't take precedent over the more Important tasks. And the Important but Less Urgent tasks should be delegated appropriately to get done after the Urgent tasks are completed.

Simply using the Box will help show your people that you care about not wasting their time, while also showing that you're not losing sight of what's important and urgent for your organization.

That's good leadership.

I like to break it down even further, specifically for corporate executives.

If you are the corporate executive and the task is truly urgent and important, then you need to do it personally, and you need to do it right now. But only *you* can determine what's urgent and what's important, and that's where people are getting confused.

If it's important but *not* urgent, you, as the corporate executive, should just schedule it for when it's convenient for you: three weeks from now, four weeks from now—actually put it on a calendar, and don't take it *off* the calendar. I mean, that's where people are messing up—they're putting things on a calendar in pencil, which tells you they're not committed. They think they're gonna change it anyway, which means it's clearly not important!

So if it's important but not urgent, then you just defer it to when it's appropriate for you, but you commit to it, and you do it.

Where I spend a lot of time working with people is in the area of "urgent but not important." I mean, think about it: How the hell can something be urgent if it's not important? Well, it's probably "important" to somebody like your boss, so, now, it becomes "urgent." He wants it now, so you gotta do it now. And the best way to get through that is to delegate. You've got people on your team that you've got trust and confidence in, and, if something pops up that's urgent but it's not that important to you, just delegate. Let somebody else do it.

And if it's not urgent and it's not important, then you should just delete it. You should just take it off the list of things to do altogether. No looking back. Done.

Think it can't be done?

I was a full colonel in the Army when I mandated that all my people be present for the birth of their child and for the first two weeks thereafter, so they could bond with their newborns. My brigade executive officer at the time was a lieutenant colonel, and he showed up for work on the day that his newborn came into his life. His wife didn't give birth, but they adopted a newborn child. And on the very day that baby came into their home, he came into work.

I said, "What the hell are you doing here?"

"I've got too much to do. I can't take two weeks off," he said. "Look, I've got 152 unanswered email messages."

So I sat down at his desk, and I deleted all of them. I sent him home, and every day for the next two weeks, I deleted his email because I knew that if I didn't do that, he'd be sneaking in and working on things.

The brigade did not falter, we did not crumble, and life did not come to an end. If something was important enough to warrant a call while the Brigade XO was not answering, they would send it to me, or they would send it to somebody else on my staff. I don't know why it is so unbelievably hard for people in corporate America to delete stuff, but I'm telling you, it's the keys to the kingdom.

I wasn't a big fan of email when I wrote the first edition of this book, and what I've seen in the ten years since then is that we've become *consumed* by email.

The average number of emails my clients are getting is about 150 a day now. That's what we used to get in a week or two, because we've got this unbelievably stupid function called "reply all" on emails. People are "replying all" on all their emails, and then people who don't need to be reading those emails are taking precious time out of their days to read them. That kills any hope of time management, and what I do in my workshops is try to give people some tips on how to prioritize email so they're not reading and answering unnecessarily.

It's often as simple as going into your settings, on Gmail or whatever platform you use, and telling the computer what to do instead of letting it dictate everything to you. For example, on important emails, if I got something that I didn't respond to within five days, or I asked for something I didn't get a response to within five days, my email is smart enough to remind me that I have to ask the question again. Most email systems also have functions that will pre-sort incoming emails into different boxes, based on whatever criteria you set up. Do that! Carve out a time one day, get some help from IT if you need it, and go tackle those settings. Make them work for you instead of you working for them. Use the technology to make your life simpler instead of more complicated.

And remember, what you do as a leader trickles down to everyone else.

I had a corporate executive announce loudly at one of my training sessions that he was following my advice on work-life balance and enjoying his weekends more than ever. But then I found out he was sending emails to his people over weekends, which meant his people started turning on their computers every weekend just in case they got emails from the boss.

Look, if you feel the need to type an email over the weekend or late at night, go ahead. I get it. Sometimes after the kid is in bed and your mind is clear, you might come up with something important that you want to share with your staff. But do them—and yourself—a favor and schedule that email to hold and send on Monday—not at 9 o'clock on a Saturday. Otherwise, everyone gets the impression that they have to work on the weekend, and that sets up a vicious cycle that leads to burnout. Get your priorities straight, and manage your time—and your direct reports' time—more effectively.

Which gets us back to the Eisenhower Box. It is so clean and should be so simple to follow, but I have clients who walk away from a workshop and then put all their tasks in box number one: everything is urgent, and everything is important.

No! It's not. All you did is put everything in a box, but you didn't really do any kind of delineation, prioritization, or discrimination. And I do find it's difficult for collective bodies to do this. That's why corporate executives have to do it themselves. The leader has to be the one to say, "Okay, I'm now establishing these rules. This is urgent and important, this is important but not urgent, this is urgent but not important, and this is neither urgent nor important," and then send it out to everyone, so that everybody in the orchestra is looking at the same sheet of music when it comes to the idea of what is truly important.

Eisenhower learned about prioritization the same place I did, which was at West Point. As a reminder, what West Point taught me, among other things, is that, if you're not 10 minutes early to a meeting, you're late.

Respecting other people's time is part of good communication, whether it's in email or in person.

That takes discipline. And Vince Lombardi, the famous football coach (who was a football coach at West Point at one point) said, "There's something in a good man that *yearns* for discipline."

All these years later, I'd add that his statement applies to women, too, and to anyone, regardless of gender, who wants to take back some control and improve their life.

THE DISCIPLINE OF TIME MANAGEMENT

This whole thing we're talking about—prioritization and time management—is *all* about discipline. It's saying, "Here's what's important," and then being disciplined enough to allocate the time to do those things.

And a big part of being successful at that is being disciplined enough to set boundaries.

If you're gonna be working from home—even part-time from home in this new world we're in—then you absolutely must establish boundaries. Let people know: "This is the period of time I'm available for Zoom calls, this is the period of time I'm at lunch, and this is my quitting time." During the pandemic, some people did that, and they were fine. Other people turned on the computer as soon as they got out of bed and didn't turn it off until they *went* to bed. I tell folks, "They weren't working from home—they were sleeping at work!"

I don't want to be repetitive here. Everything I said in Chapter 12 still applies today. But we've learned something during the course of the pandemic that needs to be addressed, and that's this idea of establishing boundaries. As I started to put the finishing touches on this new edition of the book, I looked around and realized that, 18 months into the pandemic, many people's lives had been enriched because they focused on the opportunities and not the obstacles. In the absence of a two-hour commute to the office, the disciplined among us became more physically fit, because they took time for themselves for walks and physical fitness. They're more financially fit because the money they were spending on commutes and lunches at work and all that other stuff is no longer an expense. Their families are stronger because they're having meals together and actually spending time with their spouses and kids. They're more educated because they took time to read. I mean, there are people who are popping out of this pandemic truly enriched! I put together a survey that I sent out to clients, to get a sense of what was working and what wasn't working under this work-from-home model, so I can speak with some authority on what the people think. And generally, the people think that their productivity is as good or better when they're working from home—which is why I believe the most-successful companies will move to a hybrid model of part-time in the office, part-time at home, when the pandemic dust all settles. But what people say they miss about the workplace is the human contact. They're sitting at home thinking, "Man, remember the good old days, when Sally and I would have a cup of coffee?" or "Johnny and I would go have a drink after work," or "Remember the good old days, when we could talk about what we did over the weekend on Monday, before the week started?" So that's why I am a big proponent of moving toward a hybrid model, instead of getting back to "the way things were." We need both. People need a better home life *and* a better work life. And we're quickly proving that both of those things can happen simultaneously.

Having said that, there are people who were *devastated* during the pandemic. They turned into walking zombies. They lost all passion. They lost all energy because, for the last 18 months, they were continually working. By mismanaging the technology and not setting boundaries, they allowed themselves to be continually available for people to reach out to them and say, "What do you think about this? What do you think about that?" They were subject to Zoom meetings and Teams meetings that really had no purpose. They were simply being called by lonely people who wanted to have meetings with other people, and they weren't disciplined enough to say, "No, I'm not attending the meeting."

Without that discipline, work takes over your *life*. And that's not okay!

By the way: With all the technology we have at our fingertips, don't accept cold calls. That's a boundary issue, too. Just because somebody thinks, "I got nothing else to do—let me call Johnny," doesn't mean Johnny should answer. But most of the time, he does. Out of politeness, Johnny stops what he's doing, answers the phone call, and, in doing so, throws his schedule off completely. That just doesn't work. It's okay to have the discipline and establish a rhythm with your people to say, "If you need to talk to me, get on my schedule." Even with your friends. At the very least, train them to text you first, so you can decide when it's convenient for *you* to get on the phone or hop on a Zoom. And vice-versa: Don't just call someone and say, "Hey, can we talk now?" Because the answer should be "no," but it won't be "no," because the person you called doesn't want to be rude, so they'll have a conversation, and that just breaks up their whole workflow.

I'm sure you can come up with some more areas you can work on, all on your own. But one thing's for sure: The people who have come out of this pandemic enriched are the people who established boundaries. And if you want to enrich your life going forward, those boundaries are gonna matter.

PRIORITIZING YOUR LIFE

Going back to the email conversation for a moment, in some cases, there are certain emails that come in that you've *got* to answer—regardless of when they come in, because you have a boss who has an expectation that you're gonna respond, right? And if it's not working for you, you can try to negotiate some new boundaries with your boss—but that goes only so far.

I like to remind people that if you have a job, and your boss tells you to do something, and, if what they've told you to do is not illegal, immoral, or unethical, then you have a obligation to do what your boss tells you to do. To be successful in the world—not just in the military but in corporate America, too—listen closely to what your boss says to do, write it down, and do it. It's really that simple.

If your boss wants you to do something illegal, immoral, or unethical, you should not do that. And if you don't like the circumstances that your boss has placed upon you, if you can't live with them, then vote with your feet and *leave*.

That's what almost all the executives did at one organization I know of, after a new boss came in and made it clear to his direct reports that he slept only four hours a night. "I expect you guys not to sleep any more than that, too, and if I text you at 2:00 in the morning, I have an expectation that I'll get a response."

You know there are people like that out there, right? They seem to be especially common in the tech world, and startups—the Silicon Valley types—but they exist in every field, just like they existed in the military. And if you don't like it, and you can't live with it, leave! Don't stick around and ignore the boss; don't mess up the whole organization because you can't live up to the boss's expectations. And if you're the boss, well, don't be that guy. It's just not realistic, and you're gonna wind up losing some of your best people.

One of the keys to successful time management is knowing yourself and your personal biorhythms. This is one area where people, I believe, are making some big mistakes.

Everybody who knows me knows that by 2:00 in the afternoon, I am physically present but mentally absent. I've got nothing left. If you think we're having a substantive conversation after 2:00, well, you might *see* me and *think* we're talking, but I ain't listening. I'm tired.

After all these years, I still get up at 4 or 5 a.m., so by 2:00 in the afternoon, I have already worked eight or nine hours, and I'm ready to take a nap. I currently take a nap every day from 2:00 to 4:00 p.m. And that's what everybody knows: don't call me between 2:00 and 4:00, even if you're family, because Papa is taking a nap. Does that sound reckless to you? Like something you could never do? Does it sound *lazy* to you? It's not. I do it because it extends my day. I can stay up later in the evening now because I refresh myself from 2:00 to 4:00.

I've already told you about the idea of 15, 7, and 2, and I spend more time than I used to focusing on the "7" piece—to make sure I'm not only *in bed* for seven hours but have *restful sleep*. There's all sorts of information and new technology out there, including apps for your phone, that have been developed in the last ten years that can help you to improve the quality of your sleep, and you ought to. Because without good sleep, you can't do the 2, let alone the 15.

And the 15 and 2? That's your *life*. That's your *work*. It's everything.

When I first got out of the Army, I established a couple of rules. One I've already talked about: Sarah and I committed ourselves to doing meaningful work, to touching lives and making a difference. But the second thing I personally committed to doing was living my life by a rule of 30-30-40.

And let me say right up front: You do not have to "retire" or transition into a different career to do what I'm about to show you. If you're a 35-year-old executive at some company, you can use this equation *right now*. For Sarah and me, this equation has led to a truly happy life over the last decade and counting.

So, "30-30-40" means I spend 30 percent of my time making money, I spend 30 percent of my time doing nonprofit work, and then I spend 40 percent of my time doing whatever the hell I want to do. You heard me: 40 percent is my own. If that means, in a five-day week, I carve out two whole days to play golf, that's fine—because I'm making money, I'm doing good in the world, I'm accomplishing my goals in my 30-30. So the rest of my time is *mine*.

Living by the 30-30-40 rule has served me extremely well. And again: It has nothing to do with "retirement." I'm just working smarter. Overall, I'm busier than I ever was when I was in the Army (except in times of combat), but I'm doing things that I want to do—the things that I've prioritized. And in all this time, I haven't felt the need to violate either of those rules.

I've had plenty of opportunity to sell my soul and go make a lot of money seven days a week. One wealthy gentleman called me up and said, "Meet me. Let's talk about you taking over as CEO of one of my companies." And when we got together, he said, "You've got the job, but I expect you to come in before I come to work and to stay longer; I work weekends, and you'll work weekends, too." It violated my 30-30-40 rule, and I was already so happy with how things were going. The idea of making all that money wasn't all that important to me. And let me tell you, it was a *lot* of money. This was a legit billionaire who'd built his companies from nothing. His personal work ethic is what got him through it, and he wanted people who worked as hard or harder than he did. I respect that. But that's not what I was looking for.

For one, what likely would have fallen by the wayside is my nonprofit work. And for me, that would've been too big of a loss to bear—a loss that no amount of money could ever make up for.

Sarah and I are now actively involved in five different nonprofits, with the Gary Sinise Foundation being the lead one, alongside Homes for Our Troops and Operation Finally Home. All three of those are organizations that build homes for wounded warriors. That's where the tie to my work at UTARI comes in, because a lot of the technology I developed at UTARI has found its way into homes for people who have no arms and no legs, who require an adaptive lifestyle.

I also work closely with H-E-B (the Texas-based grocery chain that is the twelfth-largest privately owned corporation in America) and their Operation Appreciation, which spends a lot of time, effort, and money showing appreciation to the military and their families, both active duty and veterans, across the state of Texas. They also partner with the Gary Sinise Foundation and Homes for Our Troops to build these wounded-warrior homes, so it's a great fit all-around.

And finally, Sarah and I are still very active in the Military Child Education Coalition (MCEC), which focuses on education for our military children. We're still very active in Tragedy Assistance Program for Survivors (TAPS), which focuses on the survivors of folks who paid the ultimate sacrifice in service to our country.

I may not serve in the military any longer, but the emotions that Sarah and I experienced leading soldiers and their families has never gone away. There are still all kinds of kids out there who need our help. I'm an active mentor for twenty-two youngsters these days—twenty-two people who call me routinely and ask for insights and advice, which ties back to my leadership principle: Be a Mentor. And many of these who are wounded and need adaptive homes were wounded under my command. While I was working on this new edition of *Adapt or Die*, we were able to give a new home to a young man who'd lost both his legs in combat, riding in a vehicle where I placed him on the battlefield. He was one of those 800 kids I've talked about who came back in pieces. And when we went to the home-dedication ceremony, he showed a picture of Sarah and me with him at Walter Reed Medical Center, where I flew to present him his Purple Heart and his Bronze Star back in the day.

There is no price you can put on that experience. None.

Our mantra when we left the military was "We're only gonna do meaningful and substantive work around people with shared values," and that's the mantra that has served us for more than a decade now, even though we left without any real idea what direction God was gonna lead us in. But look where we are now! In those ten years or so, I've managed to accumulate all the toys and benefits a good income can bring, including a Corvette and a pickup truck, which are parked on my ranch property, where my daughter and her husband and one of our grandchildren live full time, and where I get to feed deer every day and take walks down by the river that runs through our land. None of that ever would have happened without our dedicating ourselves to something bigger than, "Well, I need to get a job now," when I transitioned out of the Army.

Rick Warren wrote a book called *The Purpose-Driven Life*, and I truly believe our lives cannot be fulfilling unless we are driven by a higher purpose—one higher than just making money.

If anything, the pandemic has spotlighted just how important the 30-30-40 rule is.

WHEN IS YOUR END DATE?

In March of 2020, Sarah and I were making a speech in New Jersey to a large pharmaceutical company. When we got on a plane to come home, the guy next to me was sniffling, and the lady across the aisle was coughing and hacking. And a week after we got back to the ranch, we both came down with all the symptoms of COVID-19.

I tried to soldier my way through it, but I couldn't shake this thing, and eventually we had to go see a doctor and get tested. At that point, the tests came back negative. I'm not sure about the accuracy of the tests in those early days of the pandemic, but we were both sicker than we'd ever been. It was awful. We got better in time, but it was very clear to us that either one of us could have died—just from getting on a plane and going to work.

My co-author, Mark Dagostino, came even closer to death from COVID-19 in February of 2021. After traveling for work, wearing masks, and social distancing—just as we'd all been told to do—he and his partner, Terry, both came down with severe COVID symptoms, and the test confirmed they had it. But instead of getting better, Mark's symptoms got worse and worse, until he finally went into the emergency room. His blood-oxygen level was down to 80 percent when he walked in. Actually, I take that back. He *couldn't* walk. He was too weak to walk. He needed a wheelchair to get from the passenger seat of the car to the ER.

By the way, Mark was only 50 years old at the time and in very good health before this happened.

I'll let him tell the story:

Within two hours, there were seven doctors gathered around my bed, trying everything they could to get my oxygen level up and trying to figure out a plan for what they were going to do next. As my oxygen dipped into the 70s, despite the assistance of high-pressure lines and even a C-PAP machine, they had to decide whether to put me under and intubate. What I already knew from my own research is that, with COVID, once you're intubated, your chance of death goes up by 80 percent.

I was so weak and unable to breathe at that point, I had no say in the matter. I was entirely in the hands of those doctors. And as I lay there, staring at their worried faces, I had the very distinct feeling that, if they chose to put me under, that would be it for me.

I'm not kidding. I made my peace with God. I accepted that this was it. I'd had a good life. I didn't even have time to feel sad about it, it all happened so fast.

Finally, they tried putting me on this thing called a BiPAP machine, which involved strapping my whole head into a high-pressure oxygen mask, and pumping air in and out of my nose and mouth in varying intervals—basically forcing my lungs to inflate and deflate against my body's will. It was torture. The doc who hooked me up warned that most people couldn't take it. They rip the mask off in a matter of seconds. But I was so weak that, at that point, I didn't fight it. I lay there scared and let the machine do its job.

And it worked. My oxygen level settled a bit, and an hour later, they moved me into ICU.

With so many shots I couldn't even count them, and additional treatments I can't even recall, and with prayers and support pouring into my phone from family and friends, and even long-lost colleagues whom I hadn't spoken with in twenty years, I somehow turned the corner a few days later. After eight full days in isolation, unable to receive visits from my kids or my parents or my fiancée, somehow, I survived.

It would take me months to fully recover, and I still hit walls of fatigue to this day. COVID damaged my body. It weakened me. I feel like it aged me. And when something like that happens, it changes you. You can't help but want to reprioritize how you're spending your time.

Since March of 2020, there have been 184 million cases of COVID worldwide, which resulted in 3.97 million deaths. And as this book went to print, the Delta variant was increasing those numbers all over the globe. There were 33.7 million cases of COVID and 705,000 deaths in the U.S. alone. To date, we've had 2.9 billion vaccinations delivered, which is a miracle when you think about it. The regular approval process for vaccines is about a six-year process, because the FDA is all about efficacy and safety. They want the clinical trials to go for a long period of time. But we, as a nation, said, "We can't *wait* a long period of time." So we accelerated it. We got this emergency-use authorization from the FDA. And people would ask, "Well, how long is your vaccine going to be effective?" The answer is, "We don't know, because we didn't do a six-year clinical trial. We did a six-*month* clinical trial." But to have so many people vaccinated so quickly is a miracle, and we should be thankful to the pharmaceutical companies who put rivalries aside to get it done.

Even so, seeing all this death serves as a wake-up call to us all—to think about how we're spending our time on this Earth.

In Chapter 12, I talked about work-life balance. I spoke about how having fun is one of my Leadership Principles, and how, as leaders, we need to take time to think. I spoke about "living your dash," which I re-emphasize on my leadership tours, taking executives to gravestones marking those we lost in combat, right here on our own soil—asking them how they're living the dash between their personal start and end dates. Because we've all got an end date, and we never know when that date might come.

Dealing with Time Management in these terms becomes even more pressing and important in times of crisis. It needs to be taken seriously, for your sake and for the sake of everyone in your charge.

If you sleep for seven hours and dedicate two to physical fitness (or spiritual fitness, or any sort of fitness—which is so important, and which I delve into deeply in my second book, *Work Hard, Pray Hard*), then you've got 15 hours of time to work with, every day.

Don't tell me you don't. You *do*.

You decide how to spend those 15 hours.

On workdays, I remind people all the time that I get up by 5 a.m.; I email only until 8 a.m. I'm available for calls and meetings until noon, and, at noon, I step away and have lunch. After that, I allocate time for me to think and to plan (and, more recently, to nap). At 5 p.m., I shut down my computer until I do it again the next day. In the evening, I have time to spend with the grandkids and with Sarah. We eat dinner together. We jump in the pool. Whatever we want. And we *value* that time. It sounds so unbelievably simple, and it *is* simple—but people just don't do it.

Even if you allocate 10 hours a day for work, you've still got five hours left for your family. For your *life*. It's just math. If you mess around and don't get things done during your 15, if you spend four or five hours a day watching TV or scrolling through social media, that's on *you*.

In your personal life, even more than your work life, you've got to establish boundaries. Come up with your own rules. Live by them. Tell people about them. Expect people to respect them and follow them. Most of all, respect those rules *yourself*.

How do you go about prioritizing what you want your life to look like?

Use the Eisenhower Box. Do it. Throw all your personal stuff in there, and see how it all shakes out.

But I also want you to think about Walnuts and Rice.

HOW YOU FILL UP YOUR JAR

If I give you the task of filling up a glass jar with a bunch of walnuts and rice, and you put all the rice in first, you'll find that the walnuts won't fit. But if you put in a couple of walnuts, sprinkle in some rice, then put in a couple more walnuts, sprinkle in some rice . . . next thing you know, it all fits.

In the analogy of life, the walnuts represent those things that are *important* to you, and the rice represents the things that you *have to do in order to sustain yourself.*

Unless you're independently wealthy, you *have* to go to work in order to sustain yourself, to make money. For me, running R Lynch Enterprises is what I *have* to do to support my family and my lifestyle. It's the rice—even though I love what I do, it's still work, which means it's not as important as the walnuts.

The key is you've gotta know what your walnuts are and what your rice is. So as you fill up your calendar—daily, weekly, six weeks out and six months out—a good practice is to put the walnuts in first.

For Sarah and me, our walnuts are family, friends, fitness, spiritual fitness, and having fun.

The "walnuts" are the reason we take quarterly vacations—*and* why we put those vacations on the calendar at the beginning of the year and schedule my speeches and consulting work *around* those vacations—not the other way around.

It takes discipline to do this, but I'm living proof that it can be done.

Every six weeks or so, Sarah and I sit down (usually over a cocktail) and check in to see how we're doing on our walnuts and rice. Priorities do change over time, and it's important to make sure we're prioritizing what we want to prioritize. When this book first came out, our daughter Susan wasn't married yet. Now? She's married and has a five-year-old daughter named Piper, who lives with her and her husband here on our property. My son Lucas had two children as well, Rex and J.W. Those three grandkids are our joys, and spending time with them is a walnut we didn't have ten years ago. But family has always been important to us and a priority to us, and because of that, we've always been able to carve out the time we want and need to put family first, in good times and bad.

We had a couple of our own personal crises in the last ten years. Lucas was suffering from debilitating health problems, and we eventually discovered that he had a brain tumor. Because we knew our walnuts from our rice, we were able to drop everything and make use of the connections we'd made in our professional lives and our spiritual lives to get him (and us) the help we needed. We found our way to one of the best brain surgeons in the world, and Lucas survived.

In the interim, Sarah lost her sister to cancer, but we were able to be there for her, to get her through her final days in as much comfort as possible, surrounded by loved ones.

If you haven't experienced anything like that yet, you will. The pandemic proved it. We have all these plans, but *life happens*, and we've got to be able to adapt and deal with life's circumstances.

Paying attention to walnuts and rice will help you do that.

Prioritization and time management will help you do that.

Look at the task lists that are taking up all your time, and delegate or eliminate the 60 percent of those tasks that aren't serving you and your dash, that aren't serving your 30-30-40 (or whatever time/priority allocation you determine is the right one for your life).

And please: Stop wasting time on the piddly stuff. Get the big stuff done. The important stuff. But stop worrying about things that are out of your control. I don't bother arguing about politics or debating issues that are out of my hands. That would take up too much of my time and my thoughts. And what good does it do?

Remember: You can't roll up your sleeves while you're wringing your hands.

And if you find that things aren't going right, you probably keep changing plans at the last minute and canceling plans all the time to put out one fire or another. Please recognize that something is wrong. Stop what you're doing. Re-prioritize. Make better plans. Stick to them.

DELEGATE. DELETE. DEFER.

Keep the Eisenhower box open on your desktop. Print it out. Put it on your wall.

On a daily basis, and especially in times of crisis, remember: You cannot do it all, and you cannot do it all *right now*.

At the same time, never forget: If you get your priorities straight, then you *can* do everything that you *want* to do *and* everything that you *need* to do, too.

You have to be the one to determine where to put your effort.

WORK-LIFE BALANCE

People throw around the term "work-life balance" all the time, but a lot of people I've come across in corporate America think it's just lip service. Here's the thing: It's not. You *can* be a great corporate leader, and you *can* have a functional family that you're part of at the very same time. Saying you can't is B.S.

I work with executives who do it well—they've got flourishing companies and flourishing families. I've also worked with executives who've put all their efforts into building "generational wealth," making money their first priority—and I've watched them get divorced and alienate their kids, because their priorities are messed up, and their families just don't want to be around them anymore. What good is generational wealth if the next generation wants nothing to do with you?

In my workshops, especially with new clients, people always want to talk more about how to prioritize time in their professional lives, and I refuse to talk just from a professional perspective. If anything has become clearer to me in the last ten years, it's this: You cannot separate personal from professional issues. It's impossible. What happens at home affects you at work, and vice versa.

To help you remember this, I'll leave you with this somewhat extreme example from American history, which I highlight on my leadership tours to Little Bighorn.

In 1874, General George Custer, a renowned Army general, was stationed out in the Black Hills when he got word that a young lieutenant was flirting with his wife back home in Fort Lincoln. So, what did Custer do? He grabbed fifty of his men and ordered them to follow him on a 225-mile horseback ride to check on his wife firsthand. It was a complete waste of time and resources, and it jeopardized the strength of his men and his horses. It became known as "Custer's Ride." Custer's problems in his home life *greatly* affected his work life, and because of his jealousy (and, I suppose, his doubts about his wife's loyalty), he was court-martialed, removed from command, and suspended for a year for abandoning his position on the battlefield.

Once he was back on the battlefield, things didn't get much better. He had a major named Marcus Reno under his command who was terribly troubled by his situation at home and who had grown resentful of the entire chain of command because of what had happened to him: At one point, Reno asked Custer's boss, Gen. Alfred Terry, if he could take a leave from the front and go back home to bury his wife. His wife had been sick, and she'd died, and Reno requested the leave so he could attend his wife's funeral with their 10-year-old son.

Gen. Terry said "no."

A year later, in 1876, when Custer found himself under attack and in desperate need of rescue at the Battle at Little Bighorn, Reno was one of two men who chose not to help. (I'll share more about this story in Chapter 31.)

Reno kept his men right where they were—and he left Custer there to die a horrible death.

Extreme? Yes.

Relatable? Ask anyone in corporate America who hates their boss just how far they'll go to help when that boss gets in trouble.

These leaders from American history were humans, like we're all humans, full of flaws and personal issues. Those things don't go away just because you're at work or even when you're at war. Settling our differences and dealing with human issues and human conflicts *now* will only help us and our businesses and our families to survive and thrive in times of crisis.

– 30 –

COLLABORATE OR DIE

If you want to lead a high-performing organization, all elements of the organization need to act together. No individual silo can stand alone in the complex world in which we operate today.

I've seen it in pharmaceutical companies, where market-access teams looking to open a market for a new drug cannot do so in isolation—they have no choice but to be involved in R&D, marketing, sales, and more. And I saw it in the military, when I was running Army Installation—where, for decades, a silo approach to mission accomplishment existed, but it was no longer working and simply had to change.

I controlled about one-sixth of the Army's budget at that point, which meant there were five other guys like me controlling the other parts of the budget.

Gen. George Casey was chief at the time, and he was the one who determined that the Army needed to adopt an enterprise approach. The mantra he wanted us to follow: Quit worrying about what's best for me, and start worrying about what's best for *everybody*.

The thing he was talking about in our case was resource allocation. Resources come in three shapes: People, time, and money.

What was happening in the Army is the same thing that's gone on in too many companies to count. It's a situation where those in charge of one silo insist, "I want more resources for my silo. I don't care what anyone else has. My silo is the one that matters most."

As reading through the *Harvard Business Review* or checking the histories of siloed companies will show you, whenever that happens, the larger organization is going to fail.

Our solution in the Army was to get together monthly, to sync the Army Enterprise Board. We gathered with the six of us, and Gen. Casey, along with a political leader, and we talked about what was best for the Army, and that's how we determined where we should we allocate resources.

Resource allocation matters. Why? Because vision without resources is hallucination.

It is simply impossible to accomplish your vision if your resources aren't allocated in a way that's best for the overall corporation. Nobody has unlimited resources, and, in corporate America, there is strong incentive for program managers to try to allocate as much of the resource pie as possible to their particular division.

Senior directors have multiple directors, and their VPs have multiple senior VPs and executive VPs, and then there's the CEO, and the COO . . . I thought the military ranking system was cumbersome until I got into corporate America, where each of those executives is in charge of some portion of the company's resources. If one of them says, "My segment is more important than the others, and therefore I need all the resources," the organization fails.

I see it all the time.

There are companies who've mastered the enterprise approach and are doing extremely well, even through the pandemic. In fact, a lot of my clients came out *better* through the pandemic than they went into the pandemic because of the collaboration that existed across the enterprise.

But I watched an equal number of clients fail because of their entrenched silo approach, as the pressure to try to grab all the resources for their individual pieces of the pie doubled and tripled under the pressure of a global crisis. In those organizations, there were all kinds of infighting, and productivity dropped to dangerous new lows.

There is no room for infighting when you're on the same team.

My time in the Pentagon made me realize that there is no inter-service rivalry on the battlefield. I had Army, Navy, Guard, and Reserve all working together for the common good when we were fighting common enemies in the Middle East and elsewhere.

The only inter-service rivalry I ever truly witnessed was at the Pentagon itself, where the services were competing for portions of the DOD budget. Add to that the separate silos of the Army and the silos in each service who were competing for their pieces of pie as well, and it was just a mess. Competing over pieces of the pie was not healthy. It was affecting our ability to get things done, and in the case of our military, that meant it could lead to an endangerment of our citizens' safety.

METRICS MATTER

It's hard for corporate leaders to establish metrics that reward good behavior in collaboration. For decades, going back to the beginning of corporations themselves, most metrics have been set up to reward how well you are doing in sales, or marketing, or R&D, as opposed to rewarding the question of, "How well are *we* doing?"

All the organizations I've seen flourishing in this area have established metrics based on how well the company is doing, not just to spotlight the success or shortcomings of one division or another. Which is why I train senior leaders, like CEOs, to establish metrics that can be achieved only *across* the silos—because if you give each silo their own metrics, and their only mission is to accomplish what's best for their silo, it defeats the whole enterprise approach.

That's easy to say, hard to do.

Rarely do I find a corporate executive saying, "I have enough." They *always* need more. Which tends to lead to more rivalry rather than collaboration.

Collaboration is what we need to succeed.

So here are a few techniques I teach to foster better collaboration in any organization.

The first one is simple: **share success stories.**

Tell people from the other silos what you've been able to accomplish, and then ask them how *they're* doing. That's the question that never happens. "How are you doing?" Everybody seems to like to tell the other groups how great *they're* doing in *their* silo. They rarely take the initiative to ask the other person, "How are you doing in *your* silo?"

Sharing success stories is easy to do, and it's one big step toward collaboration. Because if two people are trying to collaborate, they just might be able to say to each other, "Okay, if you did this well, and we did that well, maybe we can work together and do *all* of this even better."

Share success stories is number one.

Number two is: **think like them.**

We all have this tendency to think only about what's best for us, and we think about *our* issues. We rarely think about *their* issues, right? "How is that person doing in that silo with these resource constraints? What kind of external influences does that person have that's caused them to behave the way they are?"

In the military, one of the must-read books for all leaders is Sun Tzu's *The Art of War*. And while war is not the thing we're looking for internally in any organization, the concepts of how to stand strong and how to compete truly matter. One of Sun Tzu's most important lessons is to *know yourself.* Truly know where you stand, how you respond, how you act under pressure. The difference in an enterprise organization is that the "self" we're talking about isn't *you*—it's your organization! To know yourself in an enterprise approach is *not* just to know your silo, but to know everybody else's silo as well.

It is only then that you'll have a chance to conquer the competition.

The third thing is, you've got to **use common vernacular.** Within silos, people develop their own language, their own acronyms. They develop their own way of speaking. That doesn't always translate to other groups, and, in a collaborative environment, you all need to speak in a way that everybody else can understand. That's the only way to get to the helpful conversations: "What are those things that we're *all* working on? What are those things that we're *all* trying to understand better?"

As a leader, the next one is especially important—and it's simply a reflection of one of the most important Leadership Principles in this book: **be a lifestyle evangelist.** I'm not talking about being a Christian evangelist. I'm saying that, as leaders, we need to walk the walk and demonstrate through our words and actions that we *want* to collaborate. Which sometimes simply means showing that you care—just like I did with soldiers in my command. When talking to the leaders of other groups, let them know that you care about their mission and their issues. Ask how they're doing. Ask what they need, and then act upon what they tell you. For example, if you have additional resources—people, time, or money—go ahead and share those resources with somebody who doesn't have any. Corporate America is already involved in promoting cross-functional teams, and we do a lot of outsourcing and those kinds of things to get the job done when resources are tight. So, taking the same approach from an internal standpoint, setting up cross-functional teams between silos and "outsourcing" from various divisions of your own company in order to lift the company as a whole only makes sense. It's the right thing to do.

If you approach this enterprise environment by showing people what right looks like, by sharing the resources you have, then, instantly, you become a Lifestyle Evangelist from the Church of Collaboration.

The next one is the one I find everybody struggles with. If you want a collaborative environment, especially one that flourishes in a pandemic or in any other crisis, you've got to **build personal relationships**. You've got to know each other's personal issues. You've got to know about each other's families, their lifestyles, where they're living. You've got to understand each other as humans, not just as professional colleagues. Which means you've got to be willing to share your stories: "Oh, here's how my kids are doing. And here's where we're struggling."

If you're bristling at that thought, please ask yourself, "Why?"

Why is it that we want so badly to keep a wall up between people's professional and personal lives?

We're all human. We're all struggling. We all have needs. We're all in this together, whether you believe that or not. And we do better together by collaborating and lifting each other up than we can possibly do by standing behind walls and believing we can do it all alone.

None of us can do this alone. Not one of us.

So, let's get honest with each other. Let's tell each other the truth.

Sarah gets frustrated, rightly so, at the end of the year when we get these Christmas letters from all our friends and family talking about how great their year was. Everybody struggled with something over the course of the year. But nobody uses their Christmas letter, which is like a personal year-end summary, to talk about the struggles that they had. Why not? Wouldn't that kind of honesty bring families and friends even closer together?

I know for a fact that being open and honest about our struggles is just as important, if not more important, than sharing our success stories. Which is why, when you're trying to build a collaborative environment across silos, in addition to sharing success stories, you've got to share your personal stories as well. You cannot be afraid to say, "Man, this pandemic is kicking my ass. Working from home in 1400 square feet when my husband is also trying to work from home, with only limited bandwidth, sucks. And, oh, by the way, I got three kids that I'm trying to homeschool while I'm working from home." It's not just about complaining—it's about commiserating and understanding each other. It's good to take a load off now and then, just by talking about the loads that we carry. And the upside is that, then the other person from the other silo is probably more willing to try to help you at work because you shared that personal story, just as you may feel more inclined to help *them* because you know *their* story—and guess what? Their story probably ain't all that different from yours.

It's all about building and developing personal relationships.

And the last thing I find that's helpful when it comes to fostering a more collaborative environment is this: Be Aware of Unconscious Biases.

You know, today is all about celebrating diversity and inclusion, and everybody wants to talk about it all the time. Candidly, I think that they *intend* to celebrate unconscious biases, too—but they don't know what those unconscious biases are. If they were conscious biases, it would be a different issue. So, I'm gonna go ahead and share a very personal issue here to make this point, because there are times when I find myself in situations where I'm acting in a way that I don't want to, and the reason I'm doing that is usually because of an unconscious bias. For example, tattoos bug me. I'm sorry, but they do. When you're an older gentleman like me, raised in a certain way, you come from a culture where tattoos were something you did not do. These days, it seems like *everybody* is getting tattoos. And they're not just tattoos hidden underneath your shirt or up your sleeve where they can be hidden at work, they're *visible* tattoos—the neck tattoos and the full-sleeve tattoos that are proudly worn with a tank top. Times have changed, and it's tough for an old guy to like those kinds of changes. I'm sorry, but it's hard to undo a lifetime's worth of programming.

After I transitioned out of the military, I found myself in hiring actions at UTARI and beyond trying to make sure that I was aware of that unconscious bias. I realized some of the most talented, qualified individuals had tattoos that I didn't personally like, and I had to check myself to make sure I didn't make a hiring decision based on something as silly as "I don't like your tattoos."

We carry unconscious biases with us all the time. It's just human nature. You've got 'em, your colleagues have got 'em, and I'm sure your boss has got 'em, too. But the more we recognize them, acknowledge them, even laugh at them together if we can, the more we can communicate and collaborate in ways that don't allow those biases to negatively affect our work.

That's about all I have to say on that topic. But I cannot overstate how important it is to collaborate. Collaboration is what leads to great discoveries. It's what led to the creation of the vaccines that are now protecting my family, and my co-author, from suffering so severely from COVID-19 again. It's what leads companies to become enterprise organizations, which have the ability to grow stronger, no matter what challenges come along.

Building a collaborative environment isn't easy. There are a lot of roadblocks to it. And those roadblocks have only been amplified by the latest crisis: Collaboration wasn't easy to achieve when everybody was coming into the office, and it's even more difficult, in some ways, when you're trying to collaborate by Zoom. But in the current environment in this great country of ours, one in which divisiveness and choosing sides seems to be more important to some people than collaborating for the good of us all, our inability to resolve conflicts and build (or rebuild) trust have become two of the biggest obstacles to success, for everyone.

You cannot collaborate if you can't trust each other and can't talk to each other. And without collaboration, your chances of surviving the next crisis are near zero. So, even though these are tricky topics, we *have* to talk about 'em. We have no choice. And that's what we're gonna do next.

– 31 –

END THE CONFLICT, *NOW*

Wouldn't it be great if everybody just got along in the workplace?
Fat chance.

It's silly to imagine a conflict-free environment, because it doesn't exist. There is no such thing as Shangri-La. Funny enough, I used to call my ranch property here in Texas my "Shangri-La." But when my Lucas was staying here with us, struggling with some personal-relationship issues that were soon followed by his health issues, he said, "Dad, this ain't Shangri-La. It's Shangri-Sh*t!"

Oh, man, did I laugh. I'm sure you've had moments when you felt the same way about stuff that was going on in your life, and especially at your place of work. Like I said before, and we tell people all the time: life happens. You have this big plan, and then something comes along and messes it all up. And sometimes the thing that comes along isn't a "thing" at all. It's a person. Someone gets in your way and creates a point of friction, a conflict arises, and you find yourself wallowing in Shangri-Sh*t from that point forward.

Or . . . you get to work and try to *resolve* that conflict so you can find some peace again and get back to living your plan.

Your choice.

As far as I'm concerned, choosing to live in Shangri-Sh*t permanently is the worst choice possible. There's always a way to resolve a conflict, or to work around it, or—if there's no other choice—to walk away from it and go find your Shangri-La somewhere else.

Sometimes there are so many conflicts, you just want to give up. One CEO I deal with tells me he loves humanity, but he just doesn't like people. I can't say I don't agree with him at times! Because people are all different, and they've all got their own egos and their own baggage and their own problems. And people are resistant to change. There are times when I'd much rather hang out with my dogs or go feed the wild deer on my property than deal with anyone's conflicts. But walking away from conflict isn't a first choice, and it's definitely not the best answer. Hating people isn't the answer, either. I mean, come on. We're leaders! Let's act like it.

In corporate America, I'm struggling with the ostrich phenomenon—where people want to avoid any confrontation and hope their problems go away. Let me tell you: *It's never going away.* I think that's the first step in all of this—to accept that conflict needs to be addressed. It's not going away, especially if you're dealing with passive-aggressive people who continue to do things that make matters worse. People need to get comfortable with dealing with uncomfortable situations.

Let's get more comfortable with uncomfortable situations, so we can work through them and build trust and collaboration in our organizations. Because as I've witnessed firsthand over these last ten years, and experienced firsthand in combat zones on the other side of the world, everything is at risk if you let conflicts fester. Everything.

So, let's break it down. If you have a conflict, or see a conflict festering in your company, take these actions:

1. Clarify What the Conflict Is

Address folks directly, not behind their backs. Schedule a time to say, "We're having this point of friction. What's causing you angst? Here's what's causing me angst." Get clarity on what the disagreement is actually about, because, I swear, nine times out of ten, it has to do with nothing in the current situation, and it has everything to do with something in the past.

I work with two execs who had a friction point several years ago that they're still dealing with, even though two adult people ought to be able to put that behind them for the sake of their shared goals. But both of them are afraid that what happened all those years ago is just going to happen again. Neither of them wants to get hurt again. While it wasn't a personal thing, it's not all that different from what happens in a romantic relationship. It's just the human psyche: when people break up in a personal relationship, they're more hesitant to go back, or they're more hesitant the next time around, because they don't want to repeat the same mistakes, primarily because they don't want to get hurt. There's a direct relationship between the personal and the professional here, because it's all about trust. "Are you going to do what you said you were going to do, or not?"

Sometimes it's not even about the other person. Sometimes one party or the other is carrying around scar tissue from a relationship that went bad before this one did, and it all goes back to that old hurt. So, ask the tough questions.

Right up front, be clear: Is it something recent? Or did it happen years ago? It doesn't matter which one it is, by the way. Both can be just as damaging to your relationships and, ultimately, to your organization.

For an extreme example, let me take you back to Little Bighorn for a moment. I spoke about Major Reno, and how Custer's boss,

Gen. Terry, wouldn't let Reno go to his own wife's funeral. You can see why Reno might hold a grudge about that, and why it might have caused some conflict and mistrust in the chain of command.

In 1874, two years prior to Little Bighorn, Custer attacked and massacred 103 women and children in battle of Washita, but the Indians fought back and attacked seven people from Custer's organization, led by Major Joel Elliott, who was a personal friend of one of Custer's Captains, Frederick Benteen.

Well, rather than mounting an attack and rescuing Joel Elliott, Custer left him to die—where he was scalped and mutilated, along with seven others. Custer abandoned Elliott, and Benteen never got over it. For the next two years, it stayed on his mind.

So, at Little Bighorn, when they had the opportunity to rescue Custer and his men, Reno and Benteen got to talking about all the horrible things their bosses had done. They spent 90 minutes talking about the gripes they had with their lousy leaders rather than taking action to rescue one of those leaders. They let Custer die, in the same miserable way Custer had let Elliott die.

That's what happens when conflict festers.

So, what can be done?

Sit down with one another, one-on-one or with a mediator, and start working things out. I've acted as mediator between executives at times. If two people won't talk to each other at all, you can't expect them to resolve the conflict together on their own. They need a third party involved—and whatever the cost, whatever the outcome, it will be better than just letting it fester. Trust me. Trust history!

2. Establish Common Goals

Ask yourself (or the parties you're mediating for): "What does it look like when this conflict is resolved? What does the 'new normal' in our relationship look like?" Are they going to start talking? Are they going to work on the same team? Are they going to start hosting after-work drinks for their teams *together*, just to show that conflicts *can* get resolved? We want to know what the upside is going to be.

3. Discuss Ways to Meet Those Common Goals

Do the parties involved need to hold weekly meetings together, to make sure they're on the same page? Would it help for them to speak to the mediator on a regular basis? Does one or the other need to set up the reservation for the after-work drinks? Whatever it is, let's make some plans for how it might play out. And then come to agreements on how you're going to meet the common goals. Don't just *talk* about what you might do, but actually *agree* to do it.

4. Discuss Any Barriers to the Common Goals

Openly talk about what might get in the way of your common goals, so both parties acknowledge that this won't always be easy. Just as in combat, it's a whole lot easier to fight the enemy you know, so agreeing on a common enemy—the barriers to your goals—will help make sure you're working together to achieve your common goals.

5. Agree on How to Resolve the Conflict

This is the hardest part. Even after you've gone through the first steps and set goals together, which, in and of itself, is an act of teamwork and collaboration, getting down to the nitty-gritty of the actual fight can still be hard to get over. If you've got something like unequal salaries getting in the way, it's not even up to the parties themselves. They've got to get over it, and one of them has to realize that they're just not worth as much to the company—which might result in them leaving the company. If that doesn't happen, they've got to make a plan to get management or HR involved to come to a more equitable agreement that makes both of them feel better about the other. But that's what's so important about this next step:

6. Come up with a *Plan of Attack* to Resolve the Conflict

Coming up with a plan is an act of collaboration. Both parties must acknowledge the solution and then determine the personal responsibilities that each party has in the resolution. It probably involves both parties apologizing, and good luck with that. There's always somebody who doesn't feel it was their fault and that, therefore, there is no need to apologize—and that's where the stalemates start. But if you can get one party to apologize for an action and the other to apologize for the long-protracted reaction, that might be doable. There's almost always a solution. Maybe it means both parties going to management, together, to discuss the pay difference and see if they can ask for a pay raise for the underpaid party together. Imagine how powerful *that* would be—and how *healing* that would be. Maybe it involves seeing a counselor. Maybe it just calls for going to dinner together and breaking bread and getting to know each other better. Whatever it is, you then have to have some system of accountability to check on how you're doing—so you don't walk away from these meetings and just go back to hating each other.

I'll be honest with you. As much as I've worked on this, rarely am I successful—because we're dealing with human beings, who come in with baggage, personality issues, and frustrations that are at the source of the conflict, and they're unwilling to get into what those frustrations really are. In the Bible, James 1:19, there's a great passage that tells us, "Everyone should be quick to listen, slow to speak, and slow to become angry." Boy, how great would life be if that were the case? But in general, that's not the case at all. So overall, I give myself a C-minus for my accomplishments in this area. But that's not a failure. That's still an improvement over where these conflicts stood before I came in.

It's tough. People get their feelings hurt, and it's difficult to get over that. We're humans at work, just as we're humans at home. Conflicts involve psyche, temperament, emotions. If somebody embarrasses you in an open forum (a conflict that has happened more than once, at more than one of my clients' offices), the person who was embarrassed often shuts down and cannot let it go. In those cases, you absolutely need mediation to work it out.

In fact, getting a third party involved is a great help in almost every case. Problems don't go away by themselves or expire over time. These are relationships, and relationships need tending.

Gen. Casey made me read a book called *Getting to Yes* before I went in to negotiate with the armed insurgents in Iraq. You remember I told you the story of me and the sixteen armed insurgents, right? I mean—come on, people. If I can get them to work with each other, why can't I get *you* to work with each other? You don't bring guns to the table. You're not gonna blow up each other's houses, even if you wind up yelling at each other as a way to get it all out on the table. You don't necessarily have to like each other at the end of this process, but you've got to get to a point where you can communicate, cooperate, and collaborate. It just has to happen.

Stop sweating the small stuff. Look at the big picture. How is allowing a conflict to fester helping *anyone*, including *you*?

How about we stop being children and deal with our problems like adults?

There. I said it.

Look, it's kind of like a marriage analogy, isn't it? We sometimes spend more hours with the people we work with than we do with our spouses during the week. So, we've got to make it work. Marriage is hard work. I don't think there's anyone who doesn't agree with that sentiment these days. I've been married almost forty years, and they've not all been smooth! But Sarah and I are committed to working things out for the sake of our marriage and family.

In corporate America, for the greater good, the good of the company, the good of us *all*, let's commit ourselves to working things out as well.

The importance of this should be even more pressing for you, having just come out of a time of crisis. Because in times of crisis, it's these conflicts that are going to cause you to fail. It's hard enough when things are going smoothly, right? But I talked about the danger of unnecessary distractions in this book, and *this* is an unnecessary distraction.

A president of one of the companies I work for recently told his execs, "I'm sick of your bickering and rivalry. I need it to stop." He was fed up. It was affecting their bottom line.

But yelling at your people to stop just doesn't work.

You have to do the work, and you must do it now. Resolve the conflict expeditiously, and don't let it fester. Because if it's still festering in a rough time, forget it.

The last thing you want to do is end up like Custer.

COMMANDING LOYALTY

If you want to make sure your people don't turn their back on you and walk, that they aren't going to leave you to fail in difficult times, take care of them. I did my best to take care of my soldiers, and when times got tough, they took care of me. They kept their noses to the grindstone and did the hard work that was needed. It wasn't just because they were following orders (although that was a nice perk of leading in the military). It was because my soldiers knew that we were in this together. They trusted that I would take care of them to the best of my ability. They trusted that I was right there in the fight with them, doing the hard work, and that, if something went wrong, I certainly wasn't going to leave any of them behind if I could possibly help it. Every effort and every decision that could be made to keep them safe while we got the job done was gonna be made by *me*.

If you show people you care, then, when things get difficult, they're going to work even harder—they're not going to want to let you down.

Think about the grocery stores that stayed open during the pandemic. We, as a nation, determined that the people who work in those stores were "essential workers," and the best companies stepped up to treat those workers like they counted. There were pay raises where none had been asked for. There were bonus checks for long days worked. The workers were provided with masks, and gloves, and new protocols that were put into place to protect their health—many of which went above and beyond CDC guidelines and were put into place faster than any government agency ever mandated.

Those businesses that stepped up and took care of our essential workers through the pandemic need to be applauded. And they should also stand out as an example of what to do in the future: Let's behave like adults and not be babies; let's work through issues *before* we get into the mess of tough times, so we can take care of our people when they need it the most; let's get ahead of our problems and go above and beyond to do what's right.

Let's do everything we can to let our people know that they can *trust us* when the chips are down.

BUILDING AND RESTORING TRUST

When it comes to organizations people trust the most, the U.S. military is ranked highest, all across this nation. (Go ahead and Google it.)

Who do people trust the least? Politicians and lawyers. They fall to the very bottom of the barrel. I mean, people just assume that if a lawyer's or a politician's lips are moving, they're lying, right? It's not that way in the military—and that matters. There's a reason our military is effective, and there's a reason the military gets things done—and trust is at the very foundation of that success.

Guess who else is low on the trust list? Business executives. That's right: business executives are right down there near the bottom of the list—down there with the Congresspeople and the used-car salespeople.

Only 25 percent of Americans trust big business. Which means if you work for a large corporation, 75 percent of the people *in your own company* likely don't trust what you're doing.

That's a problem.

Why do people trust the military? Because the military is a values-based organization. In the Army, we are sworn to uphold LDRSHIP: Loyalty, Dignity, Respect, Selfless service, Honor, Integrity, and Personal courage.

What are corporate executives sworn to uphold? Not much, in most instances, other than doing their part to help a corporation make money, because corporations are not values-based organizations.

Why not? I mean truly, what is wrong with us that we can't see that so many of the problems we face as leaders could be fixed by building trust? And trust comes from upholding values. You can't have trust if it's *not* based in values—values that you live and talk about all the time.

I train my clients in establishing corporate values on a regular basis. Not just the sort of values or mission statements that fit on a bumper sticker or get pinned to a bulletin board and forgotten. But true, life-enriching, company-enhancing human values that will only make their jobs and their lives—and the jobs and lives of their employees and colleagues—better and better over time.

The senior executives I know who embrace values and who want to foster more trust keep finding that the more senior they get, the more they have to keep repeating the values to others. They have no choice but to live the values and talk about the values. And when they find people in the organization who don't respect the values and don't want to live them themselves, they have to call 'em out on it—otherwise, the values seem to fall by the wayside, quickly. It's just the nature of the corporate beast.

When we're doing evaluations, how a particular individual or division is supporting a company's values should be near the top of the list if you want it to matter, and calling people out when they're falling short must happen. But hard conversations seem to be a hard thing for corporate leaders to come to grips with. They don't want to create new conflicts. But believe me: Doing whatever it takes to bring an organization back to a place of trust is worth the fight.

In his book *The Speed of Trust*, Stephen Covey concluded that organizations are 80 percent more effective when they're built on a foundation of trust. That's a *huge* number. And from the differences I've seen both in the military and outside the military, I believe that number is absolutely true.

Can you imagine if we rebuilt these organizations in a way that led us to an 80 percent improvement in effectiveness? That sure seems like it's something worth trying, doesn't it? Even if we got only halfway there, can you imagine the profits, the rewards, and the trickle-down to the rest of our society, if our corporate organizations saw a 40 percent improvement in their overall effectiveness?

Getting even halfway there at this point is a lofty goal, because corporate America has done so much to break the trust of the people. And survey after survey shows that most people seem to believe that, once trust has been broken, it cannot be restored.

I'm an optimist. I believe trust *can* be restored—in marriage, in society, and in business, too. But it takes work. Companies must provide leadership training for their senior executives to get the ball rolling; before they can do even that, they have to deal with the above-mentioned tasks of conflict resolution. Because when I go in to coach executives on building trust, and all they want to talk about is the terrible thing some other executive did to them four years earlier, we ain't gettin' nowhere.

There are times when I feel like shouting, *"Put it behind you! Just start fresh!"*

But I know it's not that easy. In Kosovo, my job was to keep the Serbians from killing the Albanians, and vice-versa, and the only way to accomplish that was to create an environment of trust. I tried to talk it out with a senior Albanian leader one day. I told him, in the simplest of terms, "Look, if you quit shooting at them, they'll quit shooting at you." He looked at me, and he said he'd never quit. That fight goes back generations. The Serbs killed his brother, just like they killed his uncle. He would never forgive them.

Thankfully, in corporate America, we haven't resorted to killing each other—which means that none of this infighting should fester for even the next quarter, let alone for years or generations.

Resolving our issues should be a hell of a lot simpler than it is.

So where do we start? How can we start building trust?

For one thing, in the U.S. military, everybody had a clearly defined job description. The first paragraph of our evaluation reports told the whole world exactly what our job was and exactly what was expected of us.

In the corporate world, there is great hesitancy to draft job descriptions. As a result, people's lanes are not clearly defined, and people wind up thinking that their toes are getting stepped on when they're not. It's just dumb.

To build trust, everybody needs to know what everybody else is responsible for—so we can stop being so suspicious of "Why is she in my lane?"

I don't know why corporate executives have a tendency to be suspicious of each other, but they do. I listen to complaints all the time:

"He's trying to take my stuff." "That's *my* job." "She's taking credit for my work." "He stole *my* resources . . ."

Clearly defined job descriptions help eliminate the stepping on each other's toes.

So, there's one place to start. But beyond that, we just have to acknowledge that restoring trust takes hard work, and sometimes it takes a long time. And as leaders, we have to model trust, every day, so the foundation we want to build can start to grow.

What does that look like? What should we do, as leaders, to model trust?

1. Personally, be honest and supportive

In daily interactions, acknowledge that others' success is as important as *your* success. You're both in the same company. Act like it! If somebody needs assistance, support them in their efforts, and be candid and forthright if you see something wrong or something you don't agree with. At the root of trust is honesty, so let's be candid and talk things out.

2. Follow through

Do not make promises you can't keep if you ever want to restore trust. You've got to follow through and verify that you did it; *tell them* that you did it. The same thing goes for following up to see that what was supposed to be done on their end was done, too. Trust and verify. Those two things go hand in hand.

3. Be consistent in words and deeds

If you want people to trust you, you simply cannot say one thing and then do something else. Trust is a fragile commodity. It takes a long time to build it, but you can break it with one event, one misplaced word, or one misplaced action—and it might take years to re-establish that trust. So, be consistent, and model the behavior you seek. Demonstrate behavior wherever the people you work with, and work for, can *see* that they can trust you—and you can trust them.

Remember your values, and talk about them. Talk about them all the time. Constant repetition is a good thing when it comes to trust. People learn from the steadiness. They learn by your example. They learn by the example of others, too, so be sure to hold others' feet to the fire when it comes to living the values. I've been hired to explain and give values to new hires in companies where the senior executives aren't living by the company values at all. That just doesn't work. Everybody's gotta do it.

And finally . . .

4. Build in Accountability

What do you do with somebody who doesn't live the values or does the *opposite* of your values? Do you not talk about it because it's uncomfortable? Do you play the ostrich and stick your head in the sand and hope the problem goes away? You can't do that—the problem will just fester and get worse. And, like I said, if that happens when times of crisis come, it's over. The problems that you've allowed to fester will be your breaking point. Every time.

JUST DO IT

Building and re-building trust is not easy. Resolving conflicts is not easy. And that is why the best way to prepare for the future is to start getting these things right, *right now*. Tackle the challenges head on. Deal with the issues. Work on improving collaboration. Resolve conflicts. Build trust. To steal a phrase from Nike: Just do it! Yes, it's hard work. But once you've done the hard work, you can move to a place where your work isn't so hard—that powerful, sought-after place where everything starts to click, and things start to flow. Where your people are happier. You're making more money, because *everybody's* more productive. You're more successful, you're accomplishing your goals, and your company is booming, all because you've fostered an environment of true success.

So, how do you stay focused on doing all of this? How do you get it all done?

It's simple: You remember that none of this can work—none of it—if you don't take care of the people who work for you. They're the ones you need to count on to carry out your plans. Without them, you fail.

Which means you'd better set your priorities accordingly.

– 32 –

PRIORITY ONE:
TAKE CARE OF YOUR PEOPLE

Did you know that depression rates tripled during the pandemic?

As I finished up writing Part 5 of this book, after 18 months of bad news, deaths, and disruptions to our lives, it was alleged that 40 percent of adults in the U.S. were struggling with mental-health or substance-abuse issues, directly influenced by the lockdowns and isolation.

That's a lot of people who are hurting, who need our help. Mental-health and substance-abuse issues affect everything—including productivity at work.

I'm not saying this to be a downer. I'm saying it because, as a leader, I care about taking care of people, and I want to know when people are hurting so I can try to do something about it.

I also want to know why things are happening, and as I studied all of this, I came across a report that said 90 percent of pandemic-related national media stories in the U.S. were negative. Internationally, the media reported 50 percent positive stories, and 50 percent negative stories. But here? A full 90 percent of everything we saw on the news was negative.

Well, no wonder so many people got depressed! They're not only stuck in their homes, but they're being terrified into oblivion by the media.

My mantra to friends and family during the whole ordeal was, "Turn the TV off, and wash your hands." And that doesn't mean I was burying my head in the sand—it just meant that I was being careful about where I sourced my information. As leaders, it's important not to get caught up in the hysteria or the popular thoughts of the moment. It's important to get good information, so you can act upon that information accordingly and pass the correct information on to your people as you communicate (clearly and concisely).

Here are some statistics you probably didn't see on your TV.

In 2020, the number of deaths in the U.S. actually decreased by 17 percent. And the COVID deaths were only the third-leading cause of death behind heart disease and cancer, which never went away. So even though we were all told to be worried to death about dying of COVID-19, statistically there was a 17-percent decrease in deaths overall, and COVID didn't even come close to raising the same issues as heart disease or cancer.

I'm not dismissing it. COVID was, is, and continues to be a major problem in many parts of this country, and even more so in many parts of the world. But where were the positive stories to reassure us and lift us up? Where were the leaders telling us, "We're gonna get through this, and here's the good news!"

Throughout the pandemic, there were other statistics worth noting, too—positive stats that should make us proud.

For one, divorce rates fell to a 50-year low as of 2021. Part of the reason for that is that there are fewer people tying the knot. Marriage rates are down overall. But that doesn't negate the very hopeful statistic that, for every 1,000 marriages, only 14.9 now end in divorce. The rates in the 2010s were closer to 50 percent. So that's a huge improvement!

Interestingly enough, suicide rates across the nation dropped by 6 percent in 2020 as well, despite all the mental-health issues. It was the strongest drop in suicide rates in four decades. That's good news. But how do we make sense of that, and how should it affect our leadership?

If, after reading this book, you think, "Why should I even care?" then you've missed the point. Part 3 of this book was all about the idea of taking care of people, and it is a critical factor in adaptive leadership, period. Go back right now and read it again if you have to, because, if, as a leader, you're not taking care of your people, they for sure will not take care of you or your company.

I think the number-one takeaway from these striking statistics is to remember how critical it is to understand individual circumstances. Knowing that 40 percent of Americans are reporting mental-health and substance-abuse issues should prompt you to be aware. When you ask, "How are you doing?" and they say, "We're doing fine," you should probably respond with, "Really? Because pretty much half the people I know aren't doing fine *at all* through this whole ordeal."

In truth, I don't think *anybody* was doing fine. We were all dealing with things we had never dealt with before, and that's stressful even to the well-prepared and adaptable among us. Even here at the ranch, we faced challenges I never saw coming. In the middle of the pandemic, Texas experienced a week of unheard-of sub-zero temperatures. It was so cold, the diesel fuel in my tractor froze. So I couldn't plow the driveway. The ice and snow trapped us. For a week! Talk about isolation. If anybody had asked me, I would have said, "No! I'm not okay. I'm going stir-crazy here on the ranch."

But no matter where you lived, this pandemic caused everyone to experience a previously unheard-of sense of isolation and lack of human connection. Even if you broke the rules and held gatherings at the peak of it all, there was no way you had as much human interaction outside of your own home as you had at any other time in your entire life.

As more and more individuals started finding a certain level of comfort doing calls virtually, with FaceTime and all that stuff, we found that it beat the phone call or the email. But people were still striving for that human connection that exists outside of their spouses and children. They were looking for somebody else to be around.

As leaders, we can help foster that—and do a much better job of asking our people how they're doing. What I advocate to all my clients now is constant communication with individuals to understand their circumstances, which change almost daily.

I was working on this final chapter when I got a call and learned that one of my good friends had died of COVID-19. This was in July of 2021, when things were supposedly getting better. But this friend hadn't been vaccinated, and he got it, and, in less than a week, he was gone. I learned of many friends who lost loved ones that summer as well. They lost their dad. They lost their brother. So, no—they *weren't* doing okay. And even though the isolation was less than it was a year earlier, it was still important to reach out and see how they were.

The only way to be an engaged leader is to get into it, to have those detailed conversations I talked about in Part 3. Ask intrusive questions. Do what you can to understand the circumstances of the individual. You have to have a constant communication. Routinely talk to your people. Not on group calls, but one-on-one.

When someone winds up out of work for a health reason, or maybe a suicide attempt, there's always somebody who says, "Well, I just talked to the guy. How can he be having these troubles? He didn't say he had trouble."

"Well, when did you talk to him?" I'll ask.

"He was there on the conference call with the leadership team, and there were nine of us on the call, and none of us heard anything. The person didn't say, 'Hey, I'm struggling.'"

Of course, they didn't, because that's not when anybody is gonna say something like that. That's also another reason I advocate turning the cameras on, because you can see nonverbal communication if you can see what they're doing. If someone looks off, they look down, they look especially tired, I'll always follow up with a check-in call. But I'll follow up when it *isn't* obvious, too, because you just never know.

There's a quote I've seen floating around the internet that says people don't ever pretend to be depressed; what they pretend to be is *fine*. And it's true.

This need for constant communication is even more important during a crisis. You've got to emphasize the importance of human connection, and you must understand that everybody's circumstances are different. And that calls for a certain amount of empathy.

THE EMPATHETIC LEADER

I talk a lot about being humble in *Work Hard, Pray Hard* (which I highly encourage you to read if you haven't), and being humble in a crisis environment means listening and being empathetic. If someone tells you they're having problems, you can't just blow it off and say, "Okay, well, have a nice day."

Remember: You cannot dissociate professional issues from personal issues. You can't.

So, what can you do besides lend an ear, or give some time off, or any of the other responses I've mentioned already? If anything, I think that leaders should be responding accordingly to the needs of their people, and one of those needs is clearly mental-health care. Does your company plan provide coverage for mental-health and substance-abuse issues? If not, you could wind up losing a portion of your workforce when they become overwhelmed by those issues. Health plans in general are something everybody worried about through the pandemic, and while the government can only do so much, I think businesses have a real opportunity to step things up in this area and make sure their employees aren't getting sick to their stomachs every time a co-pay comes due or they're forced to meet a ridiculously high deductible.

Your people should not have to put up GoFundMe pages to pay for their hospitalizations and long-term care. If they're in that position, chances are they won't be coming back to your company or showing much loyalty to your company when they get back on their feet.

But there's so much more that strong leaders can do for their people in times of trouble. One of my clients decided to provide family meals, twice a day, to their entire staff, throughout the course of the pandemic. Another dropped big bonuses into everybody's paychecks. One of them raised the minimum wage for the lowest-level employees to $16 an hour, to make sure those employees felt good about coming to work at a time when dealing with the public was such a high-risk scenario.

The leaders at these companies didn't wait for the government to swoop in and save them. They didn't wait for some health agency to tell them what to do. They stepped up and did the right thing for their people because they cared—because they recognized how much their people meant to *them*.

I saw a CEO cut his salary to zero to make sure he didn't have to lay anyone off. I watched another agree to take 30 percent pay cuts across all of senior management so they wouldn't have to furlough anyone, either.

Guess if those companies are floundering at the end of all of it. No! They were *thriving*. Their people were okay, and, therefore, the companies were okay.

On the other end of the spectrum, I watched some leaders decide to just furlough everybody as soon as the shutdowns were put in place. "We'll just hire them back when the quarantines are lifted," they said.

Guess what? By the time the quarantines were lifted, those workers had all gone out and found other jobs. Better jobs. At companies that actually showed people that they were valued. And those leaders were left scrambling with extreme staff shortages that have not let up as of the writing of this book.

By the summer of 2021, companies across this nation were open for business—but couldn't find employees to take the hundreds of thousands of open jobs. A lot of people wanted to blame it on the government for handing out too much unemployment money in the COVID relief bills. I'm here to tell you: That's a cop-out. Some good folks at MIT studied this phenomenon, right in the middle of it, and found that the worker shortage was *not* about lazy people wanting to collect money from the government and not go back to work. That just was not true. The worker shortages were because people everywhere, having experienced life during the pandemic, were now more selective in terms of where they wanted to work and what they were willing to go back and do.

The whole idea of voting with your feet is now the predominant movement in the workforce. While certain companies are out there demanding that everyone come back into the office full-time, a lot of folks are now looking for jobs where they can continue to work from home. Even the fully employed are leaving in droves for jobs that are closer to home or work-from-home only. Whether they're aware of it or not, they've put their jobs into the Eisenhower Box and gone about reprioritizing their lives. And that means the attrition rates are high.

I personally know executives who've improved their health, improved their marriages, improved their relationships with their families, and reclaimed hours of their lives that used to be spent commuting twice a day, all during the pandemic—and just about *all* of them started to look for new jobs as soon as their companies told them they had to come back into the office. They simply aren't going to stick around and work for leaders who don't value them and their lives anymore.

Once again, I encourage leaders: Do not play ostrich and put your head in the sand and think these issues are going to go away. They're not. Rather, let's address these issues. Let's have the difficult conversations. Let's embrace the new technologies. Let's adjust our healthcare plans. Let's adjust the way we do business.

Let's adapt!

If you don't, you'll get left behind.

Just look around, and assess the terrain: While you're there twiddling your thumbs and wondering why you can't find employees to fill the massive gaps in your workforce, other companies aren't having any trouble hiring at all. Why? Because they've raised their base pay, put new benefits in place, adopted a hybrid work-from-home model, and they've let people know it. Their *people* have let people know it, too. They spread the word to everyone they know. Why? Because they're happy they work for such good companies, and they want their friends and family to work for good companies, too.

Want to know what people are talking about when they talk about *your* company? The one that's failed to do any of that and just expects workers to come back, like robots, to the same old conditions that existed before?

You don't want to hear it. Believe me.

So *do something* about it.

It's only gonna wind up helping you in the end.

And believe me, I get it. To some of you old codgers out there, like me, who started off making 60 cents an hour at your first job, a starting pay of $15 or $16 an hour sounds like a gigantic amount of money. But it's not. A full-time job at $15 an hour is only $600 a week before taxes. $2400 a month (or more than $30,000 a year) sounds like a lot of money! And it was—in the 1980s. But it's not now. Not with gas prices where they are, and food prices through the roof; not when the going rate of an apartment in any state in the nation winds up costing more than half of somebody's take-home pay. And that's just rent! Not heat, hot water, or anything else.

Looking at how much everything costs, I really don't know how people are surviving these days. Even in my own family, I know the only way some young people can get by is because of bedrooms their parents offer to them in their late 20s and early 30s. For us, it was a choice made more out of love than money, because I love having my children and grandchildren around. But the idea of kids having to move back home for financial reasons is a trend we ought not to be proud of as Americans.

Pay rates for most jobs just haven't kept up with inflation in this country, and it's up to us, as business leaders, to do something about that. We cannot wait for the government to do it. We need to stay in touch with reality—and in touch with our people—and try to make things right.

Going back to the suicide rates for a second: the number-one cause of suicide for young people is failed relationships, and the number-two cause is financial problems. And as anyone who's ever been married or in a long-term relationship can tell you, financial problems are often the *cause* of relationship problems. So don't tell me that the wages you're paying aren't an important issue, when in fact it's the dominant issue that's causing people to break up their relationships and even take their own lives.

It is definitely one reason people are walking these days. They know they've been working for too little money, and now they're acting on it.

On a lighter note, engaged leaders want their people to *have* lives, right? To have fun and enjoy their weekends or other time off, so they're more engaged and fulfilled when they come back to work. And that takes money (and benefits), too. For example, I went out and bought Sarah a little MG Midget, a 1970s convertible that she just always loved—a car that I knew would be fun for her to drive. It wasn't an expensive car by any measure. But when I went to register it, thinking all I'd have to do is pay twenty bucks or so for the license plates, it cost me $1,000. The state of Texas charged me sales tax and other fees that I just wasn't aware I'd have to pay on such an old car. That was a $1,000 surprise to me that I could handle. But I can't even think about what somebody else would have done if they had walked up and been faced with that same surprise. For a worker who makes $15 an hour, that's like half a month's pay! How in the hell is somebody supposed to live any kind of a good life, and have a good time, when their dollars are so stretched by doing something as all-American as buying an old used car to drive in the summertime? And what if that's their only car, their only means of transportation to and from work? Does it make any sense that we're asking people to give up half-a-month's pay just to register a car they *need*? How does that add up?

If I wasn't an engaged leader, maybe I wouldn't care about such things. But I do care. And I hope you care, too.

None of us can solve all the world's problems. But the world does need us to solve the problems we're able to solve. If we want the best workers to come to our organizations, if we want to retain them, if we want them to live their dashes and take care of their families, and we want high productivity in the workplace, then we cannot ignore the reality of what our workers need in order to accomplish and sustain those goals.

It's up to you to understand their circumstances. It's up to you to acknowledge that, if you don't make them happy, they have opportunities elsewhere. And it's up to you to acknowledge that, as a leader, you play an important part in ensuring your workers' resiliency in times of crisis.

I spent a lot of time talking about resiliency in Chapter 24—financial resiliency, emotional resiliency, spiritual resiliency, societal resiliency—and the need for resiliency of all kinds is far more pronounced now than it was when I first wrote it.

So aside from the financial aspects, how do we help our people to become more resilient, so that they aren't so consumed by a crisis that it's ruining their mental health?

Frankly, in the aftermath of the pandemic, I think we need to focus more on societal and familial fitness. Spiritual fitness, which I talk about extensively in *Work Hard, Pray Hard*, is critical, too. But I think most of that falls on the individual, more so than the organization or the leader.

As I mentioned earlier, the lack of human contact outside of the home was a big factor in increased rates of depression during this crisis. And I believe that, as leaders, we can encourage people to use visual technology as a way to connect with fellow humans outside of work, just like we do during the workday.

During the pandemic, a former battalion commander of mine fell ill, and I wanted to lift his spirits. So, all of the other captains and I who were in the unit together decided to connect with him for a Zoom cocktail hour. We all drank and talked about what happened back in 1982, and it lifted his spirits. It was a chance to hoot and holler about things we did when we were all young captains, and he was a lieutenant colonel.

That was so much fun that some of us decided to do a quarterly cocktail hour with my class at West Point, too. It's been a blast telling old stories and catching up on what everybody's doing now, and how their families are doing.

Who knows if other strains of COVID or some other virus will keep circling around the globe? I hope not. But if they do, and we're stuck indoors again, I know I'll be encouraging people to connect as much as possible. Because without human connection, life gets pretty dark, pretty fast—and home life becomes harder and harder.

Families don't always like each other. In the military, domestic violence increased significantly during the pandemic. Child-abuse rates increased at military installations as well.

I can't help but think that if more of us were doing what we could to improve our societal resiliency and finding ways to encourage each other to get together with friends and colleagues, even when we can't get together in person, then maybe some of that tension and anger at home would go away.

Our families are important too, though. If you've got a strong family support unit, you're less likely to go crazy during something like a pandemic. But I'm not just talking about your immediate family. I'm talking about your extended family.

One positive that came out of the growth of Zoom and the ease of use of FaceTime on our phones is that I have friends who now do weekly video calls with their aging parents. It took some effort to get their parents online, but once they did it, they loved it!

I used to call my parents every Sunday, and after mom passed, I called my dad every day. Those check-ins were always worthwhile. But now, with the video component, it's not just three minutes to say "Hi," but extended Zoom calls where friends are able to see their moms on camera and make sure they're doing okay. The fact that people got worried enough about their parents, and aunts and uncles, and cousins, to make those kinds of connections is absolutely a positive that came out of this crisis.

I think we're all in closer touch with our mortality now, and making time for what matters, matters more.

GETTING REAL

So, what can leaders in corporate America do to be better in times of crisis?

For one, how about not furloughing anybody? That was just a mistake. Revise budgets, take pay cuts at the top, whatever you have to do—just don't let your people go at the very moment they need stability. That's not only a failure to them, it's a major failure for you.

Do the opposite. Show people that you care and that you aren't going to throw them under the bus. Don't wait for the government to help with their crisis-induced financial problems. Help them out yourselves.

If you've got $500,000 in the budget, and you don't need it—I mean truly *need* it—take that money and give to those who do. Not to a charity or some outside fund but to your *own people*.

When offices closed down, and monthly overhead expenses dropped to near zero for a while, all of that money could have gone to help your people. All of it. Because that personal investment in the people who've invested their time and their very lives in your company is the most important investment of all.

I also think every company could learn something and follow the lead of one of my clients by setting up an emergency fund designed specifically to help individuals in times of need. During regular times, a fund like that can help a team member with a medical emergency or a housing crisis (after a fire or flood, for instance). And during times of crisis, that fund can be spread around to make sure your workforce isn't decimated.

It's not only a good thing to do, it's a prudent thing to do. It's an insurance policy against attrition. It's also the sort of thing that keeps people from voting with their feet and leaving you when times get tough.

What else can leaders do in times of crisis?

By now, I don't think I need to give you specifics. You have the tools you need to think with and come up with ideas yourself.

It's simple, really: Just do *better*. Do the right thing. Forget about what everyone else thinks, or what other companies are doing, or what the current trends are telling you to do. Stop, slow down, and take time to think. Pray on it, if that's something that resonates with you. Look inside, be a human being, and you'll know what the right thing is.

Then, once you know what that right thing is, do *that*.

Lead by example. Lead with pride. Adapt and adopt change as needed. Be a Lifestyle Evangelist. Do the things that make your people smile, which encourages them to want to do better and be better, too. It is the only way—the *only way*—you can be sure that the people you're leading will be there for you and your company the next time the chips are down.

And there will be a next time.

You can count on it.

SUMMARY

In closing, I just want to thank all of you who have come along on this journey with Sarah and me over the last ten years and counting. We've made some great friends in our post-military years, and we've been involved in doing so much meaningful work—I can hardly believe how good God has been to us.

And to those of you who just picked up this book for the first time, who just learned about our journey for the first time, thank you for coming along and joining this mission, too.

Never forget: You have the power to change lives for the better—including your own.

No matter what position you're in, you're in a position to take care of people, and to make a difference in the world—whether it's on a large scale or a small scale.

The decisions you make matter. The choices you make matter. How you choose to live your life, and the preparations you make for the future, *matter.*

If you have questions, or if you want to get more involved in the life-altering discussion of Adaptive Leadership by arranging to see me in person (or via Zoom)—please don't hesitate to reach out.

WEBSITE: www.rlynchenterprises.com
EMAIL: lynchassistant1@gmail.com
LINKEDIN: www.linkedin.com/in/ltgricklynch

APPENDIX I
LYNCH'S LEADERSHIP PRINCIPLES

1. Focus on opportunities, not obstacles.
"It can be done!"

2. Have fun!
"If the boss ain't happy, ain't nobody happy!"

3. Achieve a work-life balance.
"How are you living your dash?"

4. Decide when to decide.
"Take the time to think!"

5. Look down, not up.
*"People don't care how much you know until
they know how much you care!"*

6. Be a mentor.
*"You must be accessible, you must listen,
and you must truly care!"*

7. Engaged leadership is important.
"Love your subordinates like you love your own children!"

8. Be demanding but not demeaning.

   "Everyone must perform to his or her full potential."

9. Always celebrate diversity.

   "Don't surround yourself with people like you!"

APPENDIX 2
LYNCH'S GO-TO SCRIPTURES

– JOHN 15:13

Greater love has no one than this: to lay down one's life for one's friends.

–ISAIAH 6:8

Then I heard the voice of the Lord saying, "Whom shall I send? And who will go for us?" And I said, "Here am I. Send me!"

– MATTHEW 25:21

His master replied, "Well done, good and faithful servant! You have been faithful with a few things; I will put you in charge of many things. Come and share your master's happiness!"

– 1 CHRONICLES 4:10 (THE PRAYER OF JABEZ)

Jabez cried out to the God of Israel, "Oh, that you would bless me and enlarge my territory! Let your hand be with me, and keep me from harm so that I will be free from pain." And God granted his request.

– JOSHUA 1:8

Keep this Book of the Law always on your lips; meditate on it day and night, so that you may be careful to do everything written in it. Then you will be prosperous and successful.

– PSALM 119:11

I have hidden your word in my heart that I might not sin against you.

– ROMANS 3:23

For all have sinned and fall short of the glory of God.

– ROMANS 5:3-4

Not only so, but we also glory in our sufferings, because we know that suffering produces perseverance; perseverance, character; and character, hope.

– ROMANS 8:31

What, then, shall we say in response to these things? If God is for us, who can be against us?

– COLOSSIANS 3:5-12

Put to death, therefore, whatever belongs to your earthly nature: sexual immorality, impurity, lust, evil desires and greed, which is idolatry. Because of these, the wrath of God is coming. You used to walk in these ways, in the life you once lived. But now you must also rid yourselves of all such things as these: anger, rage, malice, slander, and filthy language from your lips. Do not lie to each other, since you have taken off your old self with its practices and have put on the new self, which is being renewed in knowledge in the image of its Creator. Here there is no Gentile or Jew, circumcised or uncircumcised, barbarian, Scythian, slave or free, but Christ is all, and is in all. Therefore, as God's chosen people, holy and dearly loved, clothe yourselves with compassion, kindness, humility, gentleness and patience.

– 2 TIMOTHY 3:16

All Scripture is God-breathed and is useful for teaching, rebuking, correcting and training in righteousness.

– 2 TIMOTHY 4:7

I have fought the good fight, I have finished the race, I have kept the faith.

– 1 JOHN 1:8-10

If we claim to be without sin, we deceive ourselves and the truth is not in us. If we confess our sins, he is faithful and just and will forgive us our sins and purify us from all unrighteousness. If we claim we have not sinned, we make him out to be a liar and his word is not in us.

– PHILIPPIANS 4:6-7

Do not be anxious about anything, but in every situation, by prayer and petition, with thanksgiving, present your requests to God. And the peace of God, which transcends all understanding, will guard your hearts and your minds in Christ Jesus.

– MATTHEW 5:16

In the same way, let your light shine before others, that they may see your good deeds and glorify your Father in heaven.

– JAMES 1:2-3

Consider it pure joy, my brothers and sisters, whenever you face trials of many kinds, because you know that the testing of your faith produces perseverance.